THE LITTLE HOUSE

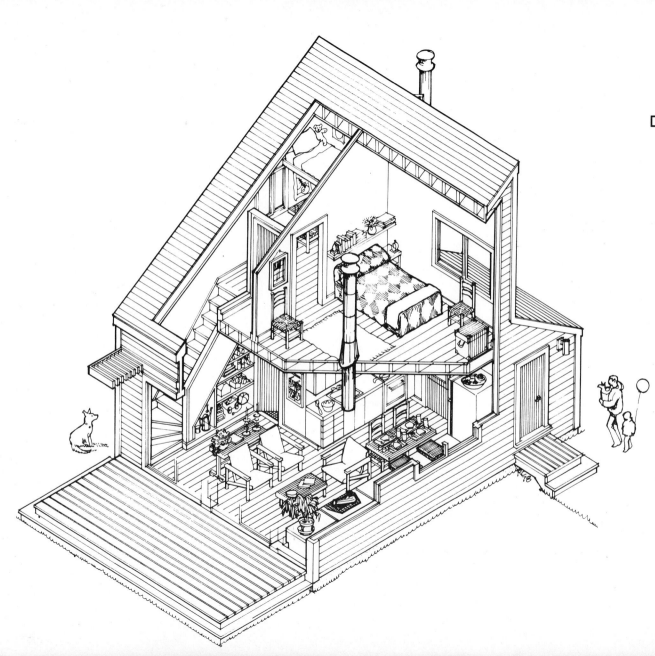

THE LITTLE HOUSE

Leslie Armstrong

COLLIER BOOKS
A Division of Macmillan Publishing Co., Inc.
New York

COLLIER MACMILLAN PUBLISHERS
London

Macmillan Publishing Co., Inc.
866 Third Avenue, New York, N.Y.   10022
Collier Macmillan Canada, Ltd.

Library of Congress Cataloging in Publication Data
Armstrong, Leslie, 1940–
    The little house.
    1. Dwellings—Designs and plans. 2. Summer houses—
Designs and plans. 3. Building materials. I. Title.
NA7125.A68   728.6   78–26641
ISBN 0–02–503230–5
ISBN 0–02–000080–4 pbk.

First Collier Books Edition 1979

Printed in the United States of America

The Little House is also published in a
hardcover edition by Macmillan Publishing Co., Inc.

For my children
Vanessa and Nino

and my quasi-children
Jenny, Ian, Becky and Lafcadio

and my friends
Annie and Michael

CONTENTS

ACKNOWLEDGMENTS

The Little House concept was born in 1970 when my friend, Annie Pfeifer, her friend Kristi Hager, and I were trying to figure out the absolute bare minimum house that each of them could build on their respective still-to-be-purchased plots of land near Wilmington, Delaware. C. Ray Smith, the architectural editor and critic, encouraged me to make drawings and models sufficiently detailed to qualify the Little House for a 1970 "Progressive Architecture" Design Award. We did not win anything, but we did have some fine ink drawings and little wood models to show for our efforts. Neither Annie nor Kristi ever bought their land, but Annie and C. Ray kept at me to find a format for making the Little House concept available to a wider audience—people like themselves. But I did not know how to begin, so I did nothing.

In 1974, James Taylor, one of the most sensitive and intelligent of my clients, came to our office apologetically asking for some information on prefab houses as he wanted to build something extremely simple for his sister. I was thrilled, told him to forget prefab, and blew the dust off the Little House plans and models. We messed with them a little, increased the house to its present size, added the shed at the rear, and talked a lot about solar and wind energy. In the meantime, his sister found a place of her own and the Little House went back in the drawer only to be half-heartedly resurrected on the occasions of Annie's periodic grumbling fits.

In the spring of 1978, my partners and I were working with Flory Barnett, a free-lance consultant, to develop a brochure to present the range of our capabilities, projects completed, and projects in the works to prospective clients. In the course of showing her our work I took out the Little House drawings and models and told her its history. Flory was fascinated and decided the vehicle for the Little House was a book. A week later off she went to Macmillan with a brochure of drawings, text, and photographs of the Little House —the brochure on the office would obviously have to wait!

Although the Little House book is one step removed from a finished building, we took it into our office as we would a bona fide architectural commission and there treated it to the full range of consulting engineers and experts that any other project would enjoy. Once we had the architectural problems worked out, we set about turning the Little House building into a book about building the Little House. I would like to take this opportunity to thank individually each person who contributed to this architecturally unconventional undertaking:

David Stein, who developed the construction drawings and details and wrote much of the text which accompanies them. Without his sensitivity both to architecture and to building, these drawings would be nothing more than an ordinary set of contract documents for an ordinary house;

Ana Marton, my architectural conscience and my right hand. Excepting the perspectives and the isometrics, almost all the final drawings which appear in this book are hers;

Russell Childs of Ives and Childs, Associated Architects, who did the renderings. His ability to capture the play of light on forms and surfaces and the movement of people through space can render the most abstract architectural concepts perceptible to anyone who cares to look;

Robert Silman of Robert Silman Associates, P.C., Structural Engineers, who has often worked harder supporting me than my architecture;

Valentine Lehr of Lehr Associates, Consulting Engineers, who contributed to the text of chapter 8, and who over the years has taught me what little I know about heating, ventilating, air conditioning, plumbing, electrical wiring, lightning rods, and the like;

Raymond Firmin of Hanscomb Associates, Cost Consultants, who researched the costs and prepared the list of materials, is the best best friend you can have if you are considering building anything from an outhouse to a lunar city;

Neil Murphy, whose clear and steady hand skillfully and patiently lettered all the drawings and charts;

Polly Eustis, who took time from her legal practice to translate my not-so-clear hand into a coherent typewritten manuscript;

Kirsten Childs and Jeremy Lang, my partners, who held the office together while the book was in the works;

Flory Barnett, my agent, who held me together while the book was in the works; and finally,

Ilka Shore Cooper, my editor at Macmillan, Helen Mills, the design manager, and Rusty Gutwillig, the production manager, who I know did not have an easy time with this first book of a nonwriter.

To each and all of you I express my warmest thanks and deepest appreciations.

THE LITTLE HOUSE

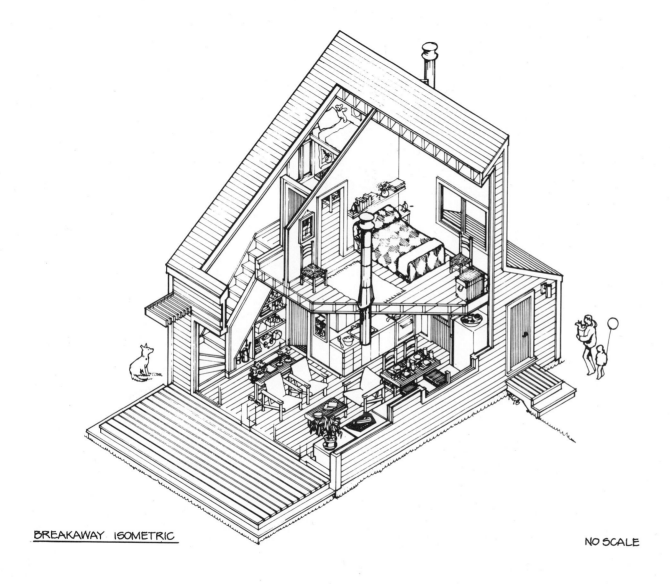

BREAKAWAY ISOMETRIC   NO SCALE

1

Introduction to the Little House

The Little House has been developed in response to the needs of young (and old and middle-aged) people who have scraped together just enough money to buy a bit of land next to a brook, by a lake, on top of a mountain, somewhere that spells peace. Then what?

The next step is to build a house, of course. But how? What will it cost? How big should it be, can it be? Who should build it? What will it look like?

If you care about design and want a part in determining your living environment, you should hire an architect. But the people for whom the Little House is conceived can afford neither the luxury of an architect nor the psychological and economic strain that accompanies the one-to-one relationship of architect and client.

The primary alternative is a prefabricated house, and many of the designs available are both sound and aesthetically pleasing. But by the time you're through modifying the prefab package, as you're encouraged to do by the manufacturer, you'll end up spending as much as if you'd started from scratch with your own architect. Furthermore, you still have had to deal with local builders for sitework, foundations, and in most cases, assembly of component parts.

The final recourse, and the one that most people take, is to go directly to a local builder. After all, he knows the area and the relevant building restrictions and regulations. More often than not, he and his competition are extremely skilled in one area or another. He knows materials and, more important, he knows what things cost. While he may not be too sensitive to the manipulation of form, space, and light, he probably has one or two stock plans that can be adapted. Perhaps he even has a registered architect working for him, or a tie-in with a prefab group. Although he may not generate an architectural masterpiece, it's a roof overhead.

The Little House book is intended to provide another alternative. It's not just a design for a house plus some "how-to-build-it" drawings; it's a process that permits you, the owner, as much participation in the design and construction of your own habitat as you are interested in and/or willing to take.

In itself, it's the absolute basic house. Its gently sloping shed roof can respond to a multitude of sites and site conditions. Within the twenty-foot square described by its four walls and shed roof, spaces to bathe, to cook, to eat, to sleep, to work, and to relax can be distributed in a number of different ways. This enclosure also includes the full complement of heating, plumbing, electricity, and ventilation. While the overall shape and dimensions of the basic Little House unit are fixed, and while we make very strong recommendations with regard to its orientation (the direction the Little House faces vis à vis the sun), and its fenestration (sizes and locations of windows), many of the critical aesthetic and functional

PERSPECTIVE VIEW FROM THE SOUTHEAST - BASIC LITTLE HOUSE

PERSPECTIVE VIEW FROM THE NORTHWEST - BASIC LITTLE HOUSE

decisions involved in designing and then building such a house are left to you, the potential owner and builder.

Your choice of materials can express your taste: the exterior can be sheathed in anything from the simplest boards and battens to sequin-studded stucco; the roof can be corrugated metal, asphalt shingles, or cedar shakes; the interior walls and ceiling can be gypsum board, rough-hewn pine strips, or, where climate permits, the studding can be left exposed; floors can be oak strips, quarry tile, or just plain linoleum; cabinetwork can be store-bought metal, custom wood veneer, or whatever you build best; appliances and plumbing fixtures can be selected from the top or bottom of the line.

The Little House is the "basic black dress" of housing. It looks as good in the morning as in the evening, with dime-store pearls or a diamond brooch.

There are several optional features you can add onto and/or delete from the basic Little House unit to adapt it to your particular site.

A small shed on the north side which protects the main door to the Little House from its northern exposure. When no basement is anticipated, the west end of the shed can be blocked off to accommodate a small boiler or furnace and a hot-water heater. In milder climates—where protection from the north is not essential—and there is no furnace or boiler to house at grade, the shed can be deleted altogether.

Add a partial or full basement under the shed or under the Little House itself, should site or soil conditions warrant, or if additional space is desired.

3

A sun screen, or "brise soleil," projects over the big sliding doors on the south facade to protect the Little House from too much summer sun. But in many applications and climates this will not be required.

In response to those sites which have either one particular view to capture or one to avoid, the slope of the roof can be reversed so that the principal spaces are oriented in a single direction.

In addition to desiring the basic space and amenities for living, you probably want a house that can grow with you. The geometry of the Little House is such that two or more units can be combined contiguously in a variety of ways to form new and enlarged structures of different shapes and configurations that relate to different kinds of landscapes and settings. Six examples are offered in chapter 4, "Combinations and Permutations." If you need more than the 880 gross square feet (81.75 square meters) of a single Little House unit plus shed, you can build two Little House units simultaneously. Otherwise you may add one later as you need. As all the utilities are concentrated in the basic unit, the second unit will be much less expensive to build than the first.

The Little House book is organized to give you as much information as possible about its design and construction and to encourage you to do as much of the work as you like or dare. The order in which the information appears parallels the conventional division of building materials and trades within the industry itself. While the drawings are to scale and as complete as any set of drawings can be, they have been done freehand.

INTERIOR PERSPECTIVE - BASIC LITTLE HOUSE

We feel that the hand-drawn line, for all its vagaries, invites you to enter a drawing, to explore its content, and to examine its detail. A hard line or ruled drawing, however impressive technically, is ultimately intimidating, particularly to the layman. As the purpose of this book is to encourage your participation in the design and construction processes, we can't afford to lose you in a display of technical draftsmanship, however spectacular.

This book does not include a set of conventional specifications that you can rip out and hand to a builder because the scale of the construction contract for one or two Little House units does not warrant such detail. However, in the great scheme of things, "specs," as they are called, are not without their purpose. They spell out controls for the purchase of materials and for the method and quality of the fabrication of the component parts of a building. But that is precisely what the text of this book accomplishes. You're warned what to look out for when shopping for materials, appliances, and the like. You're offered alternative ways of assembling parts, your evaluation of which will depend in some cases on your economic means and in others on your aesthetic ends.

In most instances, shortcuts are discouraged. Key to us, and we hope to you, are quality of construction and integrity of materials, i.e., when you use plastic, let it look like plastic and not like phony wood veneer; when you use linoleum or vinyl asbestos tile, let it read as tile and not marble. We are very big on longevity, too. The shape of the Little House has been around since Euclid;

the building itself should be able to withstand the wind and weather for several decades. Thus recommendations will focus on the most for the money over the long haul. When we shift our focus, we spell out why.

Throughout the text you're apprised of the existence of local building codes and zoning regulations, of the need to have the plans for your Little House approved by governing authorities, of the possibility that the 880 gross square feet (81.75 square meters) of a single Little House unit plus shed may be below the permissible minimum in some suburban and/or quasi-suburban communities.

There is a general discussion of foundations, drainage, and the like. Then one foundation condition is drawn up in some detail in order to give at least one picture of how the Little House meets the ground. *However, you're strongly directed not to build your foundations from these drawings but to seek local advice from a professional engineer regarding the bearing capacity of the soil, its drainage, and the type of foundation that would be suitable.* Once the Little House is out of the ground, that is, once its foundations have been designed to meet the specific requirements of your site, we have tried in our drawings to allow for all other contingencies that would affect its safety and stability, i.e., hurricane force winds along the east coast, tornadoes in the plains, earthquakes in California, super snow loads in the north. *However, we cannot have foreseen them all. Thus even if there are no zoning restrictions or apparent authorities governing building practices where you are planning to build, you*

PERSPECTIVE - UNITS A & B ONLY - COMBINATION 6

PERSPECTIVE - UNITS B & C ONLY - COMBINATION 6

must, for your own protection, have these drawings re-viewed by a local professional engineer and/or builder. In the chapter on heating, plumbing, and electricity, the specific information is presented in a similarly general fashion to compel you to take advantage of local exper-tise in these areas.

The reason for this seeming passing of responsibility from the editorial "we" to your local professional engineer and/or builder is that no one is qualified to take responsibility for the soundness and safety of a particular structure except a professional engineer or architect licensed in the state where the building is to be built. By the same token, no one can take responsi-bility for its being built in conformity with local codes except contractors, plumbers, and electricians licensed in that area.

This constitutes a disclaimer. While directives to seek local expertise will be repeated in other chapters, this disclaimer will not; however, it will be implicit through-out. If this is understood, please proceed to enjoy planning and building your Little House as much as we have enjoyed designing it for you.

2

Design for a Little House

The Little House is as small as it can be while still providing adequate space—20'0" (6.1 m.) square. It has a single shed roof sloping from 13'0" (4 m.) above the ground on the south side to 24'0" (7.3 m.) above the ground on the north. The slope is 30 degrees because it gives the Little House a strong profile without being too severe, and because it's a slope common to the roofs of many off-the-shelf components you might use in conjunction with the Little House—greenhouse connectors and the like.

The drawings for the basic Little House are presented in the conventional order. First come the floor plans, then the sections. These are vertical slices through the building at critical points. Where these slices have been taken is indicated on the plans by little flags (or they may look like arrows to you) near the margin. If more than one section has been taken, the flags and corresponding sections are labeled A and B. The elevations follow at a smaller scale.

The Little House is square for two reasons, the first being that a square is the rectangle describing the largest area with the smallest perimeter. Thus we enclose the maximum floor area with the minimum, most cost efficient wall surface. The second reason is that in plan

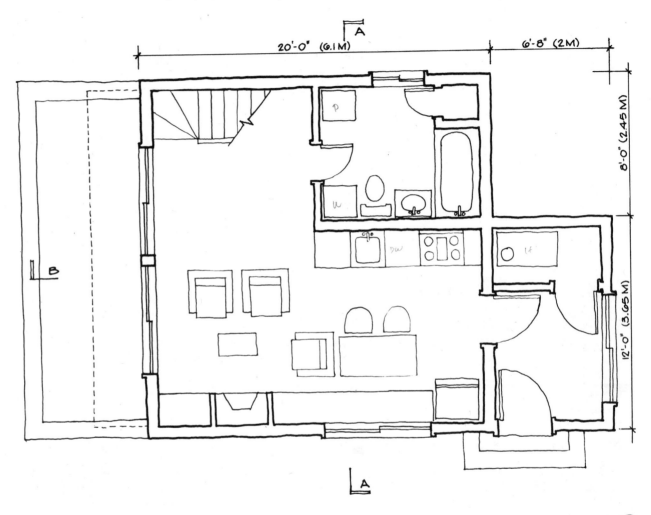

GROUND FLOOR PLAN - BASIC LITTLE HOUSE

3/16"-1'-0"

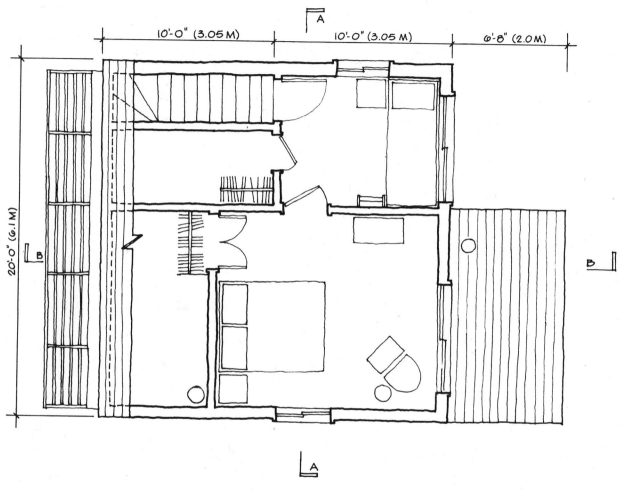

10'-0" (3.05 M) 10'-0" (3.05 M) 6'-8" (2.0 M)

20'-0" (6.1 M)

A

B

B

A

SECOND FLOOR PLAN - BASIC LITTLE HOUSE

3/16" = 1'-0"

a square is nondirectional; all four sides are equal. Therefore you can juxtapose two Little House units by butting the roofs head-on for one kind of effect, staggering them in parallel for another, or sliding them by one another in opposition for a third without drastically disrupting the flow of the floor plan—indicated diagrammatically in the last drawing in this chapter. The plan of the Little House alone or in combination with a second unit is not intended to be dramatic; it is intended to work. But the massing, the exterior profile, should have the capacity to express your own sense of what a house should be and what best becomes your site—be it subdued and intimate or outrageous and daring.

The Little House is 20'0" (6.1 m.) square because less would enclose too little space to accommodate the basic living requirements for two people, and more would involve waste in exterior cladding—most materials come in 4'0" (1.2 m.) widths. The exterior walls are approximately 8" (20 cm.) thick to allow for 6" (15 cm.) of insulation between the vertical framing members, known as studs. Therefore you have close to 19'0" (5.8 m.) clear in each direction on the inside. The gross square footage of a single unit is 800 square feet (75 square meters). If the area of the 12'0" by 6'8" (3.6 m. by 2.0 m.) shed shown to the north is included, the total is 880 gross square feet (81.75 gross square meters). Although the shed is an optional feature, we're showing it as part of the basic Little House because we can envision very few instances in which it would not be desirable, if not necessary.

As you can see from the ground-floor plan, you enter

the house through the shed, which is strictly utilitarian. If there is to be a heating system but no basement to house it (which is what we are assuming in this presentation), a partition encloses that system at the west end. The shed can also house tools, a limited supply of firewood, muddy boots, and pegs for hanging wet clothes. From here you go directly to the center of any house, namely, the kitchen. Apart from the window in the shed, there are no openings at this level on the north facade; thus cars can be parked and tools piled up on this side of the house without their being the first thing visible from every window.

The kitchen might seem large for a house this size, but it's the center of the house—and a house in the country at that. Apart from the refrigerator, shown along the east wall adjacent to the 6'0" (1.8 m.) wide window located to catch the morning sun, everything else is lined up along the west wall, which is the "wet" wall, so called because it houses all the plumbing. A full-size range, dishwasher, and 2'0" (60 cm.) wide sink are shown, as well as cabinets above and below. Needless to say you can eliminate the tray-storage unit at the end or use a smaller range if you want a larger sink. You can eliminate the dishwasher entirely. These and other alternatives will be covered in "Alternate Materials and Equipment."

To the left of the refrigerator you can see a low bench 2'1" (65 cm.) deep with storage drawers below. Like so many other features of the Little House it isn't mandatory, but it has its virtues, especially if you are building only one Little House unit to start with. In

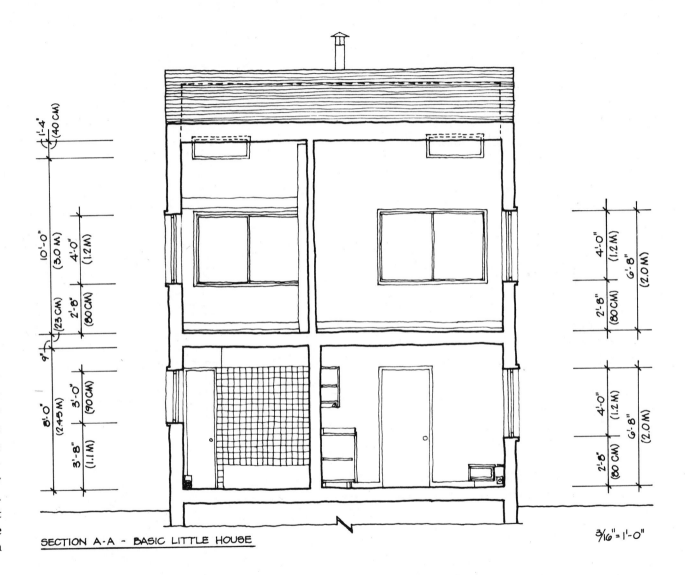

SECTION A-A - BASIC LITTLE HOUSE

3/16" = 1'-0"

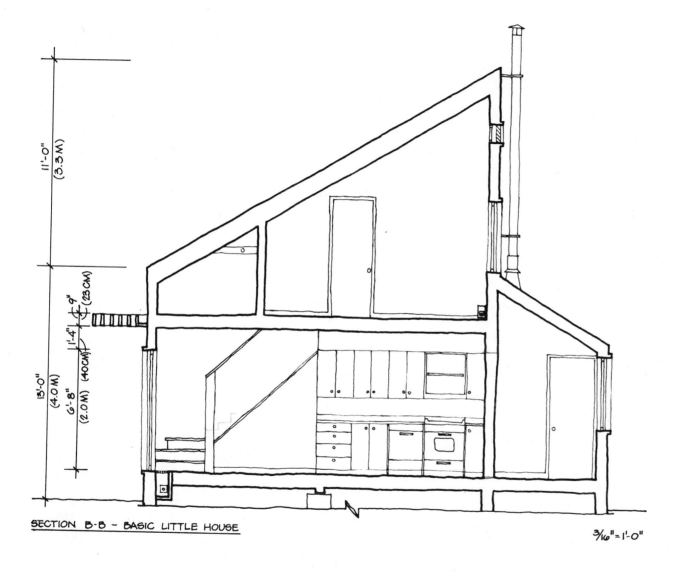

the kitchen area it serves as a banquette for the kitchen table. Combined with the adjacent section, it can double as a child's bunk. Finally, firewood can be stacked on the section to the right of the fireplace. If your preference is for a full-height wood-burning stove, you should eliminate the bench altogether, let the stove stand on a noncombustible pad on the floor, and use freestanding furniture for seating and storage.

Back to back with the kitchen is the bathroom, another seemingly oversized space given the overall size of the Little House itself. Referring to the ground-floor plan, you can see that it has the full complement of bathroom fixtures lined up along the wet wall. In addition, it can have either a stacking space-saver-type washer/dryer in the southeast corner or the washer in that corner and the dryer in the southwest corner, the dryer venting directly to the outside. A linen closet is also provided at the foot of the tub. If the shed is not built, as neither central heating nor protection from the weather at the entrance is desired, the linen closet may have to house the hot-water heater too. It could also be housed under the stair. Even if you opt not to include the clothes washer and dryer in the bathroom because you're building a basement and want them there instead, or just because you want to use the space for a vanity or a bidet, so big a bathroom is not exaggerated for a one-bathroom house. In most contemporary residential construction, bathrooms seem to be regarded only as necessary evils and are afforded the bare minimum of thought and square footage. But the fact is that we all spend a lot of time in the bathroom each day, and we

11

deserve space and accommodations commensurate with that time.

The most gracious features of the living area are the warm south light streaming through the big 6'0" (1.8 m.) wide sliding doors and the ease of access to the exterior. Our drawings show an optional 3'0" deep (90 cm.) brise soleil above these doors to protect them from the summer sun. It consists of a wood trellis created by extending some of the north-south floor joists through the exterior and running members of the same depth between them in the east-west direction (see the second-floor plan). From this trellis-cum-pergola anything from grapes to children's playthings can be hung.

Not only should this facade of the Little House face south when possible, it must also open onto the view. If you don't have a view in this or any direction, make one by defining and then enclosing the space onto which these doors give out. Use wood decking, a paved terrace, seating, low walls, and/or found objects and, of course, planting. There are many ways to create a focus, a vista, even on the smallest of plots. If this is all new to you, study how your neighbors have treated the land around their houses. Look up back issues of *House Beautiful* or *House and Garden* to see how and with what materials and plants other small houses have been landscaped in your part of the country.

Our drawings show a simple 6'0" (1.8 m.) deep deck projecting beyond the Little House to indicate this intent. But it is really up to you to design what happens on this side of the house and to select materials in

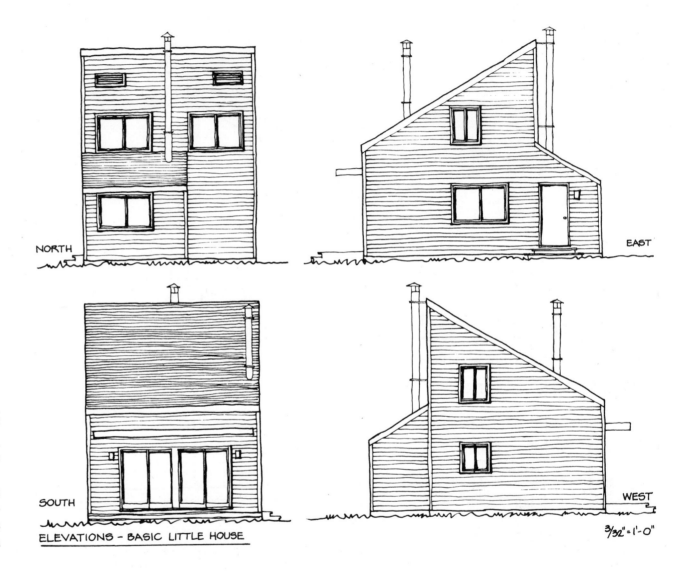

NORTH

EAST

SOUTH

WEST

ELEVATIONS - BASIC LITTLE HOUSE

3/32" = 1'-0"

NORTH

EAST

SOUTH

WEST

ELEVATIONS - UNOFFICIAL LITTLE HOUSE

3/32" = 1'-0"

response to your particular situation.

The stairs are at the west end of the living area. In order to fit a proper stair into this very short horizontal run, we have had to provide three "winders" at the bottom, i.e., steps which turn you 90 degrees. This kind of stair is comfortable, but it's also complicated to construct. If you don't mind a steeper stair—much like those found in many old colonial farm houses—and if such a stair is legal in your area, you can save yourself a lot of trouble by building it in a straight run. This alternative is shown in the ground-floor plan of the unofficial Little House.

In either case, the stairs open directly into a small room—bedroom, workroom, dressing room, or study— the exact size of the bathroom below. The main bedroom and a large storage closet also open onto this room. It has 3'0" (90 cm.) wide windows on the west wall and the potential of building a 3'0" (90 cm.) wide sleeping loft over the 6'0" (1.8 m.) wide window on the north (see second-floor plan). If you decide to build a second Little House unit and want to add a second bathroom as part of the expansion, this little room can easily be converted into a second bathroom (as discussed in chapter 4, Combination 6, unit C). However, the wide north window must be reduced to half its size and the roughing brought up from the bathroom below and capped at the time the initial Little House is built.

The sloped ceiling and the overall proportions of the main room upstairs reflect the appearance of the entire Little House. The large window on the north wall gives good light for working. However, there is plenty of space on either side (as can be seen in section A-A) to draw aside heavy curtains that will keep out the winter's cold and draft. The small window on the east wall provides cross ventilation. Storage for this room is behind the low wall to the south. Where you put the openings in this wall depends on how the room is to be used and hence furnished. The openings shown assume its use as a master bedroom.

How did the plan for the basic Little House unit evolve? How did partitions and openings come to be located where they are? The answer to both is, as a direct result of an exhaustive examination of the functions certain spaces had to perform, their requirements vis à vis the exterior, and their need to bend and flex as the area is expanded by the addition of a second unit. Further examination of where partitions wanted to fall, followed by a certain amount of gentle jiggling, led to the establishment of a design grid. This is a network of invisible lines that we have used to organize the location of secondary elements such as door and window openings, paths of circulation, and the like.

As you've seen, the Little House is based on a 20-foot square. On all four faces, a nominal 8" is allowed for each exterior wall, and another 8" (20 cm.) is allowed for an intermediate partition or support, as illustrated on the diagrammatic design grid. On the east, south, and west faces, these are located on the center lines, leaving 9'0" (2.75 m.) clear on either side. Each of these bays is then subdivided into three bays, each 3'0" (90 cm.) wide. The 3'0" (90 cm.) grid determines the precise position of window and door openings in the ex-

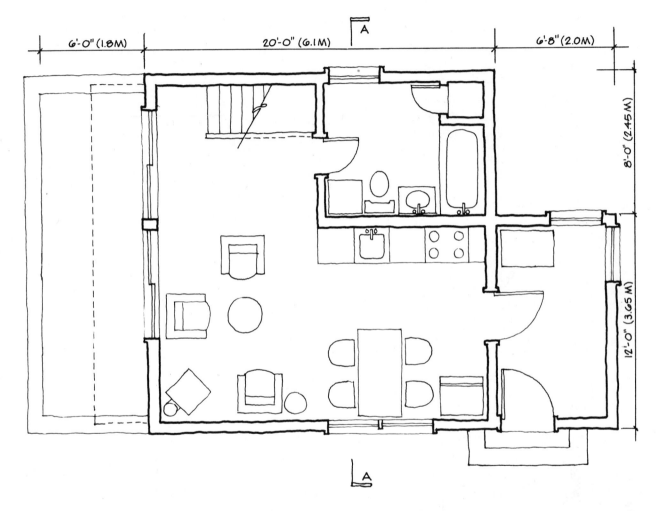

6'-0" (1.8M)   20'-0" (6.1M)   6'-8" (2.0M)

8'-0" (2.45 M)

12'-0" (3.65 M)

GROUND FLOOR PLAN - UNOFFICIAL LITTLE HOUSE

3/16" = 1'-0"

14

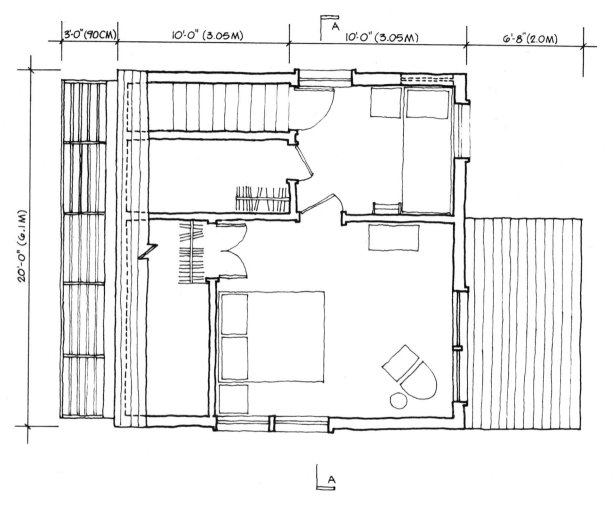

3'-0"(90CM) | 10'-0" (3.05M) | 10'-0" (3.05M) | 6'-8" (2.0M)

A

20'-0" (6.1M)

A

SECOND FLOOR PLAN - UNOFFICIAL LITTLE HOUSE

3/16"=1'-0"

terior walls. The windows and sliding glass doors we specify in our basic unit come in multiples of 3'0" (90 cm.). You may choose not to use these; those you do use may come in different sizes. But if you center the openings on these bays, you'll still achieve the order, clarity, and harmony which we feel to be vital, especially in so small a building.

The larger 9'0" (2.75 m.) bays with their 8" (20 cm.) strips on either side permit two Little House units to be built not only side by side or back to back but also staggered by half the length of one side. The intermediate 8" (20 cm.) strip of one unit takes up the thickness of the exterior wall of the other, and the 3'0" (90 cm.) grids of both units align where they interface; therefore so can common structural members and connecting openings.

There's nothing inherently magic about this 3'0" (90 cm.) grid; it's simply a convenient tool. Most doors and windows will fit within 3'0" (90 cm.) clear. When a more critical consideration arises, we're happy to put our 3'0" (90 cm.) grid aside, as indeed we have done on the north face. Had we adhered to the grid here, the kitchen and bathroom and the two upstairs bedrooms would have had to be the same size. We felt it was more important to avoid waste of exterior cladding. Thus the shed was made 12'0" (3.6 m.) wide leaving 8'0" (2.4 m.) beyond, each dimension being a clean multiple of the standard 4'0" (1.2 m.) width of siding. And the 8" (20 cm.) strip was allowed to fall within the 12'0" (3.6 m.), as indicated on the diagram of the grid. The 6'0" (1.8 m.) wide windows were then adjusted to this spacing, as is the extent to which two Little Houses coming together on the high side are staggered. This talk of staggering units will be much clearer when you get into "Combinations and Permutations."

Vertically, the grid relates to an 8'0" (2.45 m.) floor-to-ceiling height, again, a standard height for interior finish materials, and within that limit an equally standard 6'8" (2 m.) height for all door openings. Windowsill heights vary from 2'10" (85 cm.) to 3'10" (1.15 m.) A.F.F. (above finished floor), but the tops of the windows align with door openings at 6'8" (2 m.) A.F.F. Trim around doors and windows is to be approximately 2" (5 cm.) For reasons we've never understood, window and door heights generally don't align in most residential construction: windows are almost always a few inches higher than doors, and trim for doors and windows differ slightly.

Having explained the grid to you and shown you where we've cast it aside, we'd like to encourage you to take your own liberties: install the stained glass windows from your grandmother's house instead of those we specified; use an arched opening instead of a rectangular one; install the carved rosewood door you bought at auction, and so on. To illustrate this point we've prepared plans and elevations of an unofficial Little House in which we've taken a few liberties ourselves. In plan, only the suggested furniture layout differs. But in elevation, windows and doors of a multitude of sizes and shapes are jumping all over the place. Taking this and other kinds of license with its plans, sections, elevations, and materials is half of what the

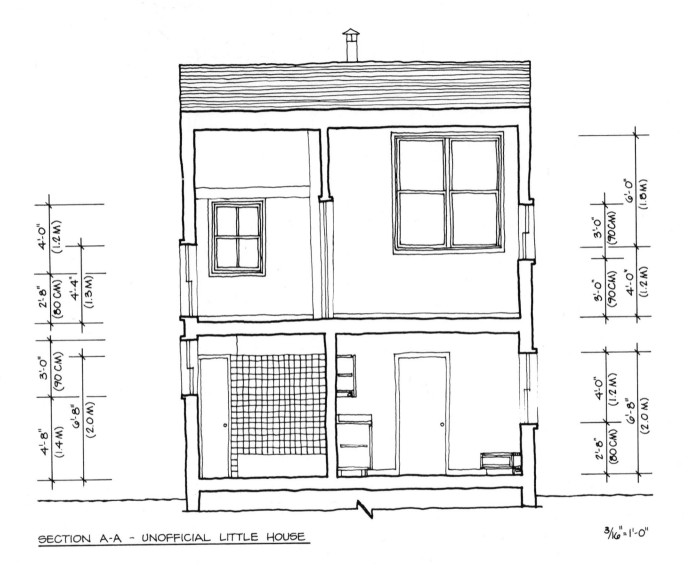

SECTION A-A - UNOFFICIAL LITTLE HOUSE

3/16" = 1'-0"

16

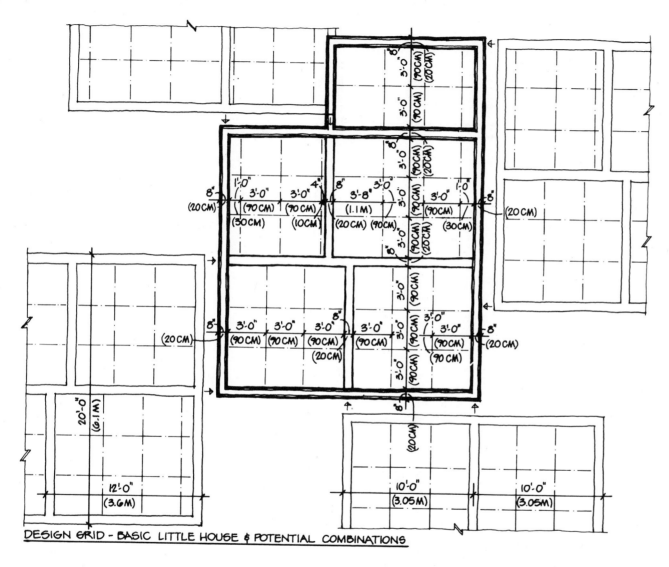

8" (20CM) 1'-0" (30CM) 3'-0" (90CM) 3'-0" (90CM) 4" (10CM) 8" (20CM) 3'-8" (1.1M) 3'-0" (90CM) 3'-0" (90CM) 1'-0" (30CM) 8" (20CM)

8" (20CM) 3'-0" (90CM) 3'-0" (90CM) 3'-0" (90CM) 8" (20CM) 3'-0" (90CM) 3'-0" (90CM) 3'-0" (90CM) 8" (20CM)

3'-0" (90CM) 5'-0" (1.5M) 3'-0" (90CM) 3'-0" (90CM) 3'-0" (90CM) 3'-0" (90CM) 3'-0" (90CM)

(20CM) (20CM)

20'-0" (6.1M) 12'-0" (3.6M)

10'-0" (3.05M) 10'-0" (3.05M)

DESIGN GRID - BASIC LITTLE HOUSE & POTENTIAL COMBINATIONS

Little House is about. But you'll have a lot more fun breaking the rules and will come up with a much better result if you understand the nature of the game you're playing in the first place.

Some mention should be made of the size and scale of the drawings as they appear here and in subsequent chapters. Most architectural plans for a house such as this would be at $\frac{1}{4}'' = 1'0''$, with the less detailed drawings at $\frac{1}{8}'' = 1'0''$. But given the page size within which we're working, normal scale is not feasible. Thus most plans and critical sections are drawn at $\frac{3}{16}'' = 1'0''$. Elevations are drawn at half that size, namely, $\frac{3}{32}'' = 1'0''$. In any case, the scale of each drawing is indicated at the lower right-hand corner together with an encircled arrow indicating which direction should be north. To facilitate your efforts, go to any drafting supply store and buy a triangular architectural ruler or scale. Both scales run along one edge. The larger scales at which detailed drawings are presented in subsequent chapters can be read off the other edges.

In this chapter and the two that follow, overall dimensions are given in feet and inches as well as in meters. The metric dimensions are approximate conversions. No effort has been made to coordinate these metric dimensions with metric building standards or construction systems. In the more technical chapters, dimensions are given only in feet and inches.

3

Variations on a Theme

While the basic Little House unit is equally suited to stand on its own or to be combined with a second Little House to form a larger house, and while its massing—its size, shape and profile—is suited to a multitude of uses and site conditions, the flexibility of its interior layout is more restricted. In our attempt to cover the principal uses and/or site conditions which require substantial adjustment to the interior plan, we've developed some variations on the Little House theme. Each involves certain changes to the elevations of the basic unit, and in some instances additional optional modifications are offered. Each such unit can be combined with a second unit, as can the basic Little House unit. As with the basic Little House, each variation is shown first in plan, then section, then elevation.

THE LITTLE HOUSE GARAGE
800 gross square feet (74.30 square meters)

The first variation is geared more toward expanding an existing setup than building the most for the least on virgin soil. It's presumed you've already bought or built a house for yourself and now wish to house—under a separate roof—your car, your kid's car, or some kind of mechanical equipment. And you wouldn't mind acquir-

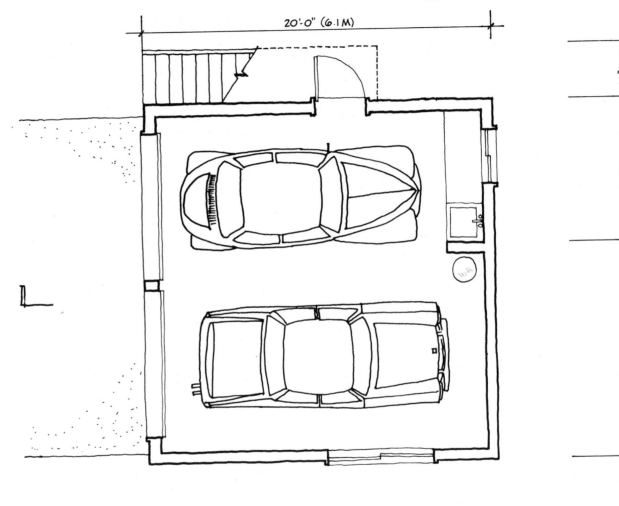

GROUND FLOOR PLAN - LITTLE HOUSE GARAGE

3/16" = 1'-0"

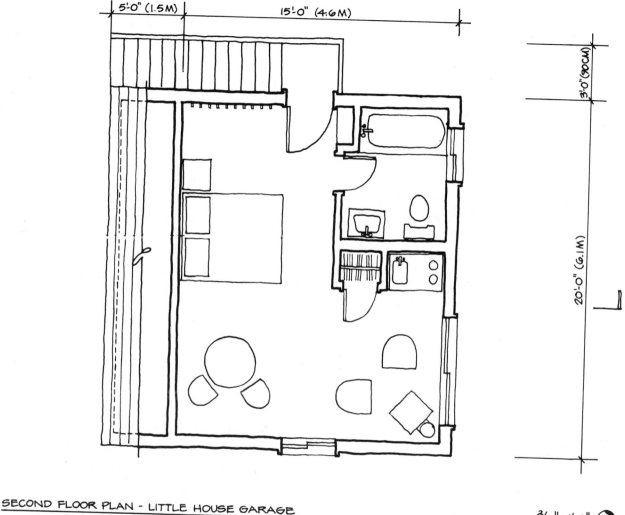

5'-0" (1.5M) 15'-0" (4.6M)

3'-0" (90CM)

20'-0" (6.1M)

SECOND FLOOR PLAN - LITTLE HOUSE GARAGE

3/16" = 1'-0"

ing some additional space for a workshop, for housing weekend guests, or just for storage. It's also presumed that you aren't trying to house a Lincoln Continental, length almost 21'0" (6.4 m.), or a Checker limousine, length in excess of 22'0" (6.7 m.) because if you are, they won't fit. If your taste runs to smaller cars, the Little House garage is the perfect answer. Its shape is simple enough to work well with any other buildings on your property whatever their architecture. You can reinforce the correlation by cladding the Little House garage in the same siding material as the other buildings, using the same kind of roofing, window and door types, trim, and exterior color scheme.

As shown in the garage's ground-floor plan, the two 6'0" (1.8 m.) wide sliding doors on the south facade have been replaced by two equally standard 8'0" (2.4 m.) wide counterweighted overhead doors. If you're sticking with the bronze anodized aluminum windows specified for the Little House unit, these doors can also be had in this finish, or they can be hinged pairs of wood doors made from tongue and groove wood boards, Z-braced on the inside, just like old barn doors.

To the north the shed has been deleted; so much heat is lost by raising the garage door that the question of building a vestibule to the north to retain the heat each time a person enters is rendered absurd. However, if additional storage is in order, it might well be included. In lieu of the stair along the inside of the west wall, a steep stair to the second floor has been provided on the exterior so as not to clutter the open floor. If you're reasonably certain that whatever car or machine you

19

intend to house in the west bay of the garage is narrower than 6'8" (2 m.), you could build a fixed stair exactly like the stair in the basic Little House unit only 8" (20 cm.) narrower, i.e., 2'4" (70 cm.) overall.

Along the north wall of the garage is a work sink and a hot-water heater which could be combined with a boiler, should this building require its own heating system. A small window is shown over the sink, and the door is located under the exterior stair landing.

In this particular variation the orientation of the Little House is of secondary importance. The high side faces north only for consistency of presentation. There's no compelling reason for the garage doors to open south, nor for the upstairs to face north. You must orient the Little House garage so that it best fits your site. If you wish to flip the east and west facades in response to the proximity of the main house, a potential view, or whatever, do so. If your revised fenestration is in keeping with the design grid explained at the end of chapter 2, you have a good chance of coming up with a functioning interior and an aesthetically pleasing exterior.

On the second floor, the plan shows an L-shaped room with its own freestanding fireplace or stove, a mini-kitchenette, closet, and full bath. You aren't required to install any of these amenities; the upper floor might just as well be a single open space. However, it's been shown this way to indicate just how much can be done with a space that seems so small.

If a second upstairs bathroom were to be added to the basic Little House unit, as suggested in the second chapter, it would have the same plan and be in the

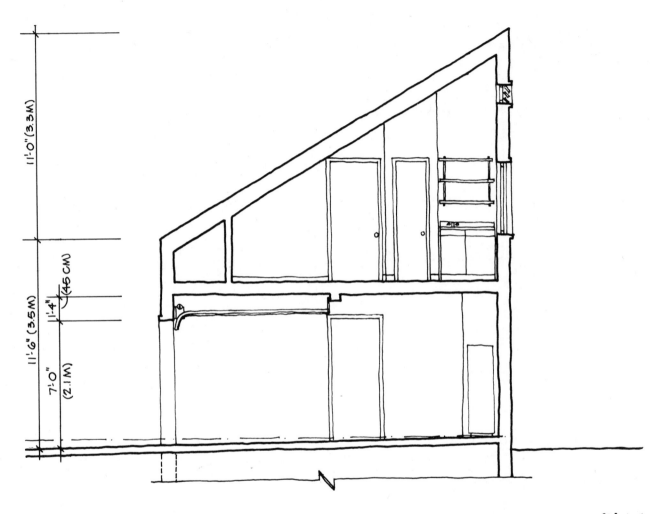

SECTION - LITTLE HOUSE GARAGE

3/16" = 1'-0"

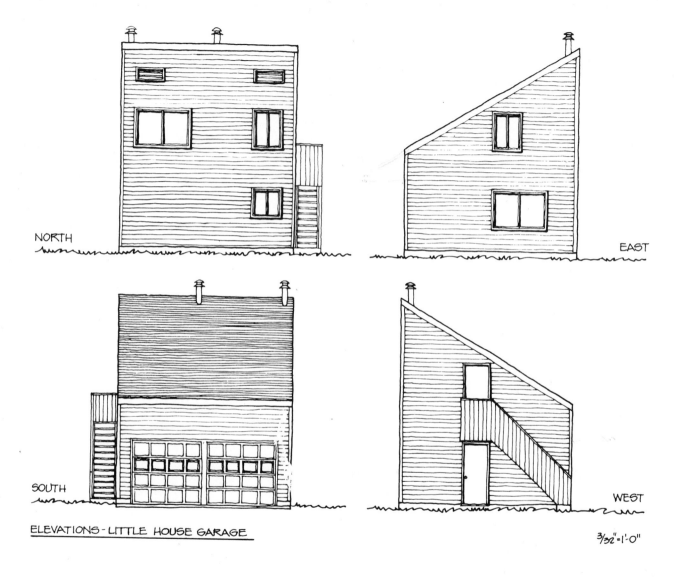

NORTH

EAST

SOUTH

WEST

ELEVATIONS - LITTLE HOUSE GARAGE

3/32" = 1'-0"

same location as it appears in the Little House garage. Furthermore, if the addition of such a bathroom is anticipated, and certainly in this case where one is shown, the 6'0" (1.8 m.) wide sliding window on the north facade should be reduced in a 3'0" (90 cm.) wide window and the 3'0" (90 cm.) window on the west facade eliminated altogether.

The second unfamiliar element in this variation is the pullman kitchen. This may not be required at all, but in the event it is, a 2'0" (60 cm.) deep pocket should be built to receive a standard-sized 3'6" (1.05 m.) long unit by Acme or Dwyer or a comparable manufacturer. These units can be bought with matching overhead cabinets. However, the cabinet tops won't align with the tops of the doors in the room because the cabinets sit above a metal backsplash, which spaces them at a fixed distance above the lower unit. This discrepancy in height looks very awkward. Thus on the second-floor plan we show open shelves above. You could as well build your own cabinets above.

THE LITTLE HOUSE STUDIO
700 gross square feet (65.0 square meters)

The ground-floor plan of the Little House studio is similar to that of the Little House garage in that it is a single open space uninterrupted by partitions or columns. The principal distinction between this and all other Little House units is that the second floor extends only halfway across the building, thus providing the

21

south half of the ground floor with a double-height ceiling and slightly reducing the gross square footage. A closet or larder and a 5'0" (1.5 m.) wide recessed pullman kitchen unit slightly larger than the one shown upstairs in the Little House garage lines the north wall. The bathroom is upstairs as with the garage and there is only one sleeping area. In this configuration the bedroom, or more appropriately the sleeping loft, and gallery leading to it open onto the main space below.

Of all the Little House variations, this seems the most spacious with its unobstructed ground floor, the loft opening onto it from above, and the slope of the roof rising overhead. (The difference is evident if you compare the studio's section to that of the others.) The seating is clustered around the fireplace or stove, this time in the northeast corner instead of the southeast. Cooking and dining areas are distributed under the loft at the north, leaving the double-height area to the south —including a reasonably large expanse of wall area to the east—free for painting, sculpting, potting, print-making, weaving, or whatever.

If large amounts of open floor area are not as important to you as ample space for sitting, cooking and dining, the full complement of kitchen cabinets and appliances can be situated against the north and west walls, until they intersect the stair, and a round table placed in the middle of this enlarged kitchen. The fireplace can return to the location in which it's shown in the basic Little House and more than enough chairs and sofas clustered around it. We don't show this configuration simply because we can't show everything. But if it

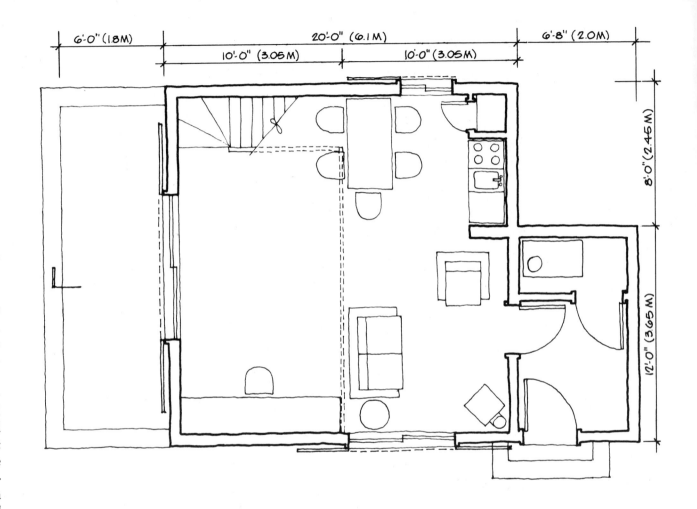

GROUND FLOOR PLAN - LITTLE HOUSE STUDIO

3/16" = 1'-0"

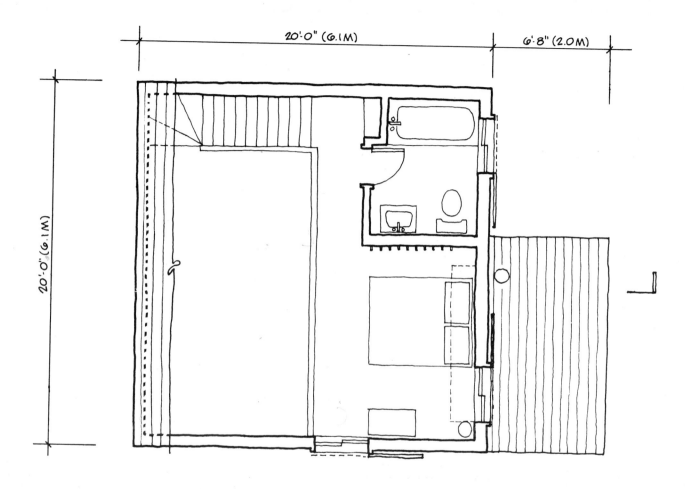

20'-0" (6.1 M)   6'-8" (2.0 M)

20'-0" (6.1 M)

SECOND FLOOR PLAN – LITTLE HOUSE STUDIO

3/16" = 1'-0"

interests you, lay some tracing paper over our drawings and from what you've already learned to be the components of a kitchen and living space, do some layouts for yourself.

As you can see from the elevations, for the exterior we've indicated a window treatment which need not be unique to this variation but can be applied to any of the Little House units, alone or in combination with each other. This is the use of sliding barn-door-type shutters at all glazed openings to reduce heat loss and protect the Little House from vandalism durings periods of extended absence. In the warmer sections of the country, instead of being opaque these shutters could be louvered, then drawn across the open windows during the hottest periods of the day to reduce heat gain. This type of shutter is used extensively in the Mediterranean and Latin American countries and might well be adapted to our southern climes.

In order to accommodate these shutters on the exterior, certain minor modifications must be made to the fenestration.

On the studio's ground floor the window on the north facade of the shed must be deleted entirely as there is no wall space above it to mount the shutter track.

A single 8'0" (2.4 m.) wide pair of sliding doors must replace the two pairs of 6'0" (1.8 m.) doors, again to leave space at the sides for the big shutters when they are in the open position.

On the second floor, both 6'0" (1.8 m.) wide windows on the north facade must be reduced to 3'0" (90 cm.). The west window would already have been reduced because of the substitution of the bathroom for the smaller sleeping area.

If you aren't interested in using shutters, the fenestration of this variation is identical to that of the basic Little House except for the substitution of the 3'0" (90 cm.) window for the 6'0" (1.8 m.) window on the north wall of the upstairs bath. The deletion of the west window in the upstairs bath and the replacement of the 3'0" (90 cm.) high window with a 4'0" (1.2 m.) high window on the north end of the west wall are as per the Little House garage.

While this variation certainly has its appeal, it has its disadvantages as well. The upstairs bath is neither as large nor as flexible as the bathroom in the basic unit. There's no space for laundry equipment. There's only one sleeping area and it isn't very large. There's almost no storage. And, as you can see in the section, in this version there's very little privacy.

These last two problems can be redressed in part by installing a series of sliding screens on top of the gallery rail, or by simply extending the partition that forms the rail up to the ceiling, or a combination of both as we show in Combination 5 in the next chapter. Space for laundry equipment and storage can be found in a full or partial basement accessible either from outside or from a stair beneath the stair up to the loft. But there is little that can be done to the bath. The final problem is that heat generated from the ground floor rises quickly and travels up along the slope of the ceiling only to get trapped in the peak above the loft. Unless a fan is installed to recirculate the warm air

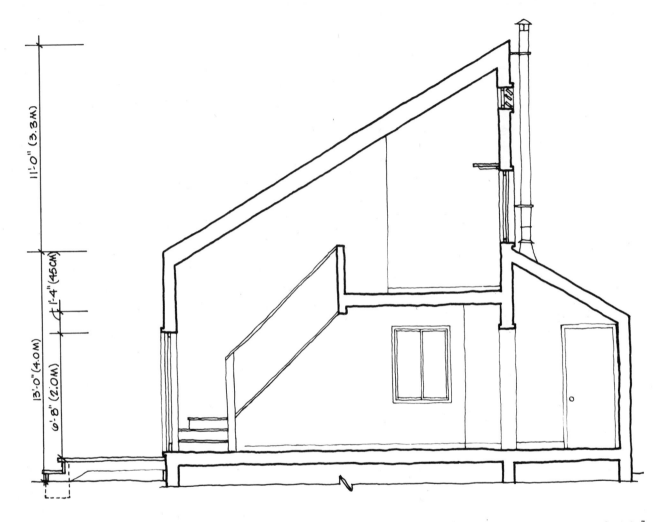

SECTION - LITTLE HOUSE STUDIO

3/16" = 1'-0"

24

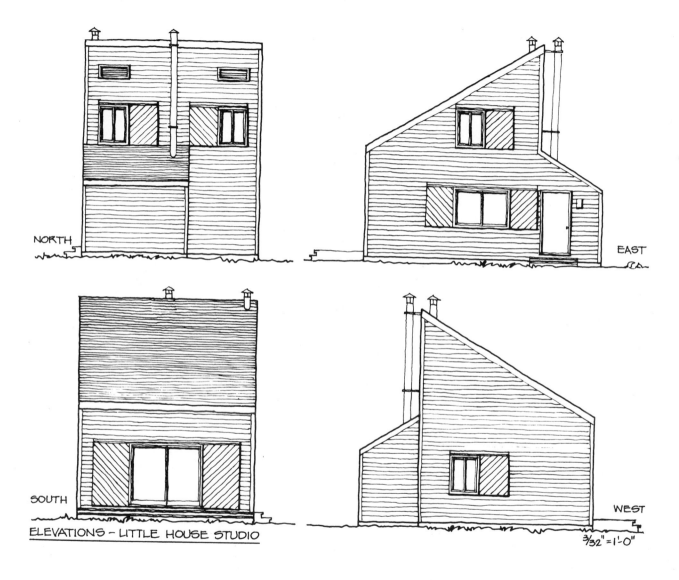

NORTH

EAST

SOUTH

WEST

ELEVATIONS - LITTLE HOUSE STUDIO

3/32" = 1'-0"

back down, neither the ground floor nor the loft will be adequately heated.

You'll notice in the next chapter that the second Little House unit suggested in several of the combinations is very much like the Little House studio except that it has no plumbing and in most cases (except unit B, Combination 6) a full second floor. It has no plumbing to save on its cost. But if the additional expense doesn't worry you, there's no reason you couldn't substitute a Little House studio—sans kitchen but with bath—for this second unit, should it suit your specific needs.

THE LITTLE HOUSE REVERSED
880 gross square feet (81.75 square meters)

For a number of reasons such as prevailing winds, a particular view, proximity of another house, or of a road, there will be some sites that demand that all the major spaces be oriented in a single direction, which for the purpose of this exercise we have selected to be south. Thus we have developed the Little House reversed, in which the high point of the roof is at the south rather than the north. As you can see in both the section and the elevations, as it slopes down towards the north, it picks up the little shed on its way, making for a kind of saltbox profile.

Needless to say, certain changes in plan result from this reversal of roof pitch, not the least of which is the flipping of the plan in the east-west direction so that the shed is at the west end of the north facade and the bathroom faces east, rather than the reverse. This isn't

25

absolutely necessary, but it permits the second window in the living area to face east, thus admitting the morning sun instead of the relentless afternoon sun that would stream through a large western exposure. Should site conditions warrant, the east-west orientation can remain as shown in the basic unit and the garage and studio variations. It should also be reiterated that should site conditions warrant, the floor plans of not only the Little House garage but also the basic Little House and the Little House studio can be flipped in the east-west direction with the understanding that in summer, the 6'0" (1.8 m.) wide window in the kitchen area will admit excessive heat from the setting sun.

The next and perhaps more critical change is the inclusion of the stair in the kitchen and dining area. If left where it is in the basic Little House, it comes out under the low section of the roof, where headroom is inadequate. With the new location of the stair, the kitchen becomes more compact and the dining area is moved south into the living area. The kitchen has also lost its large window facing east and now requires supplementary mechanical ventilation. A fan over the stove can be ducted directly under the stair to the exterior.

So that people coming from upstairs can have direct access to the bathroom without having to go through the kitchen, the bathroom door has been set opposite the entrance to the stair. This change involves shifting the tub and the basin to the south wall, opening the linen closet to the west rather than to the south, and locating the clothes washer and dryer at the foot of the

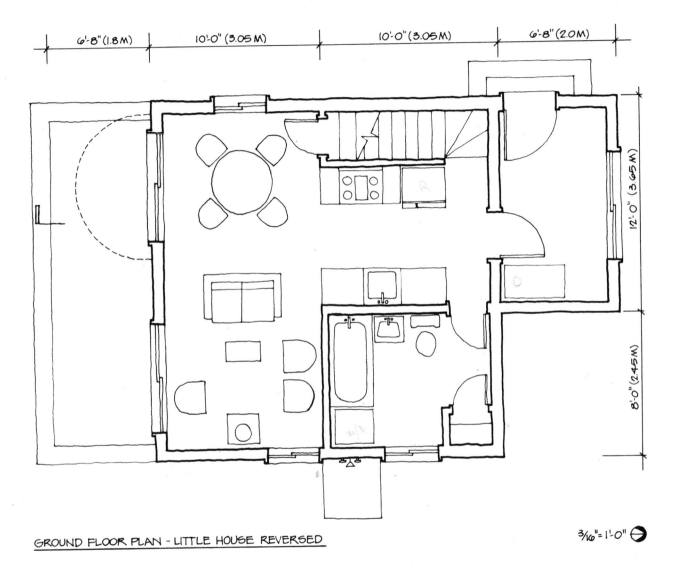

GROUND FLOOR PLAN - LITTLE HOUSE REVERSED

3/16" = 1'-0"

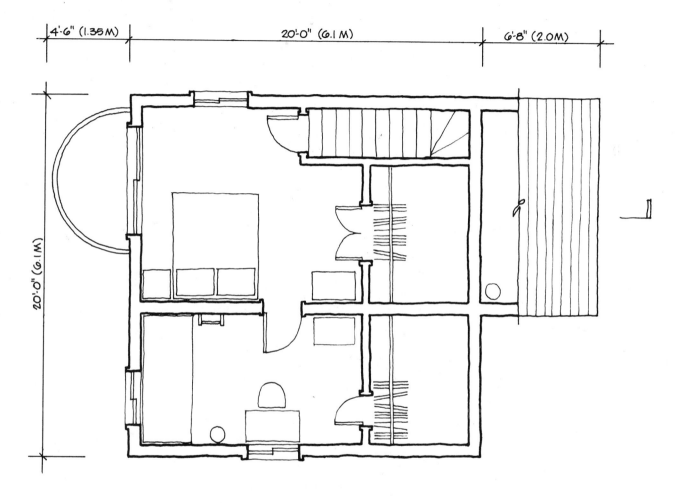

SECOND FLOOR PLAN - LITTLE HOUSE REVERSED

4'-6" (1.35M) 20'-0" (6.1 M) 6'-8" (2.0M)

20'-0" (6.1M)

3/16"=1'-0"

tub. It also involves the substitution of a 5'0" (1.5 m.) corner tub rather than the recessed tub shown in the basic Little House. These changes make the bathroom equally accessible to the kitchen and leave the dining and living room free of people "in transit."

As with the basic Little House, there are two 6'0" (1.8 m.) wide openings on the south facade. However, their spacing is taken from the grid normally associated with the north facade of the basic Little House, and only the one to the dining area is a full height door, the other being a 6'0" (1.8 m.) wide window of the type that opens onto the kitchen in the basic Little House. While this second window could indeed be a sliding door, it might render the living area less cozy.

At the second floor, the now-enclosed stair opens onto the larger of the two sleeping areas. This room has the same small window on the west facade as in the basic Little House. However, the large window facing south has been replaced with a sliding door opening onto a small balcony. This balcony serves to keep summer sun off the large door below much as the long, 3'0" (90 cm.) deep brise soleil does in the basic Little House. This balcony is not essential to the success of the scheme, although it is a pleasant amenity. The sliding door can just as well be translated into a 6'0" (1.8 m.) window and the brise soleil can run the full width of the house, as in the basic unit and as shown as an alternate in the south elevation for this variation.

If the sliding door and balcony are to be included, there is no question that the most engaging shape is a semicircle with a radius of approximately 4'0" (1.2 m.).

27

This allows just enough room for a small chair, a table, and a few plants. However, if the construction of a circular shape is beyond your abilities, as well it might be, a rectangular balcony would do.

Because the stair encroaches on the larger bedroom, the furniture has been rearranged and doors leading into the low closet repositioned. In the smaller room the large storage closet that is shown in the basic Little House has been cut back to provide more usable floor area.

In many ways, the changes in plan that result from the reversal of the roof pitch make for a much tidier, compact, and self-contained Little House than the basic Little House unit. However, the principal spaces are definitely less flexible and it might be slightly more expensive to build—more partitioning on the ground floor, a kinky balcony, and the dispersal of plumbing along two walls of the bathroom. There's no easy way to expand the kitchen should you wish to do so in the course of adding a second Little House. Finally, the fact that the stair opens onto the larger of the two bedrooms is less than ideal. If this room is used for children or guests, it means that they must travel through the master bedroom to get downstairs. But if the smaller bedroom is to be used as a study or a dressing area, passing through makes no difference.

If these drawbacks are not troublesome to you, if a more formal, compartmentalized plan is what you're after, and if you have no reason to orient any of your rooms to the north, this and not the basic Little House may indeed be the house for you.

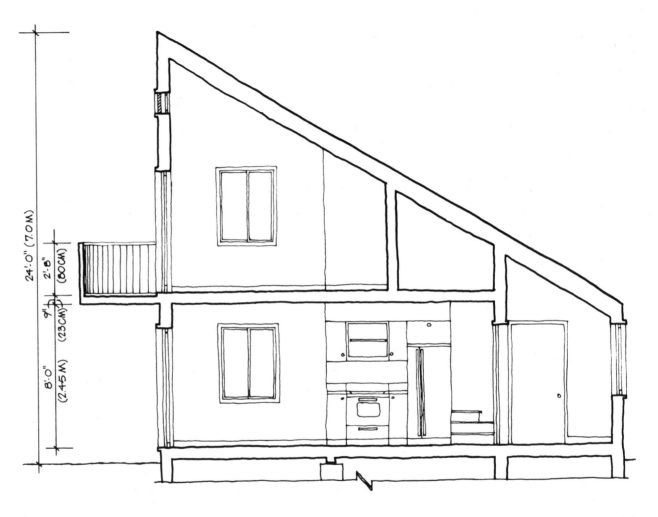

SECTION - LITTLE HOUSE REVERSED

3/16" = 1'-0"

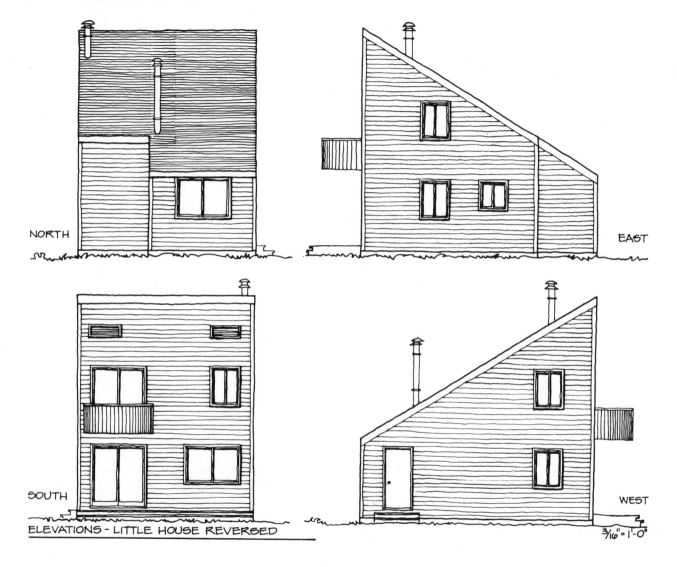

NORTH

EAST

SOUTH

WEST

ELEVATIONS - LITTLE HOUSE REVERSED

3/16" = 1'-0"

THE SOLAR LITTLE HOUSE

From the outset we had hoped to include in this book at least an economically feasible schematic solution for a passive solar Little House. In fact we have been toying with a passive approach which would be applied to a modification of the Little House reversed. But we have decided against including it because passive solar design is by nature site-specific. That is, the design must be carefully adjusted to the micro-climate of each particular site. Much the way we can't design your foundations for you, as we don't know your site, nor the bearing capacity of your soil, nor the code requirements in your region, we can't provide you with the all-purpose passive solar solution. However, we're certain that there's someone in your area who has the expertise and who can work with you to develop a solar variation on the Little House theme that's uniquely suited to your site and your needs.

4

Combinations and Permutations

So far you've been introduced to the concept of the Little House and have seen its basic plan and some of its variations. You know that additional Little House units can be added as your need for space expands. But you may already need more rooms or be aware that the 880 gross square feet (81.75 gross square meters) of a single unit plus shed is below the permissible building size for your area. What then?

You turn immediately to a combination of units each made up of a base unit, referred to as unit A, and a second unit, unit B. Unit A, either the basic Little House or one of its variations, contains all the plumbing and enough heating and electrical capacity for both units. The basic plan and the fenestration as discussed in the first chapter have been modified slightly to accommodate the addition of unit B. Unit B is also a modification of the basic Little House or one of its variations—studio, garage, or Little House reversed—but it is more drastic. In most cases two bedrooms are shown on the upper floor, and the ground floor plan is generally wide open, unless part of the space is used for still more bedrooms, as in Combination 3.

It's assumed that you'll be building both units simultaneously whichever combination you choose if only

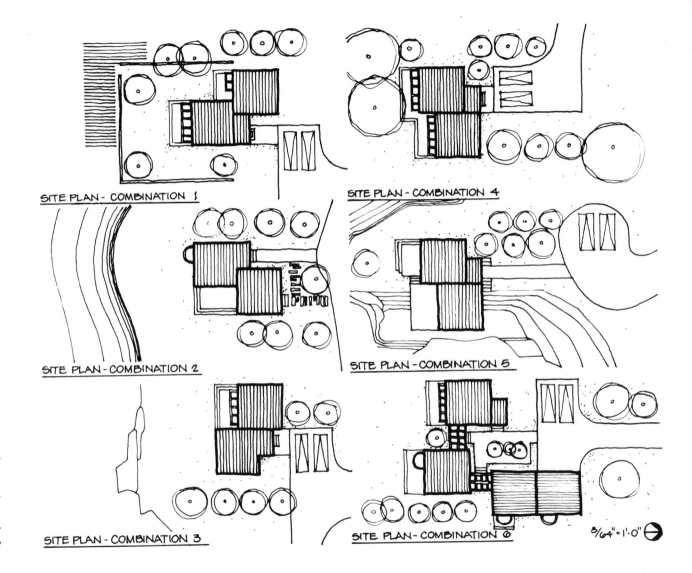

SITE PLAN - COMBINATION 1

SITE PLAN - COMBINATION 2

SITE PLAN - COMBINATION 3

SITE PLAN - COMBINATION 4

SITE PLAN - COMBINATION 5

SITE PLAN - COMBINATION 6

3/64" = 1'-0"

PERSPECTIVE COMBINATION 1

because it's both simpler and more economical to build them at the same time. If your budget can't handle both at once, don't do it. But if you plan on ultimately building more than one Little House unit, select a combination which best suits your projected needs before building the first unit. That way you can allow for modifications required to accommodate the second unit when the time comes. For this reason, the modifications to each unit required by each combination are listed below.

Hypothetical site plans are shown for each combination to give some idea of a potentially suitable context for the different forms and shapes, but more to give some indication of the many diverse ways a particular site can be treated—with walkways, decks, and planting —to enhance both the land and the house.

For Combination 1, first an exterior perspective is shown. This is followed by the floor plans side by side, flanked by three elevations and a section-elevation, that is to say, a section through one unit showing an elevation of the second unit beyond. The same complement of drawings is given for the other combinations. However, Combinations 2 and 3 are presented in parallel because, at least on the exterior, the two schemes are similar in that the roof lines are opposing. In much the same way Combinations 4 and 5 are shown in parallel because their roof lines run in the same direction. Like Combination 1, Combination 6 is shown on its own because the relationship between its components, at least between units A, B, and C, bears no similarity to the relationship between the units in the other schemes.

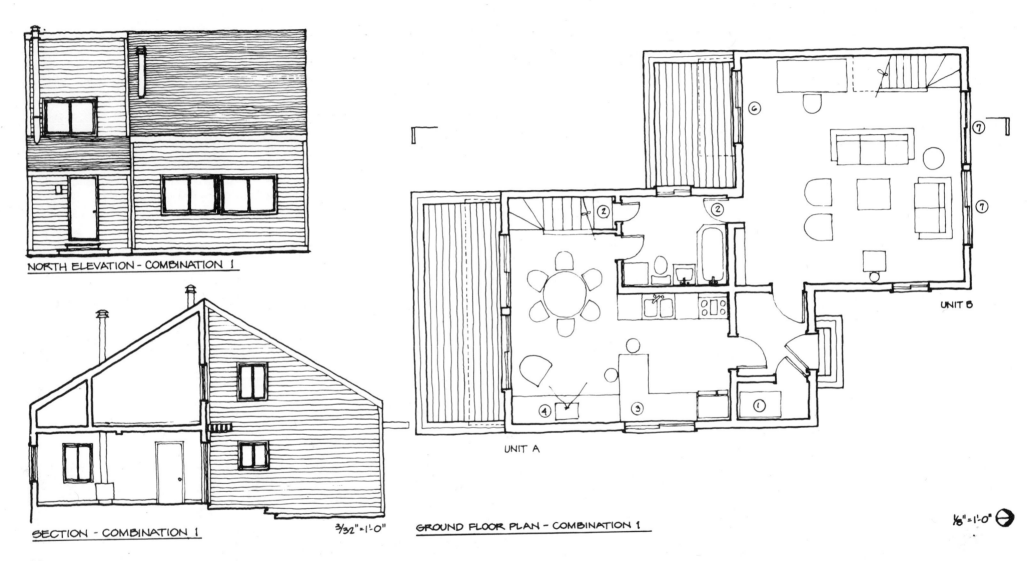

NORTH ELEVATION - COMBINATION 1

SECTION - COMBINATION 1

3/32"=1'-0"

UNIT B

UNIT A

GROUND FLOOR PLAN - COMBINATION 1

1/8"=1'-0"

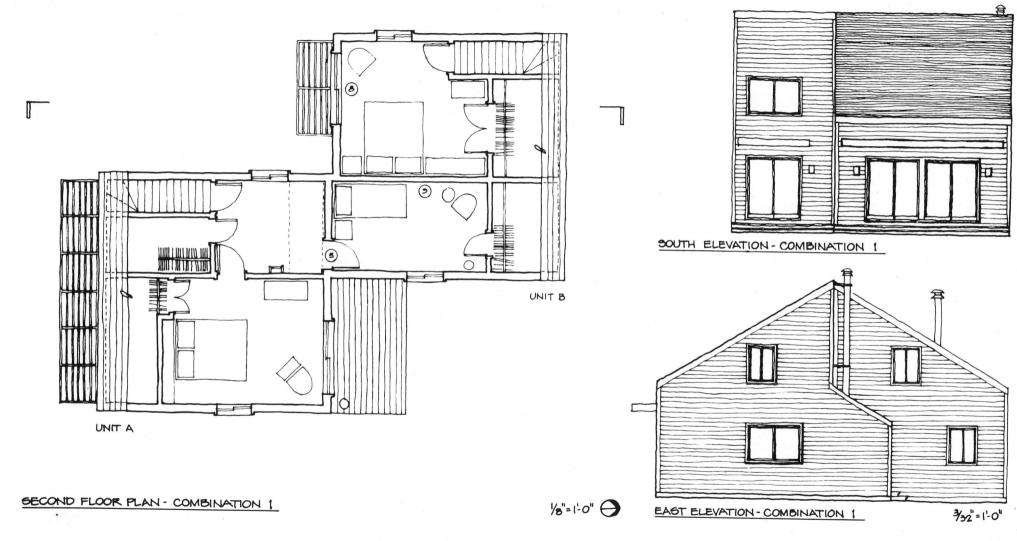

SECOND FLOOR PLAN - COMBINATION 1

UNIT A

UNIT B

SOUTH ELEVATION - COMBINATION 1

EAST ELEVATION - COMBINATION 1

1/8" = 1'-0"

3/32" = 1'-0"

33

COMBINATION 1

1680 gross square feet (156.05 gross square meters)

Of all the combinations, this is the most easily adapted to varying sites, at least visually. The two adjacent units, their high facades offset and their roofs sloping gently away from each other, fit easily into any equally gentle rural context, wooded or open, rolling or flat.

Unit A, called unit 1-A to reflect the particular combination, is a basic Little House that has been modified in the following ways (numbers key into the floor plans).

1. Because the west wall of the shed must now provide access to unit B, the furnace or boiler and the hot-water heater have been moved to the east wall of the shed. The entrance door originally on the east wall is now on the north wall, replacing the 6'0" (1.8 m.) wide window. Needless to say, if a basement is built to house the furnace and hot-water heater, none of this shifting of openings is required.

2. In the bathroom, the linen closet has been replaced by a second entrance to the bathroom from unit 1-B. The underside of the stair is then enclosed so this space can serve as a linen closet. This new door in turn necessitates the choice of a stacked washer-dryer in the southeast corner. The dryer must be vented up through the wet wall to the roof.

3. In the kitchen area the plan shows an L-shaped counter under the 6'0" (1.8 m.) window on the east

PERSPECTIVE - COMBINATION 2

wall. This counter increases the storage and working space of the kitchen substantially. The wide window is reduced in height from 4'0" (1.2 m.) to 3'0" (90 cm.) so the sill will clear the 3'0" (90 cm.) counter plus backsplash.

4.   To complete the image of the live-in, eat-in kitchen-cum-family room, in lieu of a fireplace there's an oversized television in the southeast corner plus a comfortable chair.

5.   On the second floor, the only modification to the basic Little House plan is the substitution of a door for the 6'0" (1.8 m.) window on the north wall of the smaller room. A second bathroom can be provided in this location.

Unit 1-B is a Little House reversed less kitchen and bath. The large, open living space on the ground floor can be furnished as just that or it can be fitted out with built-in settees which double as accommodations for overnight guests, as indicated in some of the other combinations. In order for unit 1-B to fit with unit 1-A, some modifications are in order.

6.   On the south wall instead of the 6'0" (1.8 m.) opening there's a small door to the bathroom.

7.   The north wall is provided with two 6'0" (1.8 m.) windows located in the same position as the 6'0" (1.8 m.) sliding doors on the south facade of unit 1-A.

8. The little semicircular balcony which so enlivens the south facade of the solo Little House reversed does not wash with the tranquil exterior of this combination. Thus only a 6'0" (1.8 m.) window is shown on the south wall, plus the 3'0" brise soleil below.

9. No connection is required between the two bedrooms on this level as the smaller room is accessible from unit 1-A. However, if a second bathroom is included don't leave out this door!

COMBINATION 2
1665 gross square feet (154.75 gross square meters)

Combination 2 is almost the exact reverse of Combination 1. Instead of the high sides of two units being face to face and offset by the length of the shed, the low sides are face to face and offset by half the length of one unit. The resulting profile is hardly one of tranquility and repose. But this kind of flamboyance has its place, perhaps not in the woods or in the rolling country but maybe in one of the resort communities by the sea.

The main living spaces open only in two directions: toward the south and the east. In most locations where this configuration would be appropriate, unless you have water frontage, there is little to see at ground level except the forest of pilings and underpinnings that support the adjacent houses. Thus you're encouraged to focus your exterior spaces inward at this level; use decking and whatever vegetation will grow to make exterior rooms out of what area you can afford to landscape. At

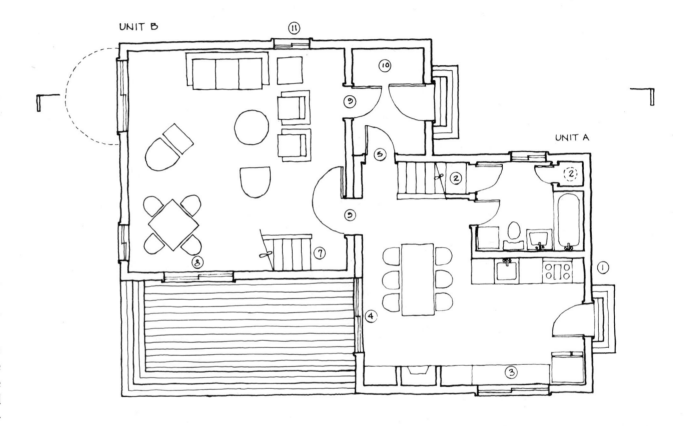

GROUND FLOOR PLAN - COMBINATION 2

1/8" = 1'-0"

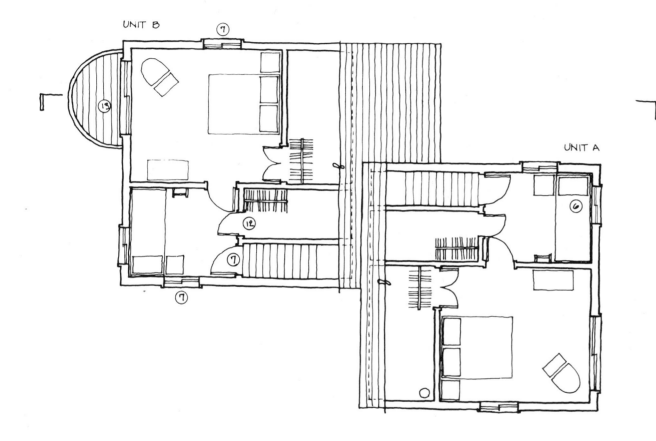

UNIT B

UNIT A

SECOND FLOOR PLAN - COMBINATION 2

⅛"=1'-0"

the same time you'll catch the best of the sun and protect yourself from the worst of the wind.

While there is often not much to see at grade, the second floor's higher altitude may yield a glimpse of the sea itself. Plus it will catch what little breeze there is on a hot and sticky night. This combination affords views in all four directions.

Unit 2-A is a modified basic Little House without a shed to the north.

1. No shed presumes that unless there is a basement, there is neither furnace nor boiler. This seems a fair presumption as this combination is most suited to a summer resort. Should you wish to provide heat for occasional fall and winter weekends, you should consider installing electric baseboard heat only in unit 2-A.

2. The hot-water heater can be located in the linen closet, and, for supplementary storage, the space under the stair can be enclosed and made to open into the bath as in unit 1-A.

3. A 6'0" (1.8 m.) length of kitchen counter is built along the east wall, and the height of the large window is reduced to 3'0" (90 cm.) accordingly.

4. Only one 6'0" (1.8 m.) sliding door is provided on the south facade. No brise soleil is included, as the shadow of unit 2-B will protect the room from the afternoon sun. In place of the second slider, a single 2′8″ (80 cm.) door opens into unit 2-B.

5. At the foot of the stair a 2′4″ (70 cm.) door opens onto a shed which is more a part of unit 2-B than unit 2-A. Both stairs in this combination are the steep straight-run type shown in the plans of the unofficial Little House. Should they be too steep to meet code requirements where you're building, eliminate the connection to the shed at the foot of the stair of unit 2-A, build both stairs with winders, and enter the kitchen either through its own exterior door or through unit 2-B.

6. On the second floor, the north window of the smaller bedroom has been reduced from 6′0″ (1.8 m.) to 3′0″ (90 cm.).

Added onto unit 2-A is unit 2-B, a Little House reversed with no kitchen or bath and with some additional modifications:

7. The stair has been moved to the east side of the unit so it opens onto the smaller of the two bedrooms above, and the east and west windows upstairs have been moved accordingly.

8. The 3′0″ (90 cm.) window on the east wall has been enlarged to a 6′0″ (1.8 m.) slider giving onto the southeast deck.

9. There are two 2′8″ (80 cm.) doors at either end of

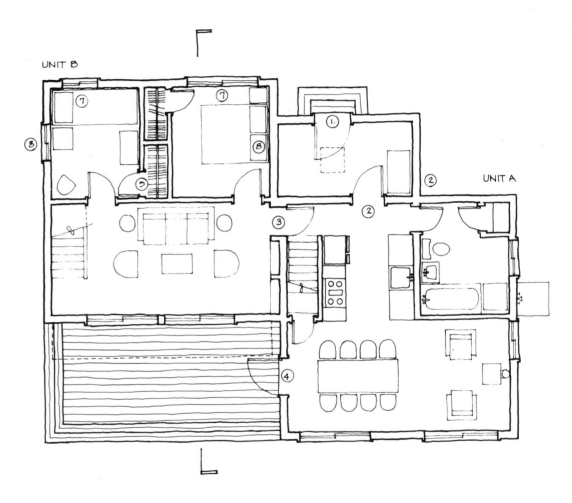

GROUND FLOOR PLAN - COMBINATION 3

⅛″=1′-0″

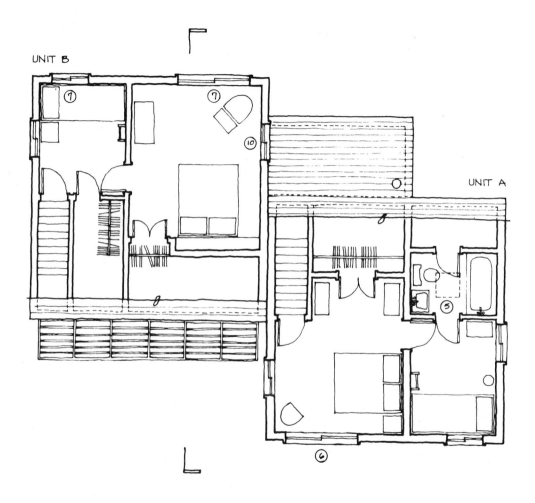

UNIT B

UNIT A

SECOND FLOOR PLAN - COMBINATION 3

1/8" = 1'-0"

the north wall, one leading to unit 2-B and the other to the shed.

10. The shed off unit 2-B isn't the full 12'0" (3.6 m.) wide but rather only 9'4" (2.8 m.), because in this configuration the midpoint of one unit aligns with the outside of the other, as compared to the smaller of the two bays aligning, as in Combination 1.

11. The small window on the west wall has been moved north by three bays.

12. Because the stair opens on the smaller of the two upstairs rooms, the storage closet can be included as part of this space.

13. You are encouraged to build the semicircular balcony off the larger bedroom with the same vehemence as you were encouraged not to include it in Combination 1.

COMBINATION 3
1680 gross square feet (156.05 gross square meters)

This combination is also a resort-type house but not exclusively. Its profile is considerably more dignified and discreet than that of Combination 2. While it would certainly do at the sea, it would also do in the mountains either on its own or as part of a land cooperative or a complex of condominiums. The ground-floor plan we show for unit 3-B includes two additional bedrooms

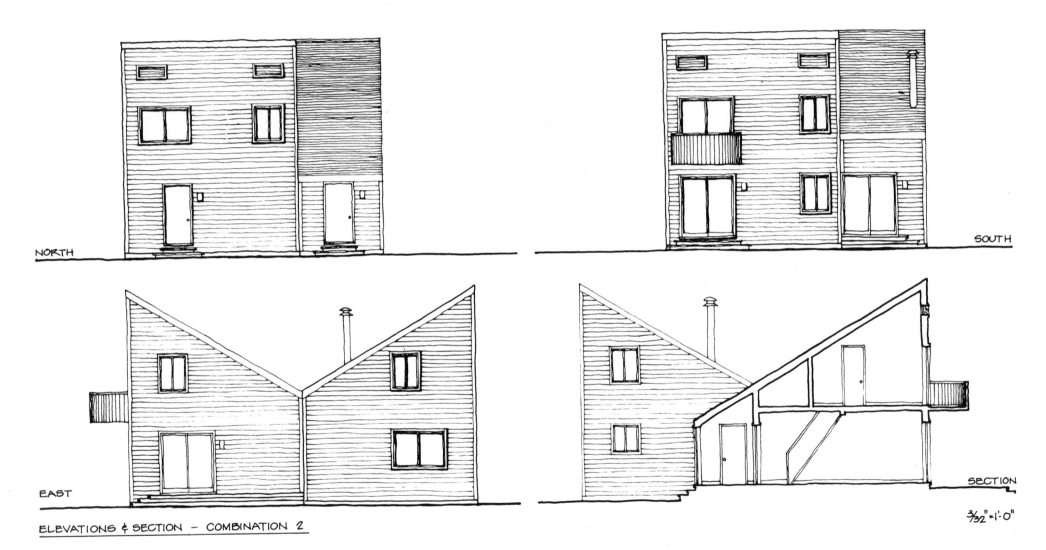

NORTH

SOUTH

EAST

SECTION

3/32" = 1'-0"

ELEVATIONS & SECTION – COMBINATION 2

40

NORTH

SOUTH

EAST

SECTION

ELEVATIONS & SECTION - COMBINATION 3

3/32" = 1'-0"

41

and a small sitting area in place of the large living room. With its total of six bedrooms—accommodating nine to twelve people—and its two baths, it would be ideal as a ski house or a hunting lodge: most of the daytime activity takes place out of doors, but space for eating and sleeping is at a premium.

Please note that in order to fit this plan on the page it has been reoriented so that north is at the top of the page rather than on the right; this change applies to Combinations 4 and 5 as well.

1. Once again the base unit, here 3-A, is a modified Little House reversed, but because of the adjacency of unit 3-B to the west the entrance must be on the north face of the shed. This can be a glass slider as shown in the perspective or a solid door as shown in the plans and elevations.

2. Because of the position of unit 3-B, the exhaust fan for the range cannot be ducted under the stair to the outside. Instead a strong exhaust fan should be mounted above the door from the kitchen to the shed, then ducted so it comes out on the east wall of the shed. To bring supplementary light to both the shed and the kitchen, a square 2'6" (75 cm.) skylight could be installed in the roof of the shed, centered on the door to the outside.

3. At the bottom of the stair in unit 3-A is a door to unit 3-B. Therefore the stair in unit 3-A at least must be the steep straight-run type to allow a level connection to unit 3-B. If such a stair is illegal in your area, you

PERSPECTIVE - COMBINATION 4

can build both stairs with winders, abandon the downstairs bedrooms in unit 3-B, and enter unit 3-B through the shed. However, if it's only the extra bedrooms that attract you to this scheme, you can work them just as well into the ground floor of the second units of Combinations 4 and 5. (See units 6-C and 6-D for yet another variation on this theme.)

4. For the 3'0" (90 cm.) window facing west we have substituted a 2'8" (80 cm.) glass door opening out onto the deck in front of unit 3-B.

5. On the second floor there's now a second bathroom, immediately above the first, to serve these two bedrooms. It's ventilated by a 2'6" (75 cm.) operable square skylight.

6. We suggest that the balcony off the main bedroom not be included.

Unit 3-B is a basic Little House that has two bedrooms and closets between them in the space usually occupied by the kitchen and bath.

7. On both stories of the north facade are two windows: one 3'0" (90 cm.) and one 6'0" (1.8 m.).

8. On the ground floor the 6'0" (1.8 m.) window on the east facade has to be deleted because this wall now adjoins unit 3-A, and on the west facade the 3'0" high (90 cm.) bathroom window gets increased to the standard 4'0" (1.2 m.) height.

PERSPECTIVE - COMBINATION 5

9. The partition acting as the west wall of the down-stairs bedroom is in the usual location and aligns with the partition above.

10. At the second floor the 3'0" (90 cm.) window on the east wall must be shifted north one bay, i.e., 3'0" (90 cm.) to align with the edge of the shed.

COMBINATION 4
1680 gross square feet (156.05 gross square meters)

Combinations 1 and 4 are far and away the most flexible of the six offered. The principal difference is that both its roofs sloping in the same direction generate a saw-toothed profile which might be considered more contemporary than the barn-shaped profile of Combination 1. But in fact, in plan and in massing it is more conservative: sliding two identical housing units a few feet past one another is not a new trick in residential construction. It is a simple but effective way of generating a varied and picturesque appearance. Here unit 4-B is slipped north of unit 4-A so that the north wall of unit 4-B aligns with the north wall of the shed off unit 4-A, and this surface now reads as a single plane.

Unit 4-A requires only very minor modifications of the basic Little House.

1. The shed must be entered on the north facade because unit 4-B is now to the east. If the 2'8" (80 cm.) door is opaque, there is no way to admit light to the shed, much less the kitchen. Thus we simply depend

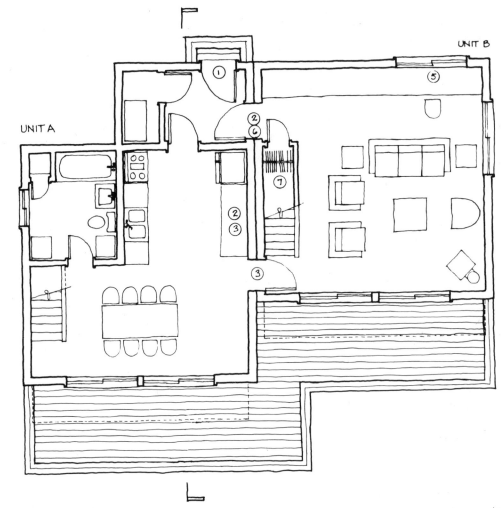

GROUND FLOOR PLAN - COMBINATION 4

⅛" = 1'-0"

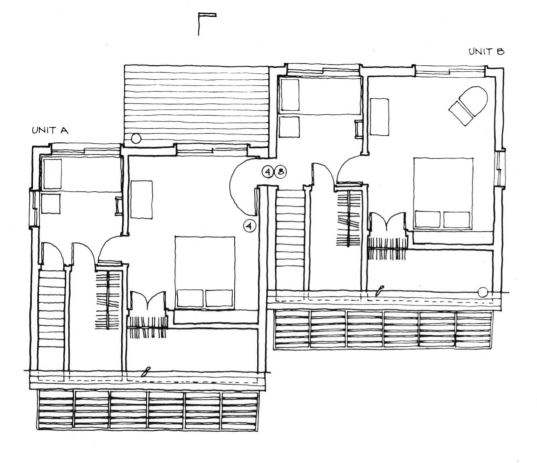

UNIT A

UNIT B

SECOND FLOOR PLAN - COMBINATION 4

⅛"=1'-0"

for light on the big sliders on the south facade, and for ventilation we use supplemental mechanical exhaust similar to that suggested for the kitchen in Combination 3. Should the straight-run stair be a problem here, simply flip the plan of unit 4-B in the east-west direction so the stairs run along the east wall and the winders can take up the corner. Then adjust the fenestration and the location of the fireplace accordingly. This suggestion also applies to the stairs in Combination 5.

2. The original entrance door to the shed now leads to unit 4-B and the 6'0" (1.8 m.) window on the east wall is deleted.

3. An additional kitchen counter with cabinets above is built along the east wall, and a 2'8" (80 cm.) door to unit 4-B is located in the 3'0" (90 cm.) bay south of the counter.

4. Upstairs the only changes are the deletion of the windows on the east wall of the large bedroom and the possibility of not providing a door between the two bedrooms, as the large room is accessible from unit 4-B.

Here, as in Combination 3, unit B is a basic Little House that has been further modified.

5. Only one 6'0" (1.8 m.) sliding window is shown at the east end of the north facade.

6. The west window is now a door opening to the shed.

7. The bottom of the stair is enclosed, and the enclosure is extended to provide a deep closet as there is little space remaining in the shed.

8. The only change in the second floor is the deletion of the window in the west wall of the small bedroom and the substitution of a door in the 3'0" (90 cm.) bay to the south leading to the large bedroom in unit 4-A.

COMBINATION 5
1500 gross square feet (139 gross square meters)

At first glance, Combination 5 does nothing that Combination 4 does not do, other than respond to a sloping site. This means that while the two Little House units are slipped 6'0" (1.8 m.) past one another, unit 5-A drops below unit 5-B so that the roof of each unit remains in the same inclined plane. This inclined plane seems to unite the two units under a single roof. In addition, the change in level gives variety and life to all elevations and responds sensitively to the topography. There is no question that this combination will be more expensive to build than Combinations 1 through 4, if only because basements or at least substantial crawl spaces are usually required to ensure that such houses sit firmly into the hillside, but you may have to make this investment if you have a steeply sloping site.

The actual level change is a function of how far past unit 5-A unit 5-B is slipped. The 6'8" (2 m.) north-south slip of this combination yields an approximate 3'8" (1.1 m.) change in level. A 3'0" (90 cm.) slip yields

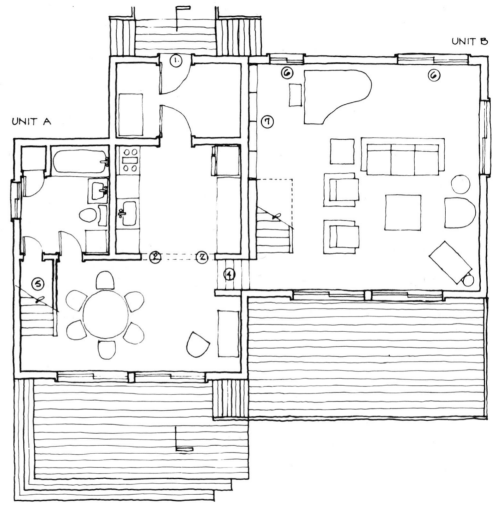

UNIT B

UNIT A

GROUND FLOOR PLAN - COMBINATION 5

⅛"=1'-0"

46

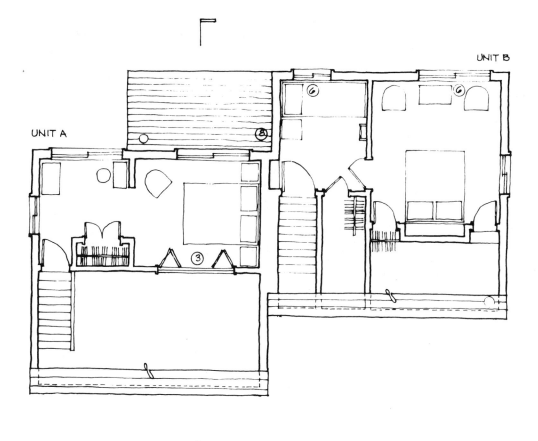

UNIT A

UNIT B

SECOND FLOOR PLAN - COMBINATION 5

⅛" = 1'-0"

slightly less than half the vertical distance and is not particularly effective visually. Should you be thinking of slipping the units more than 6'8" (2 m.) in order to achieve an even greater level change, forget it! It won't work either on the interior or the exterior. Make up a few models and see for yourself.

Unit 5-A, a Little House studio that has a downstairs kitchen and bath, is almost identical to the basic Little House.

1. Unit 5-A is entered through a single door on the north face of the shed. Again because of the position of Unit 5-B, there is no large window in the kitchen, nor a window to the shed. The skylight option in Combination 3 is a possibility but since the door to the shed and the door to the kitchen are aligned, a less costly alternative is to make both doors glass, which will bring at least same natural light to the kitchen. (This solution would not work as well in the kitchen of Combination 4 because these two doors cannot be aligned there.) Again, supplementary mechanical exhaust must be provided.

2. The east wall of the kitchen is identical to those in other units, except that it is enclosed by a cheek wall, that is, a stub of wall the same width as the kitchen counter's 2'1" (65 cm.) depth. The length of wall available for cabinetwork and appliances is reduced by the thickness of the cheek wall. The south end of the west wall of the kitchen is similarly enclosed. The opening

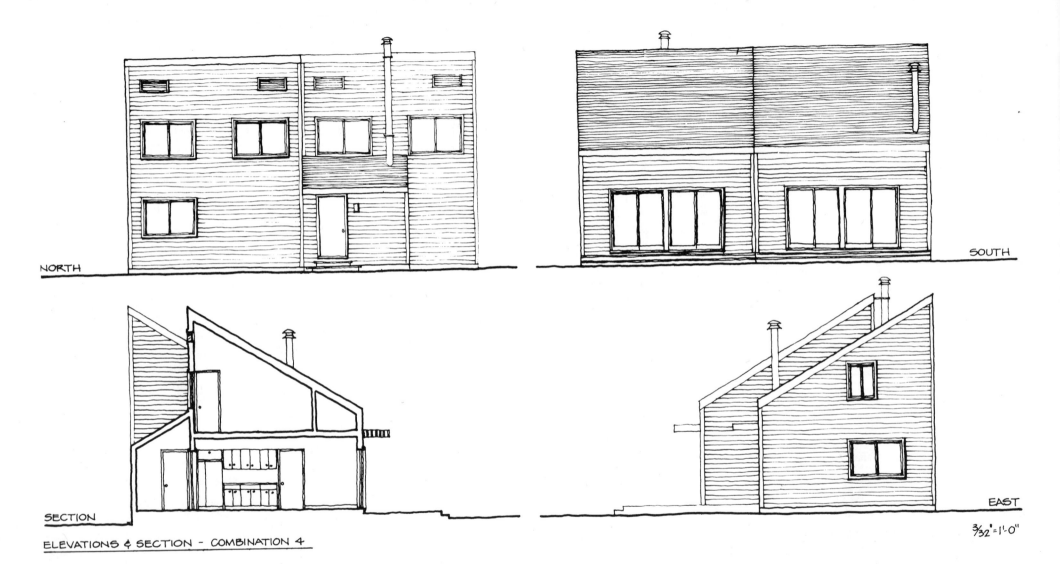

NORTH

SOUTH

SECTION

EAST

ELEVATIONS & SECTION - COMBINATION 4

$\frac{3}{32}" = 1'-0"$

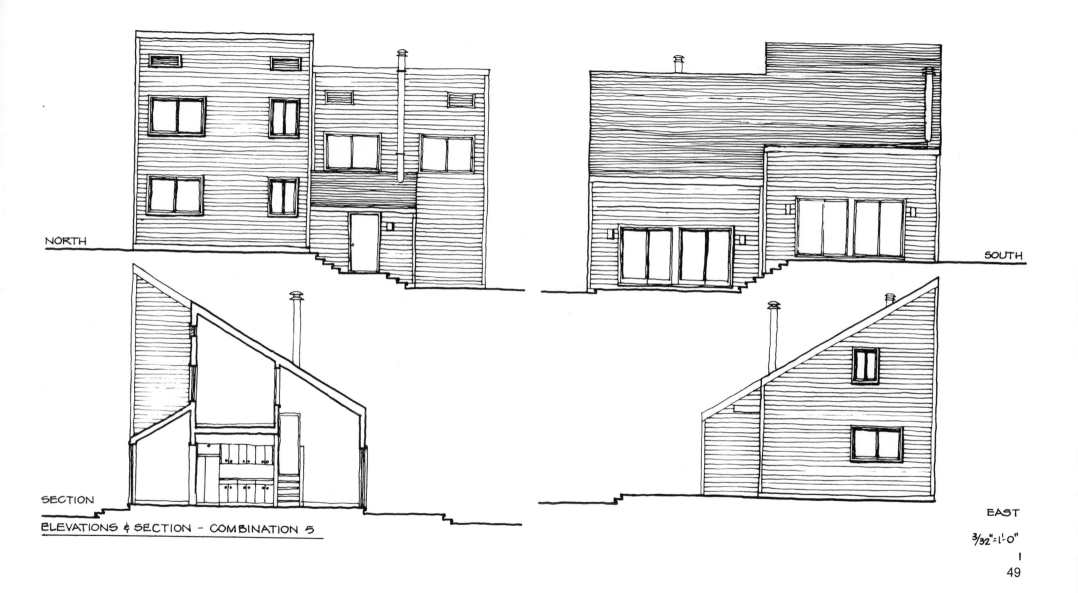

NORTH

SOUTH

SECTION

EAST

ELEVATIONS & SECTION - COMBINATION 5

3/32"=1'-0"

between these two cheek walls is 7'0" (2.15 m.) across and 6'8" (2 m.) high. It is trimmed with the same 2" (5 cm.) stock molding as the doors and windows.

3. This large opening in the lower wall is part of our device for furnishing the bedroom above with a modicum of privacy without destroying the openness and spaciousness inherent in the Little House studio section. In "Variations on a Theme" we suggested the possibility of running the parapet or partition defining the edge of the loft straight up to the underside of the roof. Here we've done both. We've run the partition up to the roof but have left an opening in it which aligns with the opening created by the cheek walls of the kitchen below. And we've made it possible to close this opening with opaque plywood folding doors the same 6'8" (2.0 m.) height as the other doors. There is a 3'0" (90 cm.) open railing in front of the folding doors. Apart from the elimination of the east window, there are no further modifications to the second floor.

4. Back downstairs: South of the kitchen along the east wall are the five steps, 9" (23 cm.) risers and 9" (23 cm.) treads, up to the 2'4" (70 cm.) door to unit 5-B. Unit 5-A must be a Little House studio in order to provide adequate headroom for this opening. Were it a basic Little House the framing for the second floor would run right across the top half of this door. Although there is adequate headroom to provide a similar connection between the second levels of the two units,

50

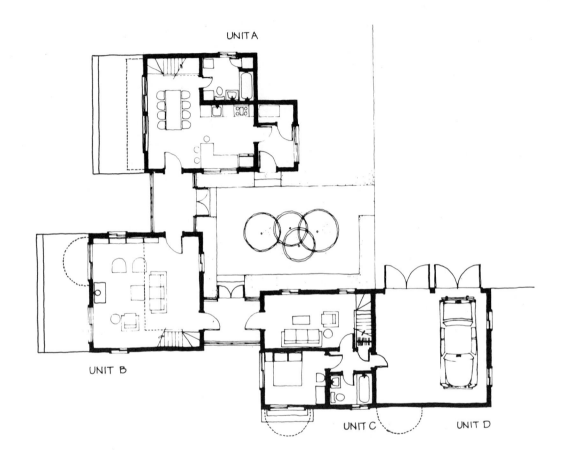

UNIT A

UNIT B

UNIT C   UNIT D

GROUND FLOOR PLAN - COMBINATION 6

1/16" = 1'-0"

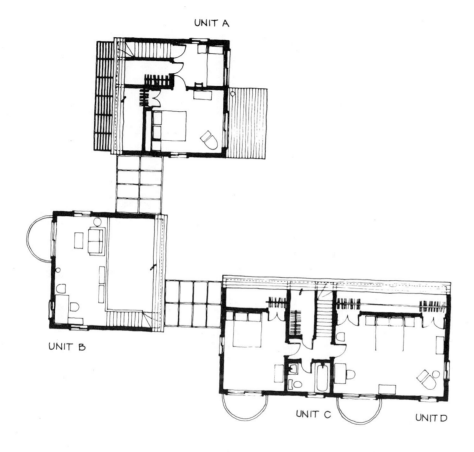

UNIT A

UNIT B

UNIT C   UNIT D

SECOND FLOOR PLAN - COMBINATION 6

1/16" = 1'-0"

it isn't recommended as it's costly to frame and the stairs eat up valuable space in the sleeping loft of unit 5-A.

5. Apart from our suggestion that the underside of 5-A's stair be fully enclosed and the space open into the bathroom to make a tidier corner for the dining room table, there are no further modifications to this unit.

The second part of Combination 5, unit 5-B, is again a basic Little House unit with neither kitchen nor bath, but some further modifications.

6. Aligned directly below the 3'0" (90 cm.) and 6'0" (1.8 m.) windows on the second floor of the north facade are identical windows on the ground floor.

7. On the second floor, the west window has been eliminated altogether.

COMBINATION 6
3260 gross square feet (303 gross square meters) of building
180 gross square feet (17 gross square meters)
greenhouse connectors

Today a Little House, tomorrow, Versailles. Why not? The fact is, the geometry of the basic Little House unit is such that by combining one with another and yet another it can shift scales upward very neatly. A group of four Little House units built simultaneously or in a sequence need not look like a child's fantasy constructed with building blocks.

This combination is made up of four Little House units. Perspectives of units A and B, and B and C are shown at the end of chapter 1, two of which are oriented east-west rather than north-south. This is the first time we see this orientation and it is shown because there are many sites which demand it for a number of reasons. If such is your situation, use a Little House reversed so all the major spaces orient east, half of them south, and only the minimum north and west.

The units are connected by two greenhouses approximately 9'0" (2.75 m.) wide by 10'0" (3 m.) long, i.e., half the length of a single Little House—one of them serves as the principal entrance to the complex. This kind of greenhouse is readily available as an off-the-shelf item in most parts of the country. The one we show has straight sides and a double-pitched roof sloped at 30 degrees, which matches the slope of the Little House roof. All these greenhouses must be set on a curb.

To develop sufficient headroom to install a single or a pair of 6'8" (2 m.) doors in one side, the curb should be built up to the height required to generate the headroom. These opaque curbs can be clad in the same material as the Little House units themselves or in a contrasting finish.

The A unit for Combination 6 is a basic Little House unit with no modification except the addition of a 2'8" (80 cm.) door on the east wall which leads through a greenhouse connector to unit 6-B.

A Little House studio reversed, with no kitchen or bath, serves as unit 6-B. Along the north wall there's

NORTH

EAST

NORTH AND EAST ELEVATIONS - COMBINATION 6

3/32"=1'-0"

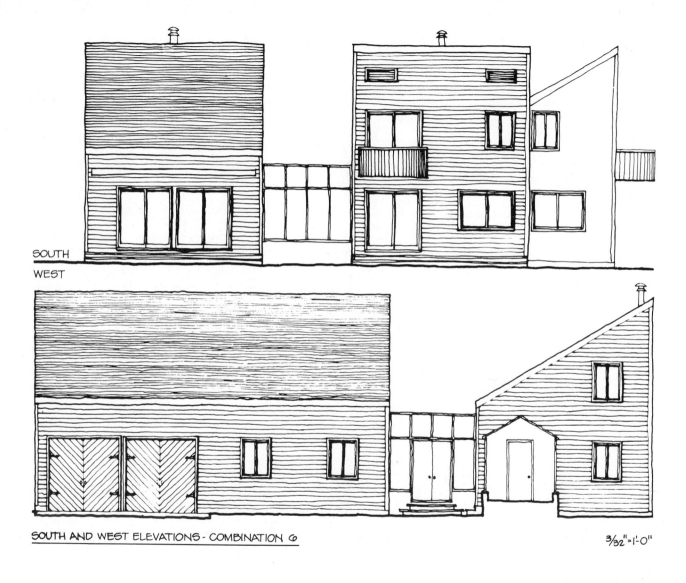

SOUTH

WEST

SOUTH AND WEST ELEVATIONS - COMBINATION 6

3/32" = 1'-0"

only one 3'0" (90 cm.) window and a 2'8" (80 cm.) door to a second identical greenhouse connector. This leads in turn to units 6-C and 6-D.

Unit 6-C is half basic Little House and half Little House reversed but with a hall, a closet, and a small bathroom located where the big bathroom is shown in the basic Little House. Because of the adjacency of unit 6-D the bathroom window is on the east wall. In place of the kitchen is a bedroom with the usual big window opening south instead of east and a 6'0" (1.8 m.) slider opening east. West of the bedroom and bath is a sitting area with two small windows facing the courtyard to the west. The stair serves both the bedroom above on the second level of unit 6-C and the bedrooms or the very large single bedroom that is shown on the second level of unit 6-D.

Combination 6 is only one of many ways of combining units. It works because the greenhouse connectors increase the apparent scale of the complex and the geometry of the individual units.

If this approach intrigues you, make up some of the models from the Appendix, and move them about on a sheet of paper representing your site until you happen on something you like. Then look at what kind of floor plan you can generate using the plans for the basic Little House unit, the variations, and the combinations. If you like it, select your finishes from the next chapter, then try to price the whole thing from the last chapter. If it checks out with your budget, your engineer, and your builder, start building!

Alternate Materials and Equipment

We are now in the stage that straddles fantasy and reality. In the last three chapters we have literally been playing house with the Little House; now it's time to be more specific. Of what is your Little House or combination of Little House units to be built? What materials and what finishes? What are your tastes? What materials and building traditions are indigenous to your part of the country?

The finishes and materials which most affect the appearance of the Little House have been organized into a basic finish group and three variations, much the way the presentation of the design is in the form of a basic theme and three variations. Group 1 is composed of the most conventional finishes in use in middle-priced residential construction. The overall effect is clean and smooth, and the price is middle range. Group 2 is less conventional, rich in texture, and more costly. Group 3 is sparse and elegant and the same price as Group 2. And Group 4 is catch-as-catch-can in the name of economy. The components of each group and the finishes themselves are listed in the first chart in the order in which they will be discussed and illustrated below. The numbers in parentheses that precede them indicate their cost relative to the same items in the other finish groups.

Many finishes and types of equipment not mentioned

FINISH GROUP		ONE (MIDDLE RANGE)	B	TWO (MIDDLE TO HIGH)	C
THE ENCLOSURE	EXTERIOR WALL FINISH	PAINTED WOOD CLAPBOARDS AND CORNERBOARDS	A	WEATHERED WOOD SHINGLES & PAINTED CORNERBOARDS	D
	ROOFING	ASPHALT SHINGLES	B	WEATHERED WOOD SHINGLES/SHAKES	C
	WINDOWS	BRONZE-ANODIZED ALUMINUM	B	PAINTED WOOD DOUBLE-HUNG	D
	SLIDING DOORS	BRONZE-ANODIZED ALUMINUM	C	WOOD	B
THE ENCLOSED	INTERIOR WALL AND CEILING FINISH	PAINTED GYPSUM BOARD	B	½" × 3" VERTICAL PINE STRIPS NATURAL FINISH	D
	FLOORING	2½" T&G OAK STRIPS WITH POLYURETHANE FINISH	D	STUDDED RUBBER RESILIENT FLOOR TILE	B
	BASEBOARD, AND DOOR AND WINDOW TRIM	PAINTED PINE ¾" × 3½" AND ¾" × 2", RESPECTIVELY	B	NATURAL FINISH PINE ¾" × 3½" AND ¾" × 2", RESPECTIVELY	B
	BATHROOM WALL AND CEILING FINISHES	WATERPROOF GYP. BD., 4" × 4" C.T. TUB SURROUND	B	½" × 3" VERTICAL PINE STRIPS FIBERGLASS TUB & SURROUND	C
	BATH FLOOR AND BASE/ WAINSCOTING	1" × 1" C.T. FLOOR, 4" × 4" C.T. WAINSCOTING 3'-8" A.F.F.	C	STUDDED RUBBER FLOOR TILE, ¾" × 3½" PINE BASE	B
	KITCHEN AND MISC. CABINETWORK	FIN. GRADE BIRCH PLYWD, HARD WD EDGES, OILED OR LACQUERED	B	½" × 3" VERTICAL PINE STRIPS NATURAL FINISH	D
	KITCHEN COUNTERTOP	PLASTIC LAMINATE WITH ¾" × 1¼" HARDWOOD EDGE	A	JOHNS-MANVILLE'S COLORLITH	D
	FIREPLACE SHOWN IN ILLUSTRATION	HEATILATOR FIREPLACE BUILT INTO GYP. BD. SURROUND	C	JOTUL COMBINATION WOOD BURNING STOVE & FIREPLACE	B

ALTERNATE FINISH GROUPS 1 AND 2

A IS LEAST EXPENSIVE
D IS MOST EXPENSIVE

THREE (MOST EXPENSIVE) D		FOUR (LEAST EXPENSIVE) A		ENTER YOUR SELECTIONS IN ORDER OF PREFERENCE
PAINTED STUCCO	C	ROUGH-CUT PINE BOARDS AND BATTENS	B	1. 2.
CLAY TILE	C	CORRUGATED METAL	A	1. 2.
PAINTED WOOD SLIDING	C	ALUMINUM OR STEEL DOUBLE HUNG	A	1. 2.
WOOD	B	ALUMINUM	A	1. 2.
PAINTED PLASTER	C	PAINTED OR PRE-FINISHED FIBERBOARD PANELLING	A	1. 2.
6" × 6" QUARRY TILE	C	VINYL ASBESTOS TILE OR SHEET LINOLEUM	A	1. 2.
PAINTED PINE ¾" × 3½" AND ¾" × 2", RESPECTIVELY	B	PAINTED PINE OR VINYL BASE, PAINTED PINE TRIM	A	1. 2.
KEENE'S PLASTER AND 2" × 2" C.T. TUB SURROUND	D	WATERPROOF GYP. BD & PLASTIC LAM OR FIBRGLAS TUB SUR'ND	A	1. 2.
6" × 6" QUARRY TILE FLOOR 3½" × 6" QUARRY TILE BASE	D	VINYL-ASBESTOS TILE OR LINOLEUM FLOOR, VINYL BASE	A	1. 2.
HDWD VENEER BIRCH PLYWD VENEERED EDGES	C	STORE-BOUGHT WOOD OR METAL	A	1. 2.
1¼" BUTCHER BLOCK	C	STORE-BOUGHT	B	1. 2.
HEATILATOR FIREPLACE BUILT INTO PLASTER SURROUND	C	FRANKLIN WOOD-BURNING STOVE	A.	1. 2.

A IS LEAST EXPENSIVE
D IS MOST EXPENSIVE

here are readily available and equally appropriate. In theory, you should feel as free to choose among them as you were encouraged to manipulate the plans themselves. However, you must be especially careful because, taken together, the finishes cited for a particular group make an integrated aesthetic whole. Before substituting one finish for another, examine the effect your substitution will have on the adjacent finishes. Does it clash? Does it make for too much texture in too small a space? If it does, do you care? And so on.

We should say at this point that we're assuming the skeleton of the Little House to be light-wood framing, as it's the most common method and material in this country for residential construction.

THE ENCLOSURE

Finish Group 1 The presentation drawings in the preceding chapter and the construction drawings in the chapter immediately following illustrate only this group of finishes.

Cladding: Painted wood clapboards and cornerboards are common throughout the United States. Imitation wood siding is made in aluminum. While we are opposed to the use of one material made to resemble another, we do concede that for those of you who are looking for a low-maintenance cladding, impervious both to rot and termites, aluminum siding does provide an answer.

Roofing: If clapboarding is the all-American siding, asphalt shingle is the all-American roofing. Shingles come in a myriad of colors, the most pleasant of which are the solid grays and browns.

Windows and Sliding Doors: Bronze anodized aluminum is a warm dark brown that will work well with any of the exterior finish combinations suggested above. Windows and doors in this finish are manufactured by Reynolds and Alcoa in the sizes we specify, and probably by other companies as well. They are neatly designed, reasonably priced, and come with screens and a choice of insulated or noninsulated glass.

Finish Group 2 Cladding: Wood shingles are a very popular cladding for both traditional and contemporary seaside architecture.

Roofing: Wood shakes are a bit of a luxury, but there's nothing like weathered cedar shakes on a roof which has weathered cedar shingles on the walls.

Windows and Sliding Doors: Wood double-hung windows are as American as apple pie. They come in sizes similar but not identical to those we require. Chapter 6 will give you the precise rough opening and sash dimensions.

In residential construction, sliding metal doors are often used in conjunction with wood windows. We don't support this mixture of materials. Instead, we suggest you go with wood sliding doors as well. They are made in sizes close to the 6'0" by 6'8" we require by both Andersen and Pella and probably by your local door and window manufacturers as well. However, they are heavy and expensive. If you want to avoid paying the price for these doors but still want to keep to the wood

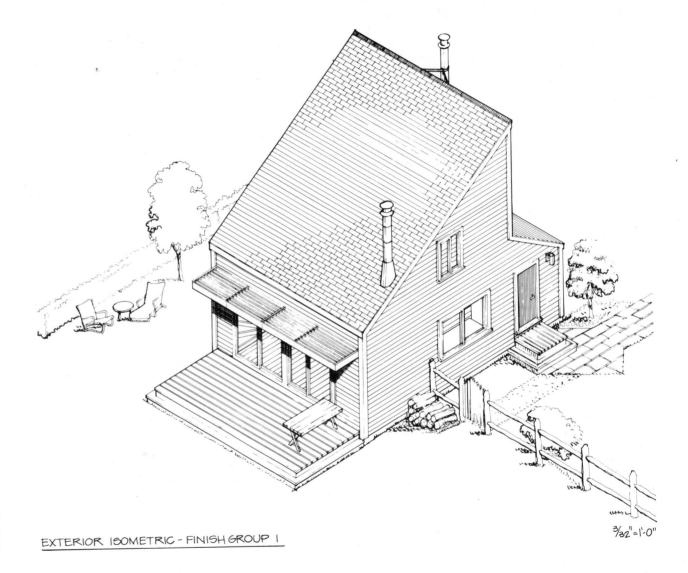

EXTERIOR ISOMETRIC - FINISH GROUP 1

3/32" = 1'-0"

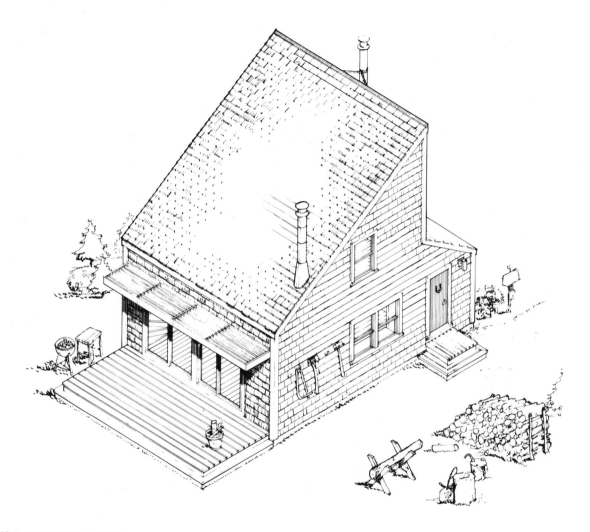

3/32"=1'-0"

vocabulary, install giant double-hung windows as we've done in our unofficial Little House.

Finish Group 3 Exterior Wall Finish (cladding not applicable): In this country, painted stucco is very popular wherever the Italianate and/or Spanish Colonial influence is pervasive or where there is a desire to capture the smooth surface of stone masonry. While it can be troweled on in many legitimate textures and can weather most climates where there is a broad range of temperature, it does tend to crack and streak, thus requiring fairly regular patching and repainting if its pristine appearance is to be maintained. The success of a stucco exterior depends entirely on the proportions of the mix and how well it is applied. This in turn depends on how deeply ingrained the tradition of plastering is in your region.

Roofing: Essential to the perpetration of the Italianate and/or Spanish Colonial image is a clay tile roof. These come in any number of patterns, all of which work within this framework. But if you're considering the use of stucco for its smoothness and crispness and not for its Hispanic associations, use asphalt shingles in a solid rich color.

Windows and Sliding Doors: As this finish group is intended to represent the top of the line, we are specifying sliding wood doors and windows. But in our opinion the substitution of wood sliding windows and doors for aluminum is worth the extra expense only if you have a real aversion to the thin frames and machine finish of the bronze anodized aluminum.

Finish Group 4 Cladding: Painted or stained and weathered rough-cut pine board and batten is the cladding of farm buildings everywhere. While no natural wood finish is cheap, pine board and battens are less costly than clapboards and wood shingles, and easier to apply. They can tolerate, at least visually, the slightly decaying appearance that results from little maintenance and infrequent painting.

Roofing: Corrugated metal is an honest, dignified, and inexpensive way to roof a minimal house. If you don't like it but it's all you can afford for now, install it anyway and replace it with asphalt shingles when you have more money to spare.

Windows and Sliding Doors: Painted steel sliding doors and double-hung windows are offered as alternatives for saving money, certainly not for their aesthetic attributes.

THE ENCLOSED

Finish Group 1 The exterior finishes and materials included in this group have been selected either because they are the most widely used or because their inherent simplicity lends scale and a modicum of elegance to this basic Little House. The selection of interior finishes for this group is governed by the same thinking.

Wall and Ceiling Finish: The most common interior finish currently in use in residential construction, gypsum wallboard, comes in 4'0" by 8'0" panels and many thicknesses. We should add that the success of a gypboard installation lies in the skill with which the hori-

EXTERIOR ISOMETRIC - FINISH GROUP 3

3/32" = 1'-0"

EXTERIOR ISOMETRIC - FINISH GROUP 4

3/32" = 1'-0"

zontal and vertical joints are taped and then concealed with taping compound and spackle.

Flooring: Whatever material you select for this surface should run uninterrupted from the kitchen through the living area. If you change materials at the invisible line separating these two areas, it will be much harder for the living area to flow into the kitchen and visa versa. The place to change finishes, if you are so inclined, is in the bathroom and on the second floor.

Our choice of flooring for this finish group is 2½" tongue-and-groove wood strips with a matt polyurethane finish. White oak is preferred over red oak for its handsome grain and durability. However, this should not be stained dark or scratches that do penetrate the polyurethane will appear white. Yellow pine strip flooring is equally common in less expensive construction, but because it's a soft wood, it wears much less well.

Bathroom Finishes: If the rest of your walls are gypboard, your bathroom walls and ceiling should be waterproof gypboard. The tub surround, the base, and the floor should be ceramic tile set in mastic. If you can afford it, ceramic tile wainscoting should run part way up the east wall behind the sink and water closet to protect the gypboard wall. Ceramic tiles come in many sizes and finishes, the most common of which are 4", 2", and 1" square, glazed or matt finish. Do not use a light colored grout; it always discolors with either mold or mildew. Mildew also forms on the surface of matt ceramic tile when used on the walls of tub enclosures. But because both the finish and the range of colors available are so handsome, you may find the added maintenance worth the effort. Our choice of finishes for this group are waterproof gypboard for upper walls and ceilings, 4" by 4" square glazed tile tub surround and wainscoting, and 1" by 1" matt-finish floor tile, all grouted in a dark gray or beige.

Kitchen Cabinetwork: There are many ways to build kitchen cabinets, but apart from the store-bought cabinets we mention in finish group 4, we are offering only one method. This is the plywood box cabinet with flush overlay doors and door fronts, a reasonably simple and contemporary approach that gives you the most storage out of the space enclosed. The doors and drawer fronts can be virtually any material or finish.

For this finish group we suggest that the ¾" plywood doors and drawer fronts be made of finish-grade birch veneer with hardwood edges, and a plastic laminate countertop and backsplash also trimmed in hardwood. The trim eliminates the ugly black line which appears any time two surfaces of plastic laminate meet at a 90-degree angle.

Finish Group 2 The finishes in group 2 are rich and varied and involve, at least on the interior, some slightly unusual juxtapositions.

Wall and Ceiling Finish: If natural finishes and warm textures are your preference, and clear pine or spruce boards ½" by 3" are available, we suggest nailing them side by side vertically on horizontal blocking between the studs and rafters. Be certain to stagger the joints between board lengths.

Flooring: Studded rubber resilient floor tile, a rubber

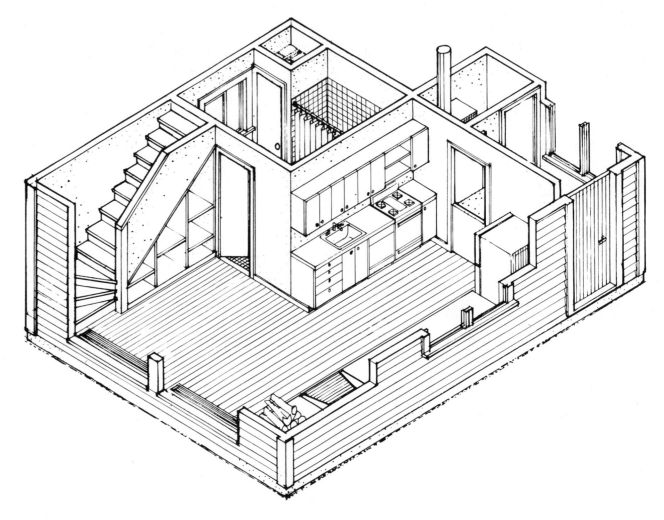

INTERIOR ISOMETRIC - FINISH GROUP 1

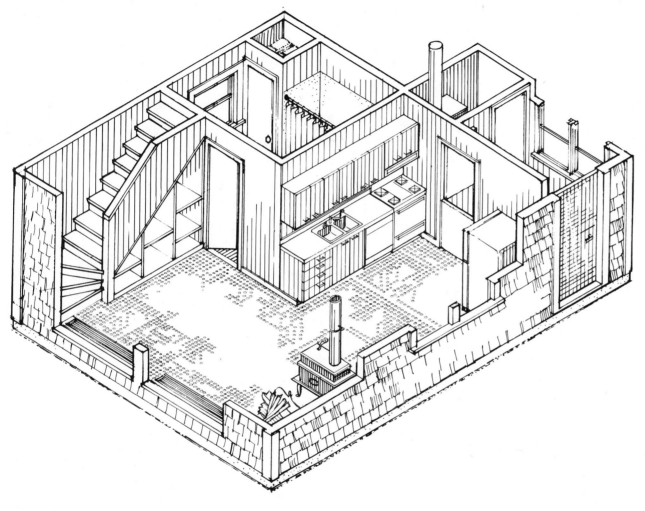

INTERIOR ISOMETRIC - FINISH GROUP 2

floor tile with a grid of slightly raised circular rubber studs about the size of quarters, is extremely common abroad and is coming more into use here. It requires no maintenance other than mopping. It was originally developed and distributed by the Pirelli Tire Corporation and has since been "knocked off" by the Hastings Pavement Company, among others. It comes in a range of thicknesses and colors. Our preference is for the dark gray, green, and chocolate brown.

Bathroom Finishes: If you use the ½" by 3" pine strips in the rest of the house, you can also use them in the bathroom if there is no insulation between the studs, or if you first apply a layer of exterior plywood to the walls and ceiling to protect the insulation from the moisture. The rubber floor tile can be run into the bathroom as well, if a ceramic tile floor is not required by law. If you wish to avoid mixing ceramic tile with these other finishes, select a fiberglass or an acrylic bathtub which is molded complete with its own enclosure.

It may seem strange to you to do the bathroom in the same materials as the rest of the house, but a bathroom so finished feels very luxurious, even when equipped with clothes washers and the like.

Kitchen Cabinetwork: Here we suggest using the same pattern of strips on the walls for the cabinet doors and drawer fronts. The tricky part is to be certain that the door and drawer fronts are hung square so the vertical stripping appears to run in straight lines from the floor to the top of the cabinets. For the countertop we are specifying Johns-Manville's "Colorlith," a simulated soapstone material that comes in a very good looking gray and brown. It has been used for countertops in science labs for decades.

Finish Group 3 The materials in this group are both more sparse and elegant than those of the preceding finish groups, but as mentioned before their net price tag is higher.

Wall and Ceiling Finish: Lath and plaster is always an expensive but elegant alternative to gypboard. But if your exterior finish is stucco, keep going and do the inside in plaster too. The cost will be close to that incurred by introducing another trade and doing the inside in gypboard.

Flooring: There are many colors and shapes of quarry tile available on today's market other than the large red unglazed flat tiles we are used to seeing in school cafeterias. Quarry tile is as elegant unadorned as used as a background for decorative rugs and floor coverings. The 6" square size it comes in is well suited to the scale of the Little House, and the maintenance is nonexistent.

Bathroom finishes: If you're using wet plaster in the rest of the house, use Keene's plaster in the bathroom. For flooring, the quarry tile can be run right through and used as a base as well, thus confining your use of ceramic tile to the tub surround. Another choice is to eliminate ceramic tile entirely by using an acrylic or fiberglass tub and enclosure.

Cabinetwork: Here we suggest the same kinds of cabinets as specified in interior finish group 1, except the edges should be veneered rather than done in hard-

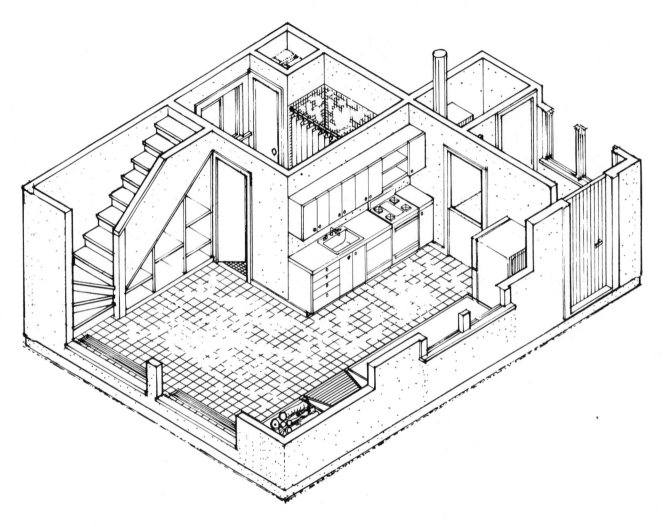

INTERIOR ISOMETRIC - FINISH GROUP 3

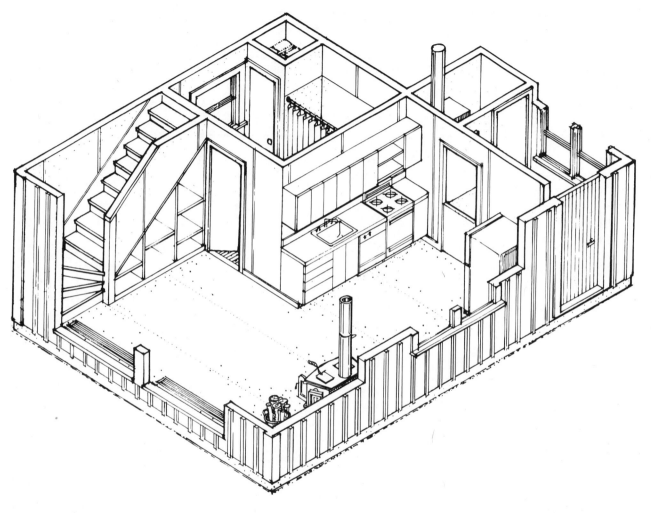

INTERIOR ISOMETRIC - FINISH GROUP 4

wood. Should you wish to pick a more expensive veneer, such as rift-cut oak or cherry or walnut, the grain can then continue from panel to panel without being interrupted by the edging.

Naturally finished cabinetwork, either oiled or lacquered, requires much less care and maintenance than painted cabinetwork unless you can afford the process of spraying the paint on in three or four coats and sanding it in between. But whatever the outside finish, the inside should definitely be left natural and oiled or sealed with a coat of clear varnish.

Dupont's Corian, made of marble dust in an epoxy matrix, would be an ideal countertop for these cabinets whether they are oiled or spray-painted because of its rich simplicity. But it's almost prohibitively expensive. Thus we have specified butcher block for this finish group. This material made of long strips of maple laminated together is every cook's dream until he/she lives with having to clean it, with its swelling from the moisture around the sink, and splitting in response to the heat of the stove. If you're building two Little House units and thus an enlarged kitchen, put the butcher block on the section of counter next to the refrigerator and use any of the other materials mentioned around the sink and stove.

Finish Group 4 The choice and combination of finishes in this group might render your Little House just-plain-folksy or extremely spartan. One thing for sure is that the finishes we suggest and the many others available at the same price will result in a less expensive

Little House than we have seen so far.

Wall and Ceiling Finishes: There are on the market many varieties of wallboards made of pressed fibers, wood chips, and so on that are then veneered with paper or wood or a texture of some sort. They are generally cheaper than gypboard and the other finishes mentioned so far, but even after painting they tend to be homelier in appearance.

Flooring: In addition to coming in thousands of textures and patterns, both vinyl asbestos tile and linoleum can be obtained in solid colors. The solid colors are harder to keep clean but in our opinion well worth the effort because decorative carpets or area rugs can be used without conflicting with some pattern the tile is trying to imitate.

Bathroom Finishes: Again, if your local code does not require a ceramic tile, you can use fiberglass or plastic laminate paneling with metal edge strips around the tub and vinyl asbestos tile or linoleum on the floor.

Cabinetwork: In this area we leave you on your own to find out who sells the cheapest ready-made wood or metal cabinets in your area, or to discover what you can do best with your own hands.

With the exception of the prefab fireplaces and the different tub surrounds, the equipment and fixtures we have selected vary not with each finish group but rather in response to the variations in floor plan. Thus we present a schedule of the fixtures and equipment already indicated in the plans for the basic Little House, in the three variations, and in the six combinations.

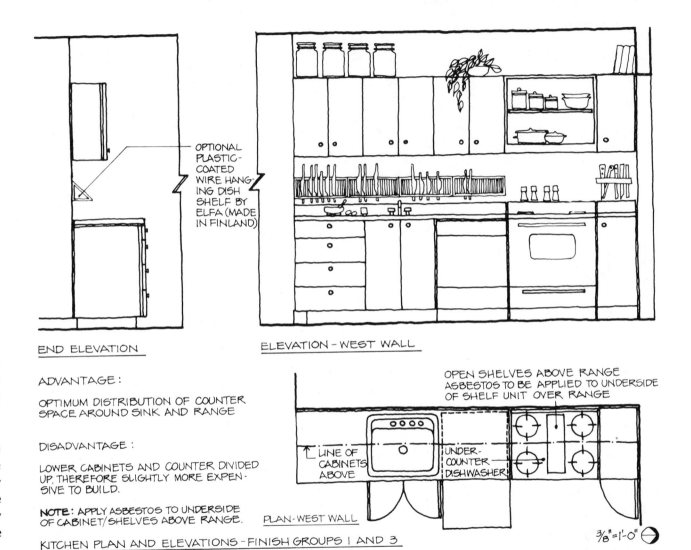

OPTIONAL PLASTIC-COATED WIRE HANGING DISH SHELF BY ELFA (MADE IN FINLAND)

END ELEVATION

ELEVATION - WEST WALL

ADVANTAGE:

OPTIMUM DISTRIBUTION OF COUNTER SPACE AROUND SINK AND RANGE

DISADVANTAGE:

LOWER CABINETS AND COUNTER DIVIDED UP, THEREFORE SLIGHTLY MORE EXPENSIVE TO BUILD.

NOTE: APPLY ASBESTOS TO UNDERSIDE OF CABINET/SHELVES ABOVE RANGE.

OPEN SHELVES ABOVE RANGE ASBESTOS TO BE APPLIED TO UNDERSIDE OF SHELF UNIT OVER RANGE

LINE OF CABINETS ABOVE

UNDER-COUNTER DISHWASHER

PLAN - WEST WALL

$3/8" = 1'-0"$

KITCHEN PLAN AND ELEVATIONS - FINISH GROUPS 1 AND 3

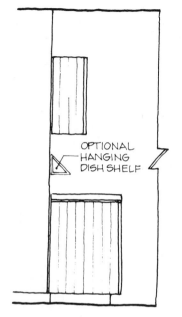

END ELEVATION

OPTIONAL HANGING DISH SHELF

ADVANTAGES:

LARGER AND/OR DOUBLE SINK. RANGE CAN BE VENTED DIRECTLY THROUGH WALL TO EXTERIOR.

DISADVANTAGE:

RANGE LOCATED AGAINST WALL IS NOT WHOLLY DESIRABLE.

NOTE: IF EXHAUST HOOD IS NOT DESIRED, MAKE CABINET OVER STOVE SAME HEIGHT AS ADJACENT CABINET.

ALTERNATE KITCHEN PLAN AND ELEVATIONS - FINISH GROUP 2

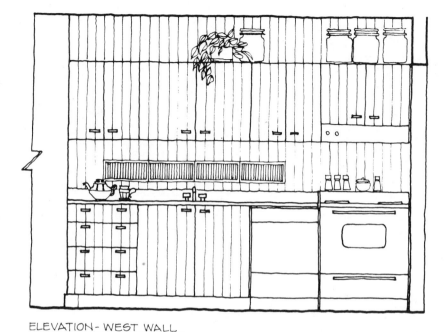

ELEVATION - WEST WALL

CLOSET CABINET PLUS EXHAUST FAN ABOVE RANGE DUCTED THROUGH SHED TO EXTERIOR

LINE OF CABINETS ABOVE

UNDER-COUNTER DISHWASHER (DOOR OPEN)

PLAN

$\frac{3}{8}" = 1'-0"$

Fireplaces: There seem to be two kinds of fireplaces: those which do some real work and those which simply eat oxygen and create drafts.

Of the hardworking types of fireplaces, we favor three Jotul models imported from Sweden by Kristia Associates. The first is a freestanding, cast-iron wood stove 1'2" wide, 2'7½" deep, and 2'6" high. It might well be able to heat the entire Little House. Because of its narrowness and great depth it's best located in a corner. A smaller version of the same stove comes 1'3/4" wide, 1'9" deep, and 2'1" high and could certainly heat the main living area without trouble. The third model, called the Combi-Fire, measures 1'7½" wide, 1'7½" deep, and 2'9" high and has a hopper-type door which opens and slides underneath so you can see the fire.

A comparable line of freestanding stoves and fireplaces is made by the Franklin Stove Company. While these are not as efficient as their Swedish counterparts, they are more readily available and less expensive.

There are many different types of the more conventional but less efficient breed of fireplaces. In the basic Little House we show a Heatilator Mark 123 prefabricated fireplace complete with screen, chimney sections, and roof termination. The surround is 3'0" wide and 2'6" high. The unit is 1'10" deep and requires some kind of enclosure above and on all three sides. Be certain that the surface below it and 1'4" in front of it is well insulated and of noncombustible material.

Kitchen and Laundry Appliances: In selecting appliances what really counts is whether a particular manufacturer will service their products where you're building. Thus, with only a few exceptions, we cite in the final chart in this chapter, simply a description of the appliance and its approximate overall dimensions.

In selecting a refrigerator, be certain the freezer and refrigerator have separate doors as such models are more efficient and require less defrosting. If you wish to conserve energy, avoid self-defrosting refrigerators, self-cleaning ovens, trash compactors, and garbage disposals.

Plumbing Fixtures: The kind of bathroom fixtures and the color you select are, like most everything else, a matter of money and taste. We feel that the finishes in a bathroom and the space itself are more important than the actual fixtures. Thus we recommend only one set of fixtures from the American Standard catalogue because American Standard products are inexpensively priced and available almost everywhere in the country. Kohler, Crane, and others make comparable fixtures which can be used interchangeably with the American Standard fixtures if you prefer.

Toilet Accessories: These are not included on the schedule because how you wish to equip your bathroom is even more a matter of taste than what kind of lavatory suits you. In any event, here are the basic requirements for a bathroom such as those shown in the various Little House configurations: medicine cabinet; three towel bars, 24" long; a semi-recessed toilet-paper holder; two semi-recessed soap dishes in the tub surround; a semi-recessed glass-and-toothbrush holder and an optional semi-recessed soap dish by the lavatory; at least two robe hooks; and a full-length mirror on the

FIXTURE AND/OR ITEM OF EQUIPMENT	BASIC LITTLE HOUSE	LITTLE HOUSE GARAGE	LITTLE HOUSE STUDIO	LITTLE HOUSE REVERSED
FIREPLACE	HEATILATOR MARK 123	JOTUL STOVE 11¾"×1'-9"× 2'-1"	JOTUL COMBI-FIRE 1'-7½"×1'-7½"× 2'-9"	FRANKLIN STOVE
CLOTHES WASHER/DRYER	PORTABLE W&D ± 24"× 18"× 30" NOT STACKED	NOT APPLICABLE	NOT APPLICABLE	PORTABLE W&D ± 24"× 18"× 30" STACKED
REFRIGERATOR	SIDE BY SIDE ± 2'-6"× 2'-4"× 5'-6" (OR TOP & BOTTOM)	INCLUDED IN 3'-6" PULLMAN KITCHEN	INCLUDED IN 5'-0" PULLMAN KITCHEN	SAME AS BASIC LITTLE HOUSE
RANGE	4 ELEMENTS, GR'LL OVEN-GAS OR EL. 2'-6"× 2'-0"× 3'-0"	AS ABOVE	AS ABOVE	SAME AS BASIC LITTLE HOUSE
KITCHEN EXHAUST	NONE	NOT APPLICABLE	NOT APPLICABLE	2'-6" WIDE DUCTED EXHAUST HOOD
DISHWASHER	KITCHENAID® 2'-0"× 2'-0"× 3'-0"	AS ABOVE	AS ABOVE	SAME AS BASIC LITTLE HOUSE
KITCHEN SINK	2'-0" × 2'-0" STAINLESS STEEL OR PORC. ENAMEL	INCLUDED IN 3'-6" PULLMAN KITCHEN	INCLUDED IN 5'-0" PULLMAN KITCHEN	SAME AS BASIC LITTLE HOUSE
BATHROOM LAVATORY	20"× 18" ROXLYN AM. STANDARD	SAME	SAME	SAME
WATER CLOSET	21"× 29"×14" ELONG. CADET AM. STANDARD	SAME	SAME	SAME
BATHTUB	60"× 30"×15" STEEL OR CAST IRON AM. STANDARD	REVERSE OF BASIC LITTLE HOUSE	REVERSE OF BASIC LITTLE HOUSE	60"× 31"×16" CONTOUR CORNER AM. STANDARD
EXTERIOR SHOWER AND HOSE BIB	HOSE ONLY ON NORTH FACADE	HOSE ONLY INSIDE	SAME AS BASIC LITTLE HOUSE	HOSE & SHOWER (OPTIONAL) ON EAST FACADE

SCHEDULE OF FIXTURES AND EQUIPMENT FOR THE BASIC LITTLE HOUSE AND THREE VARIATIONS

COMBINATION ONE	COMBINATION TWO	COMBINATION THREE	COMBINATION FOUR	COMBINATION FIVE	COMBINATION SIX
JOTUL COMBI-FIRE 1'-7½" x 1'-7½" x 2'-9"	HEATILATOR MARK 123	FRANKLIN STOVE	JOTUL STOVE 11¾" x 1'-9" x 2'-1"	JOTUL STOVE 1'-2" x 2'-7½" x 2'-6"	HEATILATOR MARK 123
PORTABLE STACKED VENT THRU CHASE TO ROOF	SAME AS COMBINATION ONE	SAME AS LITTLE HOUSE REVERSED	SAME AS BASIC LITTLE HOUSE	SAME AS COMBINATION ONE	SAME AS BASIC LITTLE HOUSE
SIDE BY SIDE ±2'-9" x 2'-4" x 5'-6" (OR TOP & BOTTOM)	SAME AS COMBINATION ONE	SAME AS LITTLE HOUSE REVERSED	SAME AS COMBINATION ONE	SAME AS COMBINATION ONE	SAME AS COMBINATION ONE
SAME AS BASIC LITTLE HOUSE	SAME AS BASIC LITTLE HOUSE	SAME AS BASIC LITTLE HOUSE	SAME AS BASIC LITTLE HOUSE	SAME AS BASIC LITTLE HOUSE	SAME AS BASIC LITTLE HOUSE
NONE	NONE	DUCTED WALL FAN OVER ENT. TO KITCHEN.	SAME AS COMBINATION THREE	SAME AS COMBINATION THREE	SAME AS LITTLE HOUSE REVERSED
SAME AS BASIC LITTLE HOUSE	SAME AS BASIC LITTLE HOUSE	SAME AS BASIC LITTLE HOUSE	SAME AS BASIC LITTLE HOUSE	SAME AS BASIC LITTLE HOUSE	SAME AS BASIC LITTLE HOUSE
2'-9" x 2'-0" STAINLESS STEEL OR PORC. ENAMEL	SAME AS BASIC LITTLE HOUSE	SAME AS COMBINATION ONE	SAME AS COMBINATION ONE	SAME AS COMBINATION ONE	SAME AS BASIC LITTLE HOUSE
SAME	SAME	SAME	SAME	SAME	SAME
SAME	SAME	SAME	SAME	SAME	SAME
SAME AS LITTLE HOUSE REVERSED	SAME AS BASIC LITTLE HOUSE	DN.STRS SAME AS L.H. REVERSED UP: BASIC L.H.	SAME AS BASIC LITTLE HOUSE	SAME AS BASIC LITTLE HOUSE	DN 1: BASIC L.H. DN 2: L.H. GARAGE UP: L.H. GARAGE
HOSE ONLY ON NORTH FACADE OF SHED	HOSE ONLY ON NORTH FACADE OF UNIT A	SAME AS LITTLE HOUSE REVERSED	SAME AS BASIC LITTLE HOUSE	SAME AS BASIC LITTLE HOUSE	HOSE N. OF UNIT A, HOSE & SHOWER EAST OF UNIT C

SCHEDULE OF FIXTURES AND EQUIPMENT FOR THE SIX COMBINATIONS

back of the bathroom door.

These can be easily obtained in a polished-chrome finish.

Alternate systems for heating the Little House are not included in this chapter because the criteria for this decision do not relate to matters of aesthetics, taste, and architectural tradition, but rather to climate, availability of fuel, and how you plan to use the house. However, in order to provide you with a meaningful and complete set of working drawings in the next chapter, we had to show heating of some kind. We chose a hydronic or hot-water system, the components of which are a boiler with a built-in coil, which heats hot water, and piping to fin-tube convectors (radiators) in each of the rooms. The pros and cons of this and two alternate heating systems will be discussed at length in chapter 8.

Building the Basic Little House

Up to this point we have talked about your right to choose what shape and quality of space you want to live in, and how to finish and equip it. Now we turn to the specific task of building the Little House of your choice. As we can't guess what that choice will be, we have elected to present a complete set of working drawings for the basic Little House in finish group one. Details relating to the variations, combinations, and other three finish groups follow in the next chapter.

In this chapter, the drawings are numbered from A-1 to A-36. They are arranged to proceed from the general to the particular and include charts and schedules where applicable. As every knob and fastener is implied, if not actually described, an experienced contractor can build the entire house from these drawings. Perhaps with some help you can too.

First you must become acquainted with the abbreviations and symbols used throughout. An uncreative but effective exercise would be to stop reading the text and start through the drawings right now. This will quickly introduce you to the language and sequence of the drawings, thus preparing you for later and more detailed discussions.

Each time you read a dimension, note what it refers to: the edge of an element, or the center, or a particular

ABBREVIATIONS

ALUM.	ALUMINUM	FIN.	FINISH	PLYWD.	PLYWOOD
AFF.	ABOVE FINISH FLOOR	FIN.FL.	FINISH FLOOR	R	RISER
ASF	ABOVE SUB-FLOOR	GYP. BD	GYPSUM BOARD	RM.	ROOM
@	AT	H.C.	HOLLOW CORE	R.O.	ROUGH OPENING
B.A.	BRONZE ANODIZED	I.D.	INSIDE DIAMETER	SC.	SOLID CORE
C.T	CERAMIC TILE	LAV.	LAVATORY	SS	STAINLESS STEEL
DN	DOWN	LB/#	POUND	SUB. FL.	SUB-FLOOR
DTL	DETAIL	O.C.	ON CENTER	T.	TREAD
DWG.	DRAWING	OPG.	OPENING	T&G	TONGUE-AND-GROOVE
EQ.	EQUAL	PT.	PAINTED	TYP.	TYPICAL

SYMBOLS

	EARTH		CONCRETE	DTL 4 / A-4	REFER TO DETAIL 4 ON DRAWING A-4
	GRAVEL		CONCRETE BLOCK	4	DOOR NO. 4
	ROUGH LUMBER		STEEL	4	WINDOW NO. 4
	FINISH LUMBER		ALUMINUM		BREAKLINE
	GYPSUM BOARD		FLASHING OR METAL FRAME	A	SECTION A
	BATT OR BLANKET INSULATION	------	OBJECT ABOVE OR BELOW	30°	SURFACE WITH 30 DEGREE SLOPE
		—··—	LINE OF FINISH FLOOR	EQ. EQ.	DIVIDE DIMENSION INTO TWO EQUAL PARTS

A-1 LIST OF ABBREVIATIONS AND SYMBOLS

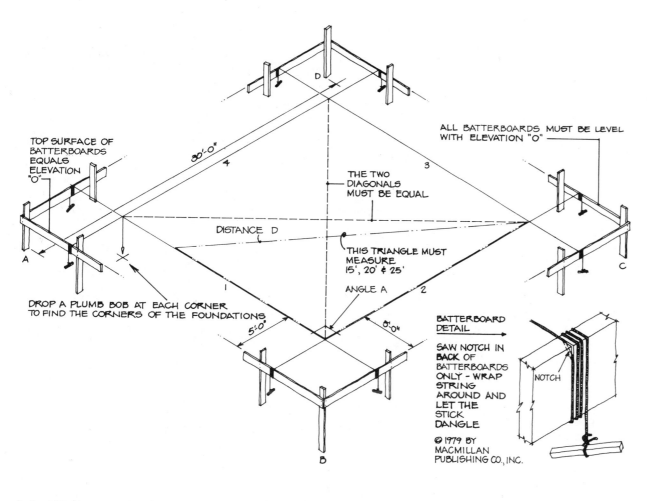

TOP SURFACE OF
BATTERBOARDS
EQUALS
ELEVATION
"O"

30'-0"

ALL BATTERBOARDS MUST BE LEVEL
WITH ELEVATION "O"

THE TWO
DIAGONALS
MUST BE EQUAL

DISTANCE D

THIS TRIANGLE MUST
MEASURE
15', 20' & 25'

ANGLE A

A

DROP A PLUMB BOB AT EACH CORNER
TO FIND THE CORNERS OF THE FOUNDATIONS

5'-0"

5'-0"

C

B

D

4

3

1

2

BATTERBOARD
DETAIL ⟶

SAW NOTCH IN
BACK OF
BATTERBOARDS
ONLY - WRAP
STRING
AROUND AND
LET THE
STICK
DANGLE

© 1979 BY
MACMILLAN
PUBLISHING CO., INC.

NOTCH

A-2   ISOMETRIC · BATTERBOARD LAYOUT

⅛"=1'-0"

layer in a sandwich of elements. On the basic plans, almost all dimensions refer to the rough framing, that is, the structural members rather than the materials which ultimately enclose them. For example, on the ground-floor plan the 20'0" dimension tells you to make the stud wall 20'0" long, outside edge to outside edge. When you add the sheathing and clapboards the wall is even longer, but the amount by which it is longer is not important in this drawing so it is not shown.

You must also know that while certain lumber products are called 2 x 4 studs or 2 x 10 joists, their actual cross sections are considerably smaller, e.g., $1\frac{1}{2}$" by $3\frac{1}{2}$" and $1\frac{1}{2}$" by $9\frac{1}{2}$", respectively. The latter are called dressed dimensions. Basically the differential represents the amount of wood that is turned into sawdust when these pieces are milled. For wood of this type, the nominal dimensions are used in the notes, but dressed dimensions appear on dimension lines. When in doubt follow the dimension lines.

To build things exact, square, and plumb is the goal of fine carpentry, and it must be yours, too. Yet try as you will, your Little House will not come out exactly square and plumb. If you can accept this without abandoning your quest for perfection, you will understand many building details which otherwise don't make sense. For example, look at the interior door details on drawing A-29. Notice that between the rough studs and the finish jamb there is a space for shimming. You might think it would be simpler just to nail the finish jamb right to the studs. But because the studs are bound to be a little bowed, space for shimming is provided so

69

you can wedge the finish jamb perfectly plumb and the door will open and close easily. You must constantly verify dimensions during construction to compensate for deviations in your own carpentry.

The best way to prepare yourself for participating in the construction of your own house is to assume you're going to do it with your own hands. If you're experienced in housebuilding, executing something as clean as the Little House will be a rewarding challenge. If you are not but wish to do some of the work yourself, reading through this chapter will give you a taste of what's involved, so you can decide for yourself what aspects of the work, if any, you want to undertake on your own.

So, for the purpose of this exercise, you're going to do almost all but the mechanical work yourself. First, devote some time to studying carpentry. Many of the do-it-yourself books and carpentry manuals on the market are most instructive. Try to spend as much time as you can around housebuilding sites in order to acquaint yourself with how things are done.

Next you should think out a general building schedule. If you are inexperienced you should start laying your foundations in early spring so you'll have at least six months to frame and close in the house before the cold weather sets in—that is, if you have cold weather where you are. While you're planning your schedule, make a list of the major materials you'll be using as well.

All your structural lumber should be what's called Hem-fir and stamped "construction grade." Hem-fir is a mix of materials; some of the stock is hemlock and some fir. They are used interchangeably when they are

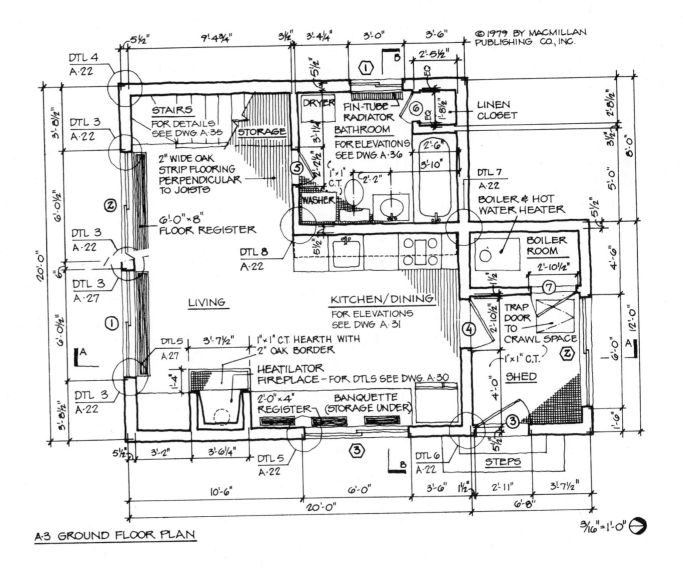

A.3 GROUND FLOOR PLAN

$3/16'' = 1'-0''$

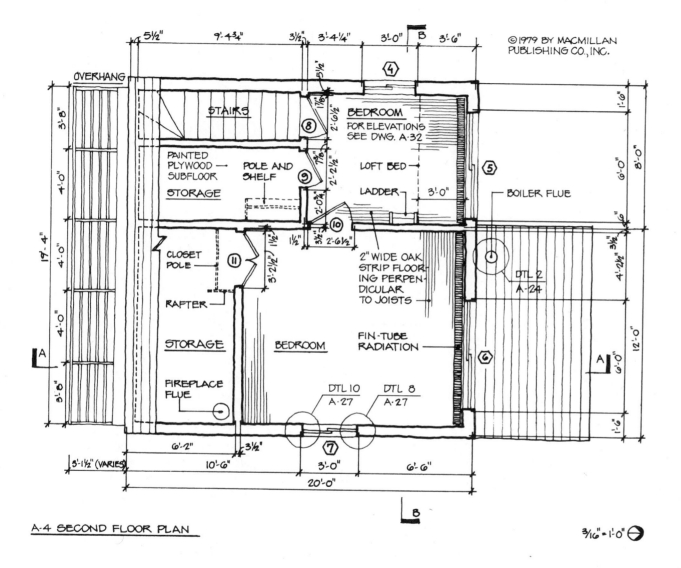

OVERHANG

STAIRS

BEDROOM
FOR ELEVATIONS
SEE DWG. A·32

PAINTED
PLYWOOD →
SUBFLOOR

POLE AND
SHELF

STORAGE

LOFT BED

LADDER

BOILER FLUE

CLOSET
POLE

2" WIDE OAK
STRIP FLOOR-
ING PERPEN-
DICULAR
TO JOISTS

DTL 2
A·24

RAFTER

STORAGE

BEDROOM

FIN-TUBE
RADIATION

FIREPLACE
FLUE

DTL 10
A·27

DTL 8
A·27

5'-1½" (VARIES)

A·4 SECOND FLOOR PLAN

3/16" = 1'-0"

classified Hem-fir. Beams and girders should be made of Hem-fir graded No. 1; rafters, joists, and 2 x 6 studs should be Hem-fir No. 2; and the plates and 2 x 4 studs can be Hem-fir stud grade. Be certain that all the lumber you buy is grade-stamped and that it is kiln-dried. The required thickness for plywood sheathing depends on the distance it must span. It should be APA (American Plywood Association) grade-stamped accordingly. The layers should be laminated with exterior glue. Take copies of your list around to the local lumberyards and suppliers and ask them to fill in their prices. Check prices outside your area. You can sometimes cut costs by buying materials at a distance and trucking them in. If prices seem fairly uniform, deal with those suppliers who have time to talk to you. Their advice can be invaluable.

So you can use electric tools, try to acquire a gasoline-fueled generator or better still get the utility company to run in their wires and tack a meter and some temporary outlets onto a pole. See if the telephone company will install a temporary outdoor phone so you can keep in touch with the world as the work progresses.

If you really are a novice, you should hire at least one experienced carpenter to work with you at first. He will advise you as to what tools to buy, and how to store and care for them. He can also tell you about ordering and storing materials. He may know off-hand what items must be ordered well in advance. He may be able to suggest alternatives to those items which are either unavailable or extra-high priced. Later on, as you become more adept, he might only work part-time. In any case it is essential to have someone expert in construction continually checking your work. If you enlist the support of your local building inspector from the outset, you may find that he can be very helpful in this regard. However, in more remote areas you probably won't see an inspector more than once or twice during construction.

FOUNDATIONS

When you have established how you're going to orient your house and precisely where it is to be sited, dig a test pit at that location 3'0" by 3'0" by 4'0" deep and have samples of the soil at the bottom tested for its percolation (the rate at which liquid flows through it) and its bearing capacity. If its minimum bearing capacity is 4000 psf (pounds per square foot) and if your footings will be resting on undisturbed soil, you're ready to begin. By contrast to the flat and abstract world of architectural drawings, the reality of your not-so-flat land will come as a shock. Take your rented transit, some 4'0" stakes cut from 2 x 4's, batterboards, and some string, and following drawing A-2 begin to inscribe a 20'0" by 20'0" square on a predetermined portion of your site.

Pace off a 30'0" by 30'0" square and drive in a stake at each corner. Make a mark on the stake, which will serve as a benchmark or elevation zero. With the transit and measuring rod, locate elevation zero on the other three corner stakes. The four marks establish a horizontal plane hovering above the uneven ground.

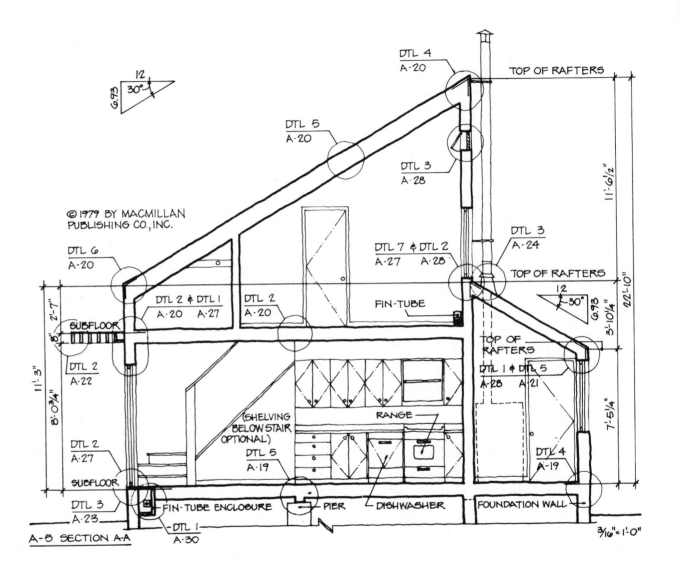

A-5 SECTION A-A

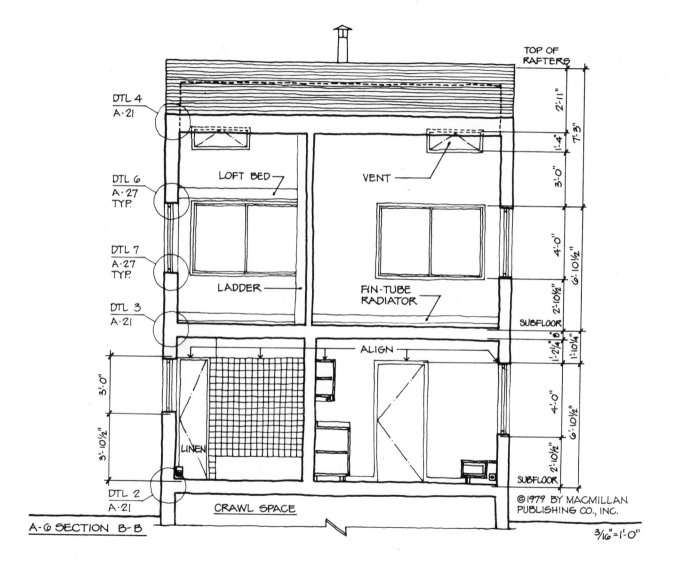

DTL 4
A·21

DTL 6
A·27
TYP.

DTL 7
A·27
TYP.

DTL 3
A·21

DTL 2
A·21

LOFT BED

VENT

LADDER

FIN-TUBE
RADIATOR

LINEN

ALIGN

CRAWL SPACE

A·6 SECTION B-B

3/16" = 1'-0"

TOP OF
RAFTERS

2'-11"

7'-3"

1'-4"

3'-0"

4'-0"

6'-10½"

2'-10½"

SUBFLOOR

1'-2¼"

1'-10¼"

3'-0"

3'-10½"

4'-0"

6'-10½"

2'-10½"

SUBFLOOR

The next task is to inscribe a 20'0" by 20'0" square within that horizontal plane. Drive in two more stakes at each corner as shown. Then nail batterboards horizontally, as shown, making sure to level their top edges accurately at elevation zero. Stretch string 1 tight and fasten it. That string is the first side of the 20-foot square. Stretch string 2. That's side two of the square.

Now you must adjust string 2 until angle A is a right angle. We know from the Pythagorean 3:4:5 right triangle that a triangle with sides 15'0", 20'0", and 25'0" will also be a right triangle. So with a tape, mark out 15'0" on string 1, and 20'0" on string 2. Adjust string 2 until distance D is exactly 25'0". Now the two strings are at right angles.

Measuring 20'0" along string 2 marks the second corner of the building. Stretch string 3 over that mark and square it to string 2. Then proceed to string 4. There's the square.

To check your work, measure both diagonals of the square and all four sides. Each side should be exactly 20'0" long, and the two diagonals should be equal. Do not eliminate this step. It is absolutely vital to have a square and level foundation. The foundations for the shed should be laid out the same way. You may have to go through the whole process several times before it's right.

Now it's time to hire a backhoe and driver to dig your foundation trenches, your septic field, and septic and water line trenches, plus the hole for the oil tank.

While we insist that you have your foundations designed specifically for your Little House and that you build them as they're designed, we'll take you through the building of the foundations we indicate to give you an example of what can be involved.

Footing forms, the next step, are easy to build. The sides of the forms can be the same stock as the 2 x 12's you will use for the rafters. Paint them with oil so the cement won't stick, and reuse them later on. Nail the oiled 2 x 12's to stakes driven in every three feet or so. Order five cubic yards of concrete from whoever sells ready-mix concrete in your area. If possible, prepare the footings for any steps and decks you wish to include and do them all together. This should be 1" diameter stone aggregate concrete whose minimum compressive strength will be 3000 psi (pounds per square inch) at 28 days. If this concrete is to be subject to freezing and thawing, it should be air-entrained as well. It is beyond the scope of this book to explain what all this means in detail. If you're curious, consult a good manual on building materials and construction. In most instances all we can do is tell you what you'll need.

The concrete block you use for your foundations should be hollow load-bearing units conforming to ASTM (American Society for Testing Materials) C90, Grade N-1. The mortar, which you'll have to mix yourself, should conform to ASTM C270, Type S. This is made up of 1 part Portland cement, ½ part lime, and 4½ parts sand. In laying the block, follow the foundation plan carefully. It is designed so that no block cutting is necessary.

The beam pockets allow the large beam to notch into the foundation wall. Use a 4 x 8 x 16 block at these loca-

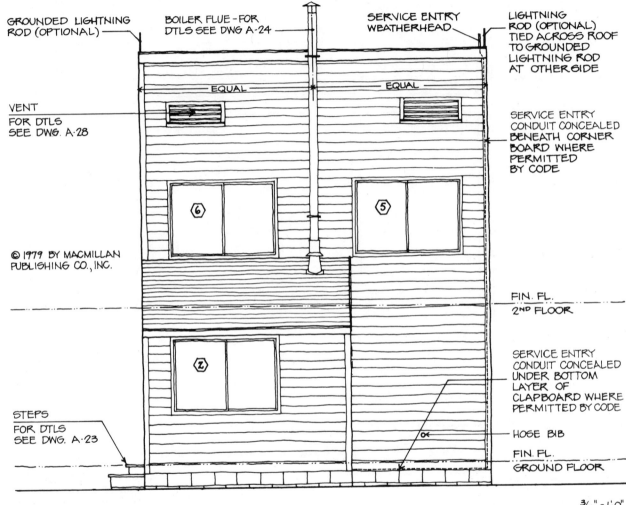

GROUNDED LIGHTNING ROD (OPTIONAL)

BOILER FLUE - FOR DTLS SEE DWG A-24

SERVICE ENTRY WEATHERHEAD

LIGHTNING ROD (OPTIONAL) TIED ACROSS ROOF TO GROUNDED LIGHTNING ROD AT OTHER SIDE

EQUAL EQUAL

VENT FOR DTLS SEE DWG. A-28

SERVICE ENTRY CONDUIT CONCEALED BENEATH CORNER BOARD WHERE PERMITTED BY CODE

© 1979 BY MACMILLAN PUBLISHING CO., INC.

FIN. FL. 2ND FLOOR

SERVICE ENTRY CONDUIT CONCEALED UNDER BOTTOM LAYER OF CLAPBOARD WHERE PERMITTED BY CODE

STEPS FOR DTLS SEE DWG. A-23

HOSE BIB

FIN. FL. GROUND FLOOR

A-7 NORTH ELEVATION

3/16" = 1'-0"

74

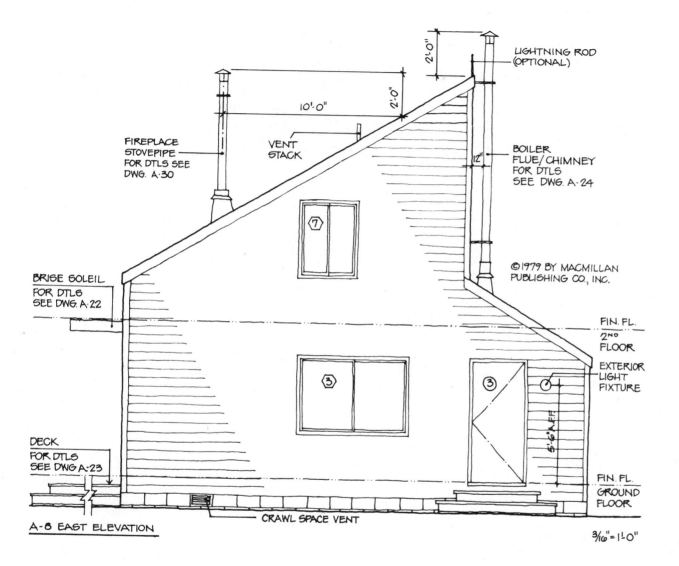

LIGHTNING ROD
(OPTIONAL)

2'-0"

2'-0"

10'-0"

FIREPLACE
STOVEPIPE
FOR DTLS SEE
DWG. A·30

VENT
STACK

12"

BOILER
FLUE/CHIMNEY
FOR DTLS
SEE DWG. A·24

⑦

© 1979 BY MACMILLAN
PUBLISHING CO, INC.

BRISE SOLEIL
FOR DTLS
SEE DWG. A·22

③

③

EXTERIOR
LIGHT
FIXTURE

FIN. FL.
2ND
FLOOR

DECK
FOR DTLS
SEE DWG A·23

5'-6" A.F.F.

FIN. FL.
GROUND
FLOOR

A·8 EAST ELEVATION

CRAWL SPACE VENT

3/16" = 1'-0"

tions. This will allow space for the beam to rest on the foundation wall. Use some bricks and a 2 x 4 under each beam end to shim it up. The anchor bolts should be spaced about 6'0" on center and about 1'0" away from the corners of the building. Sink the anchor bolts into the mortar which is supported by screening, as shown in detail 4, drawing A-19. Leave about 3" exposed. Let the mortar harden. It should take about a day.

The pier will be carrying a heavy load. It is built of concrete blocks 16 x 16 x 8 filled solid with mortar and gravel. All the blocks under the beam pocket and under the post between the sliding doors should also be filled solid with mortar.

Depending on soil conditions, you may need to install foundation drains to carry groundwater away from your foundation walls. To prevent minor seepage through the foundation wall, apply a bituminous coating.

Ventilation of crawl spaces is required by most codes. The block vent shown is extruded aluminum and can be easily mortared in like an ordinary concrete block.

Begin installing the 2 x 8 plates by boring holes for the anchor bolts. Make the holes larger than necessary to allow for some adjustment. Then lay a bed of mortar all along the top of the foundation, and bolt down the 2 x 8's (don't forget to use washers). Use the transit to insure that everything is level. If not, adjust the anchor bolts as necessary.

Don't start shoveling dirt back in the trenches yet. The framing and subfloor must be in place to prevent the foundations from cracking under the pressure of the earth.

Concrete work is so brutal and exacting; you might consider subcontracting the whole foundation package. Professionals can do it faster, and you can use the extra time organizing other aspects of the work.

FRAMING

Framing is the most enjoyable part of housebuilding. The work goes fast, and the house springs almost magically into existence. When the lumberyard delivers your lumber, have it set where it's most convenient to the work and sort it into sizes. You will notice that most of your lumber is bowed a little. Choose the straightest pieces for your beams and edge members.

Now look at drawing A-13—the ground-floor framing plan. It consists almost entirely of 2 x 8 stock. The one important exception is the center girder which is made up of three 2 x 12 beams.

To begin, set a 2 x 8 on edge on all four sides of the 20′0″ square. Nail them together at the corners and toenail them into the sill all along the sides. If you need advice regarding what kind of nails to use for this and all the other tasks, consult any carpentry manual. Then build the big girder of 2 x 12's. This is actually made up of an 8′0″ long beam and a 12′0″ long beam butted together at the center pier. Spike the components of each piece at 12″ intervals and at opposing angles. Set the beams in place and nail them in.

When you place the floor joists, set them so that they camber upward. The load of the flooring, furniture, and people will render them horizontal. Using joist hangers,

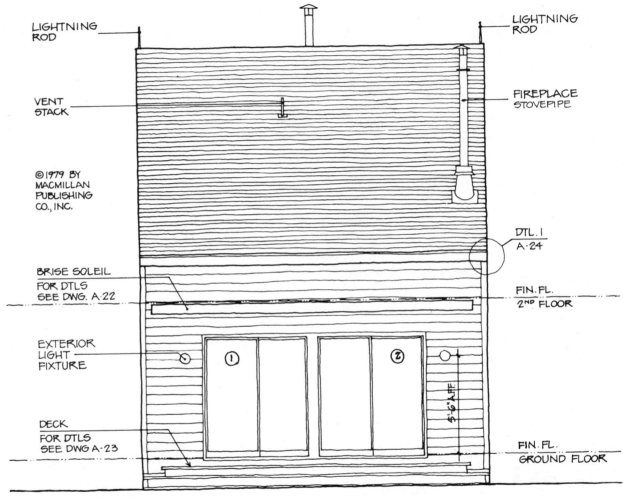

LIGHTNING ROD

VENT STACK

© 1979 BY MACMILLAN PUBLISHING CO., INC.

BRISE SOLEIL
FOR DTLS SEE DWG. A-22

EXTERIOR LIGHT FIXTURE

DECK
FOR DTLS SEE DWG A-23

LIGHTNING ROD

FIREPLACE STOVEPIPE

DTL.1
A-24

FIN. FL. 2ND FLOOR

5′-6″ A.F.F.

FIN. FL. GROUND FLOOR

A-9 SOUTH ELEVATION

3/16″ = 1′-0″

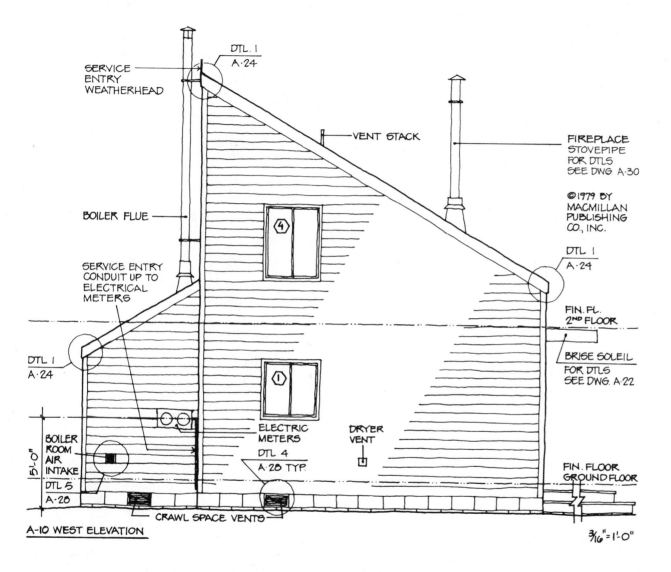

SERVICE
ENTRY
WEATHERHEAD

DTL. 1
A·24

VENT STACK

FIREPLACE
STOVEPIPE
FOR DTLS
SEE DWG. A·30

©1979 BY
MACMILLAN
PUBLISHING
CO., INC.

BOILER FLUE

④

DTL. 1
A·24

SERVICE ENTRY
CONDUIT UP TO
ELECTRICAL
METERS

FIN. FL.
2ND FLOOR

DTL 1
A·24

BRISE SOLEIL
FOR DTLS
SEE DWG. A·22

①

BOILER
ROOM
AIR
INTAKE

ELECTRIC
METERS

DRYER
VENT

DTL 5
A·28

DTL 4
A·28 TYP.

FIN. FLOOR
GROUND FLOOR

5'-0"

CRAWL SPACE VENTS

A·10 WEST ELEVATION

3/16"=1'-0"

install the joists 16″ on center. Do not deviate from the 16″ spacing except where indicated on the framing plans or you will have difficulty installing the plywood sub-flooring later.

At this point whoever is going to install the piping for your plumbing and heating system should begin while the crawl space is open to the sky.

Once the piping is in, you're ready to install the fin-tube enclosure under the south wall and insulate the floor joists. Usually this is not done until after the roof is on and the exterior walls are sheathed. But lying on your back on the ground clothed from head to toe to protect yourself from falling glass fibers just to staple batt insulation between the joists by the light of a drop light is so miserable a task we are proposing this alternative.

Cut some ¼″ thick sheets of plywood into 14″ or 14½″ strips. Set some nails into the sides of the joists towards the bottom. Leave ½″ to ¾″ of each nail head exposed. Lay the strips on the projecting nails, then install 6″ thick reflective-foil-backed insulation shiny side up. The foil will pay for itself by reducing your overall heat loss. You can't knock off for the day once the insulation is installed. It may rain during the night, and insulation, once wet, is less than useless. Press on with the subflooring.

Plywood is stronger if it spans in the direction of its face grain. For extra rigidity, glue-nail, that is to say both glue and nail the panels down as shown in draw-ing A-14. Use B.F. Goodrich PL400 APA (American Plywood Association) approved elastomeric construc-tion adhesive. Then stretch plastic over the whole floor, tape the full length of each joint or overlap the plastic so water can't get between the plastic and the subfloor and ultimately into the insulation below. Staple the edges down over the sides of the framing, trim them neatly, and there you are, standing on the future floor of your new house.

When you return in the morning, it will be safe to back-fill the foundation trenches. Have the earth sloped slightly upward against the walls so rainwater will run away from the house.

The exterior walls and the interior wet wall are framed with 2 x 6's spaced 24″ on center rather than the conventional 2 x 4's spaced 16″ on center. This is slightly more costly but it permits the installation of 6″ rather than 4″ thick insulation. Other interior partitions are framed with 2 x 4's spaced 16″ on center.

To find vertical stud length, you always have to calculate a little. For example, find the stud length for a wall frame 8′0¾″ high: there are two top plates and one bottom plate, each 1½″ thick for a total of 4½″. So 8′0¾″ minus 4½″ equals 7′8¼″. You can either cut these to this length or order them precut from the lumberyard. Study the door and window details before framing the openings. Note the special framing detail 1, drawing A-28, at the top of the window in the shed. We did that to make all the window frames line up. Don't forget the blocking for the recessed medicine cabinet in the bathroom, or for the boiler room vent.

When you're ready to start, cut the studs, headers, and sills to the proper lengths, saving the scraps for blocking or for firewood. Lay them out on the floor just

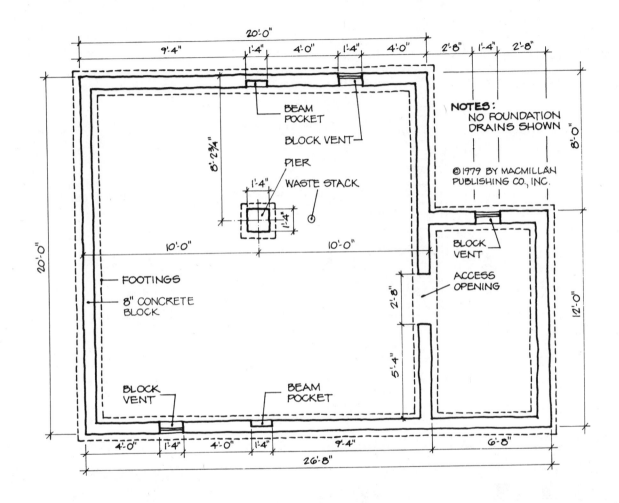

NOTES:
NO FOUNDATION
DRAINS SHOWN

© 1979 BY MACMILLAN
PUBLISHING CO., INC.

A-11 FOUNDATION PLAN

3/16″ = 1′-0″

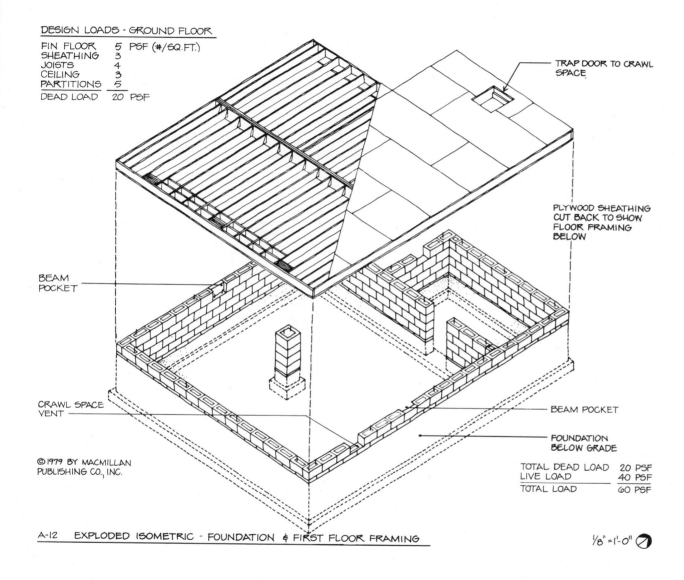

DESIGN LOADS · GROUND FLOOR

FIN FLOOR	5 PSF (#/SQ.FT.)
SHEATHING	3
JOISTS	4
CEILING	3
PARTITIONS	5
DEAD LOAD	20 PSF

TRAP DOOR TO CRAWL SPACE

PLYWOOD SHEATHING CUT BACK TO SHOW FLOOR FRAMING BELOW

BEAM POCKET

CRAWL SPACE VENT

BEAM POCKET

FOUNDATION BELOW GRADE

TOTAL DEAD LOAD	20 PSF
LIVE LOAD	40 PSF
TOTAL LOAD	60 PSF

A-12   EXPLODED ISOMETRIC · FOUNDATION & FIRST FLOOR FRAMING

⅛" = 1'-0"

as they will be in the wall, nail them together, tilt them up carefully, and brace them so the assembly stands plumb. (You may need another person to help you tilt them into place without their wobbling loose.) Nail the wall panels together hard at the corners and overlap the top plates to reinforce the corners. To position interior partitions, follow the rough dimensions indicated on the plans.

As you are framing, you will notice that at several places along the exterior walls three- and four-way framing occurs. (See details 2 and 3, drawing A-21, and details 6 and 7, A-22.) Once the framing is complete, there is no way to insulate these pockets. So keep a roll of fiberglass nearby and loosely pack these pockets as you come across them.

Thanks to your own foresight or to the advice of your professional carpenter, you will have long since ordered the steel flitch plate with the requisite ¾" bolts, nuts, and washers, and you will be ready to start framing the second floor. We think it only fair to mention that this flitch plate is not absolutely essential. Instead you can install a deeper built-up girder made up of three 2 x 12's, as is the one designed for the ground-floor framing.

We elected to use the flitch plate beam in spite of its additional expense because we felt that a break in the ceiling between the living area and kitchen would seriously interrupt the flow of space much as would the change in floor finish which we mentioned in the previous chapter. The second reason for using the flitch plate here is to prepare you for the fact that you'll have to use one if you build a second unit and you want the ground floor to be completely open, or should you want to build a Little House studio or garage.

Use good straight Douglas fir for the flitch plate beam and bolt it tightly according to the drawings. Make sure the built-up columns which support it are well spiked together so they can carry the load.

Double up the joists where indicated on the drawings. These support the dead load, that is to say the weight of the lumber and finish materials of the partitions above. Note that every third joist overhangs the south wall by 3'0". These carry the 2 x 8 louvers supported on ledger strips which make up the brise soleil.

Nail down the subfloor as before. Staple plastic over the subfloor as you did on the floor below. This time your purpose is to provide a temporary roof overhead. The plastic need not be removed when the finished floor is installed except if moisture has gotten beneath it, or when there is no finished floor. Begin framing the second-floor walls. The highest walls will need at least one course of blocking between the studs.

While framing the second-floor walls may come easily as you've become more proficient, the angles of the roof framing may set you back a bit. But if you cut the joists or rafters to the measurements shown, and you cut them so they camber upward, and you don't forget to drill the vent holes, you'll do fine. The vent holes are required to ventilate the space between the roof and the finished ceiling below. If they are omitted, condensation will collect and cause mildew on the gypboard ceiling. If it's still just you and the hired car-

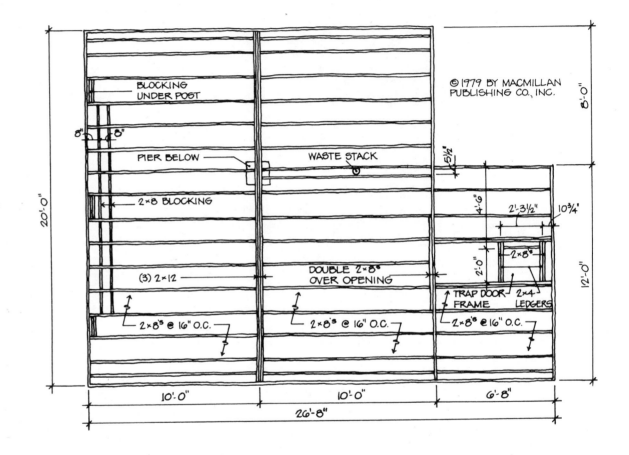

A-18   GROUND FLOOR FRAMING PLAN

3/16" = 1'-0"

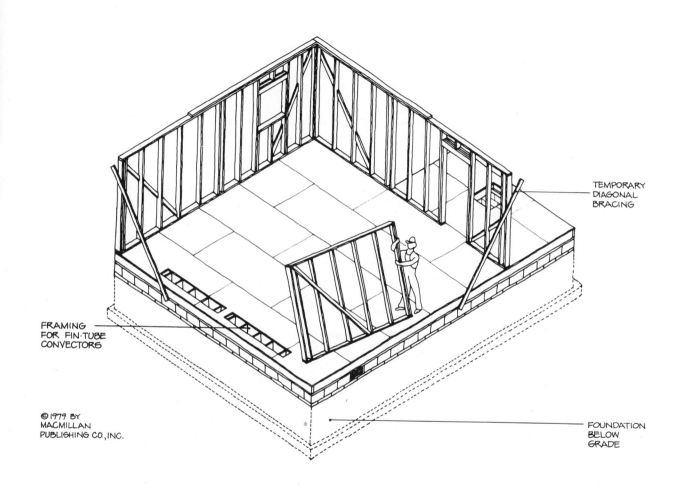

TEMPORARY
DIAGONAL
BRACING

FRAMING
FOR FIN-TUBE
CONVECTORS

© 1979 BY
MACMILLAN
PUBLISHING CO., INC.

FOUNDATION
BELOW
GRADE

A-14   ISOMETRIC - FIRST FLOOR WALL FRAMING

⅛"=1'-0"

penter working, find some help. The two of you will have a rough time setting joists this heavy this high off the ground. From here on in things will get easier because instead of having only abstract drawings, you have a full-scale model to refer to. Much of what seemed confusing when you began will now be very clear.

Sheathing the walls and roof is easy. Starting at the bottom, cover the exterior walls with ⅝" exterior plywood. Stagger the plywood joints. Span the top grain of the plywood perpendicular to the studs and rafters wherever possible. Remove the temporary diagonal braces as you go. Staple #30 saturated felt, better known as building paper, over the entire surface before it rains.

ROOFING

The need to shed water determines most exterior details. If you think of every element of the exterior surface as a shingle, that is to say overlapping the element below it and being overlapped by the one above, it will help you understand why things are placed as they are. Bear this in mind while you install all the edge trim. This must be installed before the roof shingles because it is overlapped by them. If you study details 4 and 6 in both drawings A-20 and A-21, you'll see that the edge trim consists of a 1 x 6 pine trim board which runs all around the roof edge. Underneath it is a 1 x 4 blocking strip. Together these pieces form an overlap for the top course of clapboards. Notice the ¾" vent holes drilled just below the 1 x 4 and the little pieces of insect screen stapled over the holes. Use clear pine, free of large knots, for this and other finish trim. Neatly cut and join the pieces and sand smooth any rough spots.

Begin at the peak, then do the eave and finally the sloping sides. The roof trim elevations show a tidy way to handle the corners. Install safety boards on the roof to catch you or anything else that's falling, or at least wear a safety belt whenever you work on a slope this steep.

Next you must cut holes in the sheathing to accommodate all the items which penetrate the roof. Assuming the Metalbestos chimney parts have been ordered and have arrived, cut a hole in the sheathing and build the Metalbestos roof support for the boiler chimney right into the shed roof. Then cut a hole for the Heatilator chimney pipe, as per the details on drawings A-24 and A-30 and the instructions that accompany the Metalbestos and Heatilator components. Be certain to leave 2″ clearance around each chimney. Finally cut the 3″ diameter hole for the plumbing vent. If your plumber doesn't supply a flashing collar for the vent, get one from a hardware or plumbing supply store. It isn't included as a detail because it's a stock item requiring no particular talent to install.

Now you're ready to work on the roof itself. First, nail on the eave flashing or drip edge. This is aluminum or galvanized metal which comes in 8′0″ or 10′0″ lengths. Snip it with shears and butt the ends.

Next cover the roof with the 15-pound asphalt

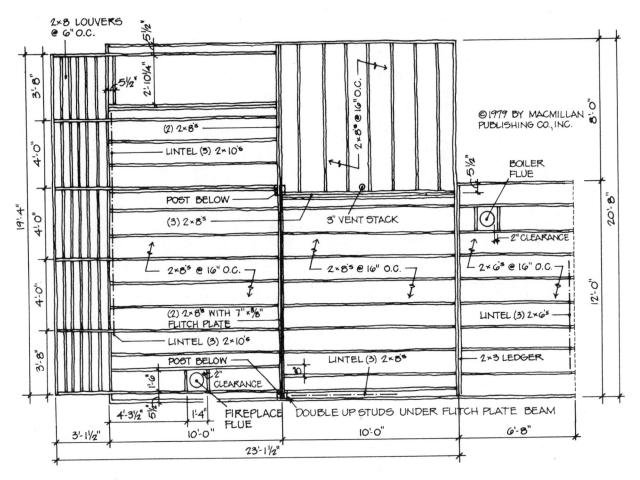

A-15 SECOND FLOOR FRAMING PLAN

$\frac{3}{16}″ = 1′-0″$

82

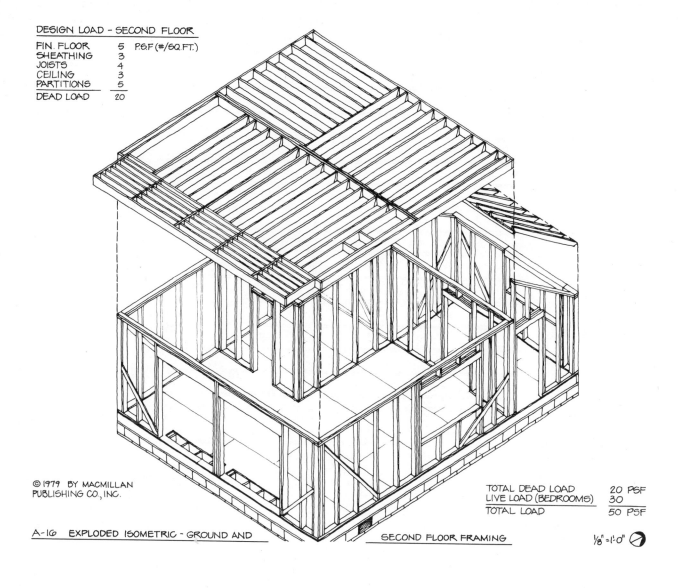

DESIGN LOAD - SECOND FLOOR

FIN. FLOOR	5	P.S.F. (#/SQ.FT.)
SHEATHING	3	
JOISTS	4	
CEILING	3	
PARTITIONS	5	
DEAD LOAD	20	

TOTAL DEAD LOAD	20 PSF
LIVE LOAD (BEDROOMS)	30
TOTAL LOAD	50 PSF

A-16   EXPLODED ISOMETRIC - GROUND AND   SECOND FLOOR FRAMING   ⅛" = 1'-0"

saturated felt. Start at the lower edge of the roof and roll the paper out to cover the pine edge trim and drip edge. Cut and staple it neatly. Overlap the next course 6" and repeat until you've gone all the way up the roof overlapping the Metalbestos roof support on the way.

Now you can begin to apply the shingles themselves. Start at the bottom again and work toward the top. Use the 235-pound asphalt organic felt 3-tab self-sealing strip type. Carefully follow the manufacturer's directions using 1¼" roofing nails with annular rings to nail the shingle strips in place.

When you get to the Metalbestos chimney pipe, study the detail on drawing A-24. Notice that the adjustable roof flashing overlaps the shingles below, and is overlapped above. Apply roofing cement under the flashing to make it watertight. At the Heatilator fireplace pipe, follow their instructions for installing the "cap for 30-degree roof." At the 3" plumbing vent, the flashing overlaps the shingle below, and is overlapped above. Use roofing cement as before. Shingle right up to the peak of the main roof. Finish the roof with 4" peak flashing as shown. Repeat the process for the shed and your roofs will be complete.

WINDOWS AND SLIDING DOORS

Your immediate goal is to get the house closed in so you can proceed with the more painstaking interior finishing safe from the rain and cold. Thus the next step is to install the windows, sliding doors, and exterior trim. Carefully study the head, sill, and jamb details on drawing A-27. You'll notice that the opening afforded by the rough framing is slightly wider than the window and/or sliding door itself. This allows you to shim it level. The best device for shimming is a pair of cedar shingles wedged against each other.

The best instructions for installing, flashing, and caulking the sliding doors and windows will be those of the manufacturers. Go slowly, particularly with the sliding doors. Don't try to install them alone. Pay attention to right- and left-handedness, that is to say which side slides and which side is fixed. Be certain that every element is level and plumb. Force neither the frames nor the screws; screws strip and doors break. Replacement panels can take weeks to arrive.

The exterior window trim is ¾" by 2" (actual dimensions) all around. The sill piece is routed out to overlap the clapboards below. The head trim is overlapped by a length of standard cap flashing. You will notice that some of the exterior door trim consists of wide pine boards which must be ripped to the proper width and placed with finish nails.

As you get further into finish work you may want to consider renting or buying a small table saw. Finish work requires care and accuracy if it is to look anything but makeshift. Your task will be much easier and less time-consuming if you make this nominal investment.

WALL VENTS

Following details on drawing A-28, place the wall vents in the framed openings high on the north facade. Need-

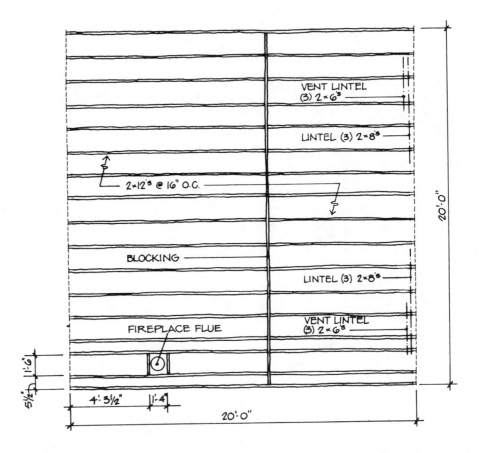

A-17 ROOF FRAMING PLAN

3/16" = 1'-0"

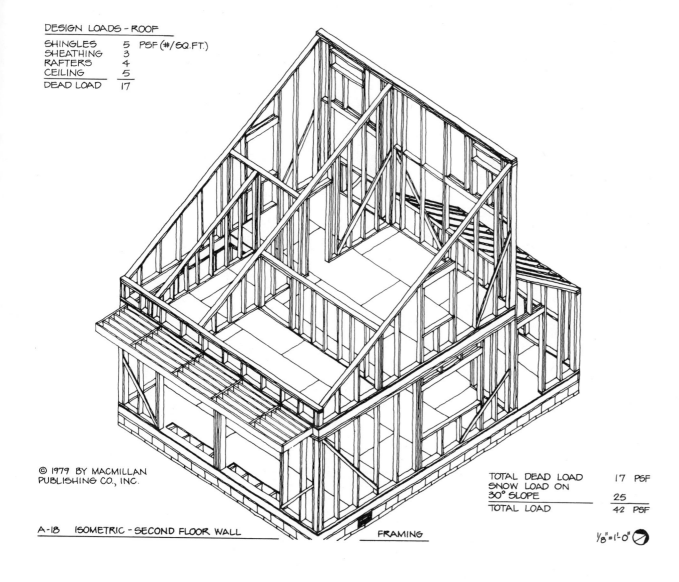

DESIGN LOADS - ROOF

SHINGLES	5	PSF (#/SQ.FT.)
SHEATHING	3	
RAFTERS	4	
CEILING	5	
DEAD LOAD	17	

TOTAL DEAD LOAD	17	PSF
SNOW LOAD ON 30° SLOPE	25	
TOTAL LOAD	42	PSF

A-18 ISOMETRIC - SECOND FLOOR WALL

FRAMING

⅛"=1'-0"

less to say, these should be the same bronze anodized finish as the sliding doors and windows. Trim them as you would a window. Seal in the vents with clear silicone caulk. Install the boiler room vent as well.

ENTRY DOOR

Hanging doors, prehung or not, is tricky business. If you are not familiar with what is involved, buy doors premortised for hinges and locksets, or consult your carpentry manual. The necessary instructions are far too detailed to be included here.

When you have a feel for it, study our exterior door details on drawing A-29. We show a door frame custom-built from $1\frac{3}{8}$" stock. Like all the other sills in the house, the exterior sill is oak. However, to install so wide a sill, you must cut down the 2 x 8 framing underneath. Use countersunk screws to fasten down the sill and then plug the holes with $\frac{1}{4}$" dowel.

You must also undercut the door itself to accommodate the weatherstripping. The extent of the undercut depends on what type of weatherstripping you buy. Once the door is hung, apply adhesive-backed foam rubber weatherstripping at the head and joints.

CLAPBOARDS AND SIDING

Your Little House is now closed in and is it ever ugly with that black building paper all over it! So on with the siding.

The first step is to nail on the cornerboards or trim. If each side of the corner trim is to look as though it is

$3\frac{1}{2}''$ wide, you can use a 1 x 4 for one side and rip another 1 x 4 down to $2\frac{3}{4}''$ wide for the other side, or order the exact size needed from the lumber yard. They stock #1 common pine in many sizes just for this purpose. Tuck these cornerboards up under the 1 x 6 roof trim, nail them with aluminum nails (to prevent rust) to the plywood and to each other. Insert a bead of silicone caulk in the butt joint. Saw off the bottoms 1" below the plywood sheathing.

You should aspire to make your clapboards line up with the tops and bottoms of the door and window frames. It not only makes a world of difference visually, it eliminates a lot of fussy cutting and fitting as well. You will probably have to vary the exposure widths as much as $\frac{3}{8}''$ to achieve this. Recommended exposures for both shingles and clapboards vary from region to region depending largely on the wind and the weather. We show approximately 6" "to the weather."

The first course of clapboarding is the bottom course. It should be double and should hang 1" below the edge of the plywood. Snap chalklines from the cornerboards to mark each course. Butt the clapboards tight against the cornerboards. Stagger the joints.

At the window sills, push the clapboard edges tight up into the routed space. Whittle them a little thinner there if you have to. Apply a bead of silicone caulk under there to insure against rain seeping behind the clapboards. Cap flashing should be inserted over all exterior doors and windows.

Push the final courses of clapboards up under the roof trim, but be sure to notch them out a little for the vent

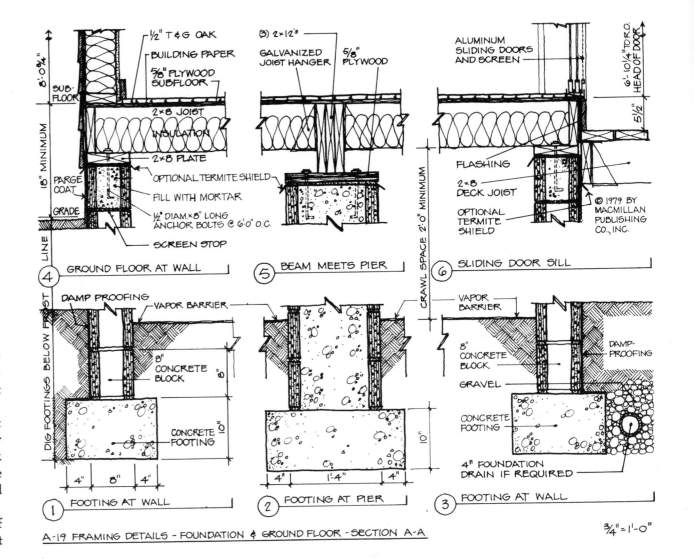

A-19 FRAMING DETAILS - FOUNDATION & GROUND FLOOR - SECTION A-A

$\frac{3}{4}'' = 1'-0''$

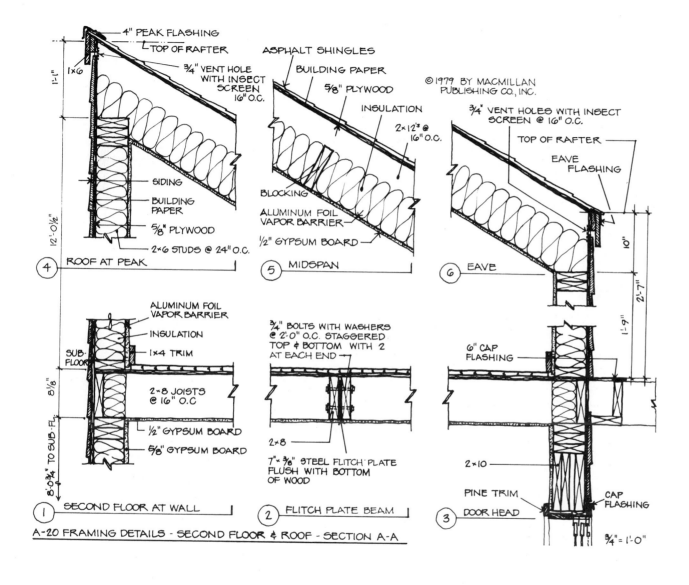

4 ROOF AT PEAK

4" PEAK FLASHING
TOP OF RAFTER
1×6
3/4" VENT HOLE WITH INSECT SCREEN 16" O.C.
1'-1"
12'-0½"
SIDING
BUILDING PAPER
5/8" PLYWOOD
2×6 STUDS @ 24" O.C.

5 MIDSPAN

ASPHALT SHINGLES
BUILDING PAPER
5/8" PLYWOOD
INSULATION
2×12's @ 16" O.C.
BLOCKING
ALUMINUM FOIL VAPOR BARRIER
1/2" GYPSUM BOARD

6 EAVE

© 1979 BY MACMILLAN PUBLISHING CO., INC.
3/4" VENT HOLES WITH INSECT SCREEN @ 16" O.C.
TOP OF RAFTER
EAVE FLASHING
10"
2'-7"
1'-9"

1 SECOND FLOOR AT WALL

ALUMINUM FOIL VAPOR BARRIER
INSULATION
1×4 TRIM
SUB-FLOOR
2×8 JOISTS @ 16" O.C.
1/2" GYPSUM BOARD
5/8" GYPSUM BOARD
8½"
8'-0¾" TO SUB-FL.

2 FLITCH PLATE BEAM

3/4" BOLTS WITH WASHERS @ 2'-0" O.C. STAGGERED TOP & BOTTOM WITH 2 AT EACH END
2×8
7"×3/8" STEEL FLITCH PLATE FLUSH WITH BOTTOM OF WOOD

3 DOOR HEAD

6" CAP FLASHING
2×10
PINE TRIM
CAP FLASHING
3/4" = 1'-0"

A-20 FRAMING DETAILS - SECOND FLOOR & ROOF - SECTION A-A

holes. It's a good idea to have previously marked on the sheathing where they are located.

Clapboarding your house will take about a week depending on your own proficiency and how many people are working with you. It's an ideal time to schedule the electrician to begin and the plumber to return to complete the roughing in as you and your crew will not be underfoot.

Using the electrical plans in chapter 8, the electrician should be able to complete his work in a few days. He comes with a big fast drill, his use of which must sometimes be restrained. Don't let him drill through major beams and posts. At wall studs and floor or ceiling joists, make sure he drills through the *center* of the member in question. A hole at the center won't weaken the member much. Have him install the lightning rods while he's there.

The plumber also comes with a drill. He will partially obliterate the stud wall between kitchen and bath. Don't worry about this as it isn't a load-bearing partition. Just make sure his vent stack passes by the joists as shown on the plumbing drawings in chapter 8. Make certain he sets the bathtub in place because it's too large to go through the finished bathroom door opening and because both the wall and floor finishes must overlap its edges.

Most of the ground-floor roughing for the heating should have been done following the completion of the ground-floor framing. Now the plumber can install the second-floor piping, the boiler, and the boiler chimney, following which you can frame the partition separating the boiler from the rest of the shed.

The electrical and plumbing inspectors should be called in to certify that the wiring and roughing-in have been done according to code. It is illegal to close in the walls until their approval has been obtained. If you bypass this step, not only do they have the authority to make you reopen the wall, they exercise it.

INSULATION

Now you're ready to complete insulating the interior. For the ceiling, use fiberglass batts 16″ wide and 8″ deep with aluminum foil backing. Staple them up between the rafters with the aluminum foil facing down. Fit them snugly, but leave an air space above them to ventilate the roof. Don't block the vent holes.

Before you begin the walls, take a large red crayon or piece of red chalk and mark on the face of every stud those locations where holes have been drilled through which live wiring passes. Later these marks will warn you where not to nail in the gypboard, but if you wait until later to make the marks, you will have lost the wires behind the insulation. On the exterior walls, staple fiberglass aluminum-faced batts 2′0″ wide and 6″ deep between the studs. As before and as always, the aluminum foil faces into the house. At the one location a heating pipe occurs at the exterior wall, be certain that insulation is stuffed behind it. Should the plumber have moved other pipes to the outside walls, be certain they are similarly insulated. Where the floor joists meet the walls, loosely pack insulation into the end space between

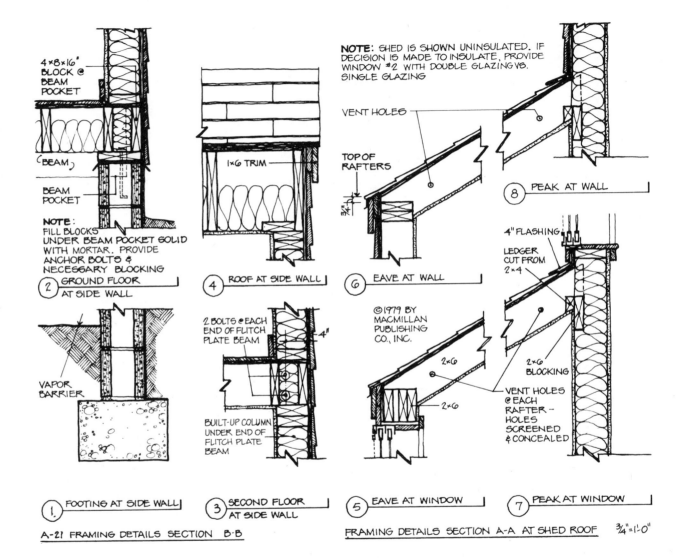

4×8×16″ BLOCK @ BEAM POCKET

(BEAM)

BEAM POCKET

NOTE: FILL BLOCKS UNDER BEAM POCKET SOLID WITH MORTAR. PROVIDE ANCHOR BOLTS & NECESSARY BLOCKING

2 GROUND FLOOR AT SIDE WALL

VAPOR BARRIER

1 FOOTING AT SIDE WALL

A-21 FRAMING DETAILS SECTION B-B

1×6 TRIM

4 ROOF AT SIDE WALL

2 BOLTS @ EACH END OF FLITCH PLATE BEAM

4″

BUILT-UP COLUMN UNDER END OF FLITCH PLATE BEAM

3 SECOND FLOOR AT SIDE WALL

NOTE: SHED IS SHOWN UNINSULATED. IF DECISION IS MADE TO INSULATE, PROVIDE WINDOW #2 WITH DOUBLE GLAZING VS. SINGLE GLAZING

VENT HOLES

TOP OF RAFTERS

6 EAVE AT WALL

© 1979 BY MACMILLAN PUBLISHING CO., INC.

2×6

2×6

5 EAVE AT WINDOW

8 PEAK AT WALL

4″ FLASHING

LEDGER CUT FROM 2×4

2×6 BLOCKING

VENT HOLES @ EACH RAFTER - HOLES SCREENED & CONCEALED

7 PEAK AT WINDOW

FRAMING DETAILS SECTION A-A AT SHED ROOF   ¾″=1′-0″

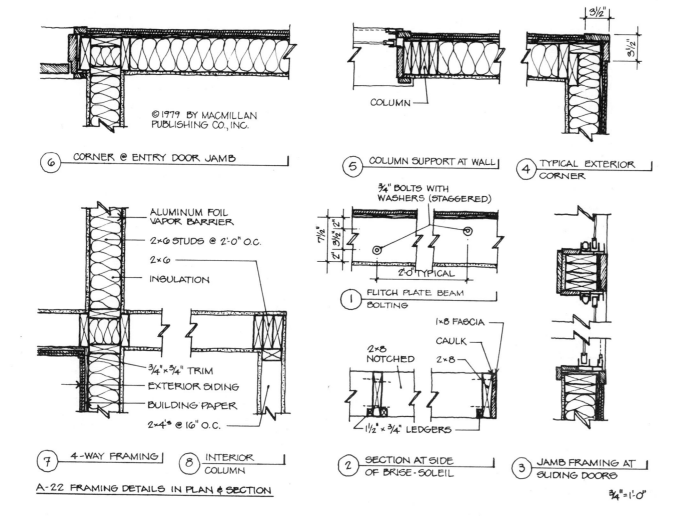

© 1979 BY MACMILLAN
PUBLISHING CO., INC.

⑥ CORNER @ ENTRY DOOR JAMB

⑤ COLUMN SUPPORT AT WALL

④ TYPICAL EXTERIOR CORNER

ALUMINUM FOIL VAPOR BARRIER
2×6 STUDS @ 2'-0" O.C.
2×6
INSULATION
¾"×¾" TRIM
EXTERIOR SIDING
BUILDING PAPER
2×4's @ 16" O.C.

⑦ 4-WAY FRAMING

⑧ INTERIOR COLUMN

A-22 FRAMING DETAILS IN PLAN & SECTION

¾" BOLTS WITH WASHERS (STAGGERED)
2'-0" TYPICAL

① FLITCH PLATE BEAM BOLTING

2×8 NOTCHED
1½"×¾" LEDGERS

② SECTION AT SIDE OF BRISE-SOLEIL

1×8 FASCIA
CAULK
2×8

③ JAMB FRAMING AT SLIDING DOORS

¾"=1'-0"

COLUMN

each pair of joists. Finally, insulate the interior bathroom walls. (Foil backing is not required here.) This will improve the sound isolation so you don't hear the toilet and laundry machines in the living room.

Excited by the enclosed space, the presence of live electrical outlets and a single water faucet, you may be tempted to move in. Resist the temptation if you can afford it. Continuous exposure to the screaming saws and sawdust, not to mention the inconvenience of no kitchen, no toilet, and no furniture, lessens both your energy and your enthusiasm for completing the job. But if you must move in, buy a refrigerator and get the bathtub hooked up so you have running water and a vessel to contain it. Then, most important, set about completely finishing the upstairs bedroom. The process will give you a sample of each of the remaining tasks which await you, and the finished product will be your only refuge from the grit and chaos below.

GYPSUM BOARD

Using ½" gypboard, start with the ceiling. Gypboard is heavy, fragile, and unwieldy. You'll need at least one person to help you. Score the gypboard with a matt knife and break it. Cut the paper hinge that forms. You'll need some scaffolding for the high part of the room. Using the gypboard nails, fit the ceiling gypboard close to the walls so that later the wall pieces can help support their edges. You'll have to balance and hold the gypboard in place with your hands (and head) while your partner does the nailing. Install whatever minor blocking seems necessary.

Use ⅝" gypboard on the walls. This is strong enough to span the 2'0" spaces between the studs. Be certain to avoid banging nails into those places marked with red crayon. Even so, keep one light bulb burning on each electric circuit so that if someone does drive a nail through a wire, the light will go out and you'll know which of the hundreds of nails it was that did the damage. Carefully measure the holes for your electrical outlets and switch plates.

Stop the gypboard a little short of the edges of the door frames as indicated in details 4 and 5, drawing A-29. Nail ⅝" blocking strips all around. This will give strength to the door frame later.

When you are done nailing, you must tape and spackle the corners and the joints between boards. There are many different ways of doing it, of which this is one: with a flexible wide-blade putty knife, first knife a flat layer of compound over the joint, then flatten the tape down smoothly into this layer, and knife another flat layer of compound over the tape. The center part of this layer should look smooth and even. The tape should be slightly buried, or it will bubble up as it dries. Scrape off the edge globs and feather the joint to the wall.

This will dry as an uneven white scar. Sand it even with medium grit sandpaper, without penetrating the tape, and feather on another flat layer of compound. Sand this layer with medium and fine paper. A third layer and more sanding should render the joint invisible when painted. Corners should be taped and can

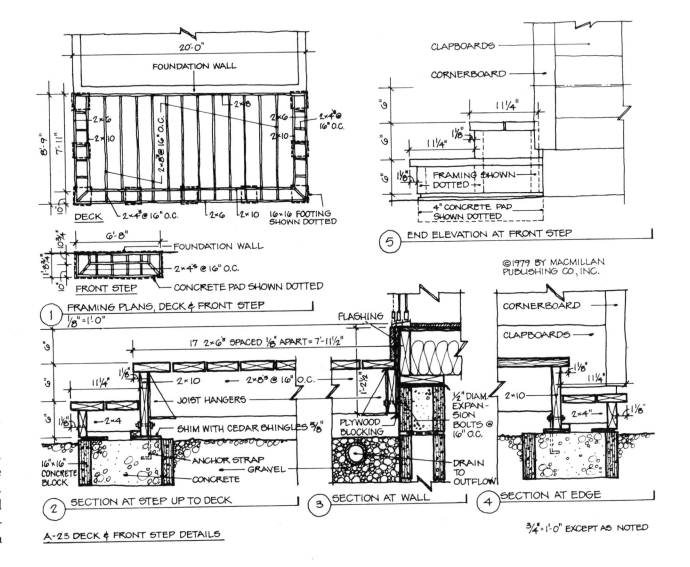

© 1979 BY MACMILLAN PUBLISHING CO., INC.

90

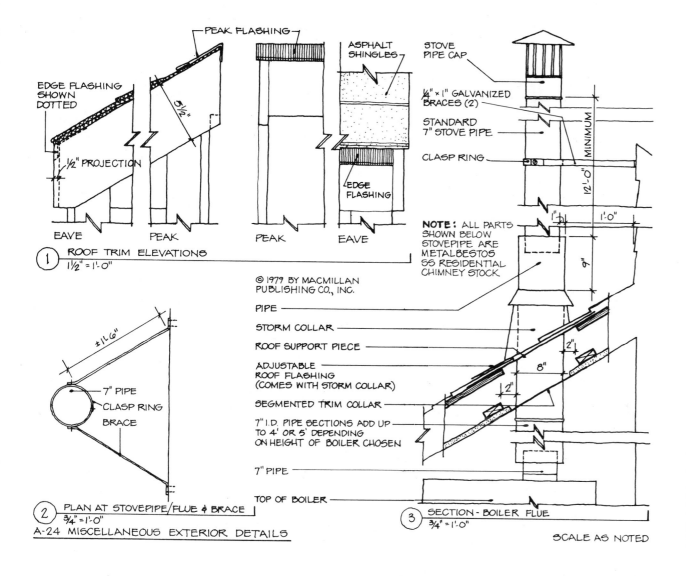

PEAK FLASHING

EDGE FLASHING SHOWN DOTTED

½" PROJECTION

EAVE   PEAK

PEAK   EAVE

ASPHALT SHINGLES

STOVE PIPE CAP

¼" × 1" GALVANIZED BRACES (2)

STANDARD 7" STOVE PIPE

CLASP RING

EDGE FLASHING

① ROOF TRIM ELEVATIONS
1½" = 1'-0"

© 1979 BY MACMILLAN PUBLISHING CO., INC.

NOTE: ALL PARTS SHOWN BELOW STOVEPIPE ARE METALBESTOS SS RESIDENTIAL CHIMNEY STOCK

12'-0" MINIMUM

1'-0"

9"

8"

2"

2"

PIPE

STORM COLLAR

ROOF SUPPORT PIECE

ADJUSTABLE ROOF FLASHING (COMES WITH STORM COLLAR)

SEGMENTED TRIM COLLAR

7" I.D. PIPE SECTIONS ADD UP TO 4' OR 5' DEPENDING ON HEIGHT OF BOILER CHOSEN

7" PIPE

TOP OF BOILER

7" PIPE

CLASP RING

BRACE

② PLAN AT STOVEPIPE/FLUE & BRACE
¾" = 1'-0"

A-24 MISCELLANEOUS EXTERIOR DETAILS

③ SECTION - BOILER FLUE
¾" = 1'-0"

SCALE AS NOTED

be done as perfectly as flat joints. Nail holes require at least two layers of compound. The first layer must be allowed to dry before the second is applied.

Although the bedroom has no outside corners, downstairs you will discover two of them. To make a sharp, straight outside corner you need a length of corner bead. This is a metal corner that you fit over the rough butted gypboard corner. You will also need corner beads around the boiler room vent and any other opening that does not have some kind of trim covering the rough edges.

INTERIOR DOORS

The frames we show are pine, the sills oak, and the hardware finish we have suggested is brushed chromium or stainless steel, as we think polished brass is a little precious for this particular house, but the final choice is yours. If you refer to the door schedule on drawing A-25, you will notice that the bedroom door, number 10, has sill type C. Referring to drawing A-29, you see that sill type C can't be installed until the oak flooring is down. So be sure to hang door 10 high enough to clear the sill once it's installed.

Cut the pair of doors, number 11, to the closet from a sheet of ¾" paint grade birch plywood or particleboard, an equally strong but heavier composition board. Trim the edges with ⅝" hardwood and hang them on hinges designed for doors of this size and thickness. Install bullet catches at the top of each door and inactive or dead knobs to match as closely as possible the knob on the latchset to door 10.

To fabricate the cover for the upper wall vent, see detail 3, drawing A-28. Use exterior plywood. Spread white glue over the two sheets and C-clamp them together. Glue ⅝" hardwood edge strip all around the panel as shown. The hinges are face-mounted as this will give the most strength for this application. You can mortise them flush if you like. We are verging on cabinetwork here. Read up on this as well as the art of hanging doors; it's the same family of work only fussier. The edging process requires a few bar clamps 4'0" long. If you undertake your own cabinetwork later on, you will find these essential.

INTERIOR TRIM

You can now install the pine trim around all the door, window, and vent openings. Use finish nails. Countersink them with a nail set, putty the nail heads plus any hammer marks, and sand smooth.

In trimming a window, install the sill first. Notice that it notches out past each jamb trim and the nosing returns to the wall.

The rounded nosing on the window sills is easy to make. Set the table saw blade at a 45-degree angle, run the sill edge through both ways, plane it rounder, and sand it rounder still.

OAK FLOORING

Tongue-and-groove oak flooring should span the joists

DOOR SCHEDULE

						FRAME			HARDWARE		REMARKS
NO.	TYPE	MAT.	FIN.	DIMENSIONS	ROUGH OPG.	MAT	FIN	SILL	HINGES	LOCKSET	
1	C	ALCOA #6068		6'-8¼" × 6'-0⅛"	6'-9¾" × 6'-0⅝"	ALUM	BA	G	–	INTEGRAL WITH UNIT	OPTIONAL: ALCOA SCREEN #30586
2	D	ALCOA #6068		6'-8¼" × 6'-0⅛"	6'-9¾" × 6'-0⅝"	ALUM	BA	G	-	INTEGRAL WITH UNIT	OPTIONAL: ALCOA SCREEN #30585
3	A	SC	PT	6'-8" × 2'-8" × 1¾"	6'-10½" × 2'-11"	PINE	PT	A	2¼" × 4"	MORTISE LOCK	
4	A	SC	PT.	6'-8" × 2'-8" × 1¾"	6'-10½" × 2'-10½"	PINE	PT	B	2¼" × 4"	LOCKS FROM BOTH SIDES	
5	A	SC	PT.	6'-8" × 2'-0" × 1⅜"	6'-10½" × 2'-2½"	PINE	PT	E	2" × 3½"	PRIVACY LOCK BATHRM SIDE	
6	A	¾" PLY.	PT.	6'-8" × 1'-6" × ¾"	6'-10½" × 1'-8½"	PINE	PT	F	CABINET HINGES	MAGNETIC CLOSER	DEAD PULL + EDGE TRIM ON DOOR
7	A	H.C.	PT.	6'-8" × 2'-8" × 1⅜"	6'-10½" × 2'-10½"	PINE	PT	F	2" × 3½"	LOCKS FROM OUTSIDE	INCLUDE SAFETY KNOB ON INSIDE
8	A	H.C.	PT.	6'-8" × 2'-4" × 1⅜"	6'-10½" × 2'-6½"	PINE	PT	DTL 3 A-35	2¼" × 4"	NO LOCK	CENTER R.O. ON FINISHED WIDTH OF STR
9	A	H.C.	PT.	6'-8" × 2'-0" × 1⅜"	6'-10½" × 2'-2½"	PINE	PT	D	2" × 3½"	NO LOCK	INCLUDE SAFETY KNOB ON INSIDE
10	A	H.C.	PT.	6'-8" × 2'-4" × 1⅜"	6'-10½" × 2'-6½"	PINE	PT	C	2" × 3½"	PRIVACY LOCK BEDRM. SIDE	
11	B	¾" PLY.	PT.	±5'-0" × 3'-0" × ¾"	±5'-2½" × 3'-2½"	PINE	PT	D	CABINET HINGES	MAGNETIC CLOSERS	DEAD PULLS + EDGE TRIM ON DOORS
WALL VENTS		DTL 3 A-28	PT.	1'-2¼" × 2'-10¼" × 1½"	1'-4" × 3'-0⅛"	PINE	PT	–	2" × 3½"	MORTISED LIFT RING	SEE DETAIL 3 DWG A-28
TRAP DOOR		DTL 2 A-30	C.T.	1'-11½" × 2'-3"	2'-0" × 2'-3½"	SS	–	–	NONE	MORTISED LIFT RING	SEE DTLS 2 & 3 DWG. A-30

A-25 DOOR SCHEDULE

©1979 BY MACMILLAN PUBLISHING CO., INC.

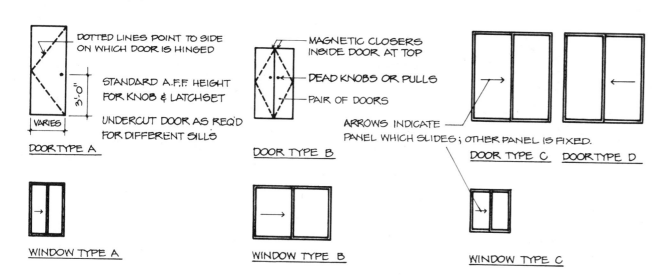

DOOR TYPE A
- DOTTED LINES POINT TO SIDE ON WHICH DOOR IS HINGED
- STANDARD A.F.F. HEIGHT FOR KNOB & LATCHSET
- UNDERCUT DOOR AS REQ'D FOR DIFFERENT SILLS
- VARIES / 3'-0"

DOOR TYPE B
- MAGNETIC CLOSERS INSIDE DOOR AT TOP
- DEAD KNOBS OR PULLS
- PAIR OF DOORS

DOOR TYPE C DOOR TYPE D
- ARROWS INDICATE PANEL WHICH SLIDES; OTHER PANEL IS FIXED.

WINDOW TYPE A **WINDOW TYPE B** **WINDOW TYPE C**

GENERAL NOTES

1. SLIDING DOORS: ORDER ONE 'RIGHT OPENING' & ONE 'LEFT OPENING'
2. ALUMINUM DOORS & WINDOWS ARE AVAILABLE IN SAME SIZES FROM REYNOLDS ALUMINUM
3. FLASH AND CAULK ALUM. UNITS AS PER MANUFACTURER'S INSTRUCTIONS.
4. ALL ALUM. DOOR AND WINDOW UNITS TO HAVE BRONZE ANODIZED FINISH.
5. HINGES, LOCKSETS & OTHER HARDWARE TO HAVE STAINLESS STEEL US 26D, OR BRUSHED ALUMINUM FINISH, US 28
6. 1½ PR BUTT HINGES PER FULL-SIZE DOOR

A-26 DOOR AND WINDOW TYPES AND WINDOW SCHEDULE

WINDOW SCHEDULE

NO	TYPE	MODEL	DIMENSIONS	ROUGH OPG.	GLAZING
1	C	ALCOA #3030	2'-11½" × 2'-11⅞"	3'-0" × 3'-0⅛"	DOUBLE
2	B	ALCOA #6040	3'-11½" × 5'-11⅞"	4'-0" × 6'-0⅛"	SINGLE
3	B	ALCOA #6040	3'-11½" × 5'-11⅞"	4'-0" × 6'-0⅛"	DOUBLE
4	A	ALCOA #3040	3'-11½" × 2'-11⅞"	4'-0" × 3'-0⅛"	DOUBLE
5	B	ALCOA #6040	3'-11½" × 5'-11⅞"	4'-0" × 6'-0⅛"	DOUBLE
6	B	ALCOA #6040	3'-11½" × 5'-11⅞"	4'-0" × 6'-0⅛"	DOUBLE
7	A	ALCOA #3040	3'-11½" × 2'-11⅞"	4'-0" × 3'-0⅛"	DOUBLE

below. Sweep the floor perfectly clean. Then, starting at one wall, staple down a course of building paper. Lay down an oak strip and drive either a spiral nail or a cut nail at a 45-degree angle through the tongue of the oak strip at 12" intervals along the length of the strip. Rent a nailing machine to set the nails. Fit the strips as tightly as you can. Alternate long and short strips. Stagger the joints.

Halfway across the floor you'll notice that in spite of everything the front line of oak is starting to curve. This is the result of an accumulation of invisible errors, and you have to start correcting for it or the errors will compound further to the point where you cannot force the next strip to fit. Begin correcting the curve, but don't feel badly about the feather-thin gaps, you can always fill them in with oak paste or plastic wood.

When you get to the opposite wall, you must rip the last strip and face-nail it. It is not bad practice to set the last strip ¼" or so back from the wall to allow for expansion. The last step of this phase is to nail on the 1 x 4 baseboard.

In the interest of economy we suggest that in the storage closets you leave the plywood subfloor as is, and simply paint it. By the same token, you can leave off finishing the walls and ceiling with gypboard as well. If you do elect to finish the walls, be sure to nail in the 2 x 6's which support the clothes pole beforehand.

When you get around to installing the downstairs flooring, don't oak over the hearth in front of the fireplace. Lay out the shape of the hearth including the oak trim and work up to it.

PAINTING

While you're waiting for the plumber to hook up the fin-tube convector, start to apply a primer coat of paint to the walls and the raw wood doors and trim. The latter will be especially thirsty and cannot be deprived of this base coat if the finish coat is to come out smooth and even.

The conventional approach is to do the walls in flat paint and the doors and trim in semigloss—colors are entirely up to you. Our preference is to do everything in eggshell. This may sound like a color, but it's actually a generic name for a particular finish slightly duller than semigloss but brighter than matt. We recommend it because walls and ceilings do not soil so easily and when they do they can be washed down. The best of these paints are oil based as opposed to water based. In the long run we think they're well worth the extra time and effort it may take to apply them.

Don't screw in the outlet and switch plates until the room has been painted and the paint is dry. If your preference is to paint these plates to match the walls do so, but don't paint them in place. Lay them out on a newspaper and prime and finish them separately; then screw them on; should you need to reach the wires behind them, you won't have to crack the paint. If you aren't going to paint the plates, select a finish which relates to the finish of the door hardware.

Now that you have a habitable sanctuary, start gypboarding the smaller bedroom and work your way downstairs, then install the window, door, and base trim just as you did in the bedroom.

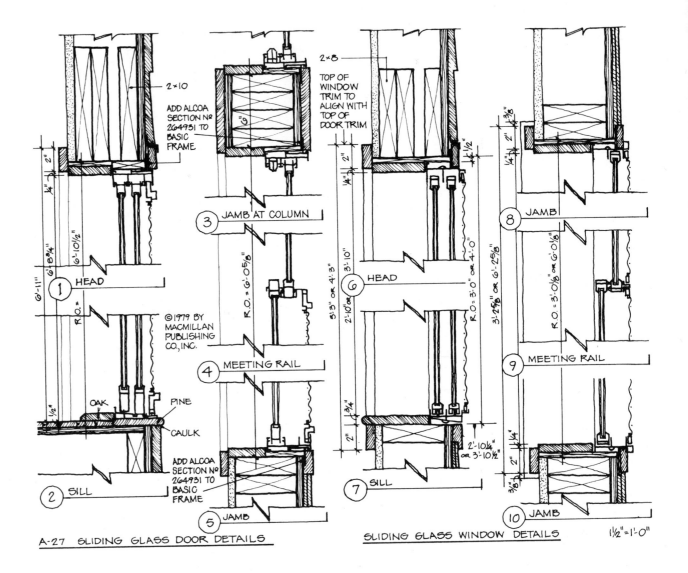

A-27 SLIDING GLASS DOOR DETAILS

SLIDING GLASS WINDOW DETAILS

94

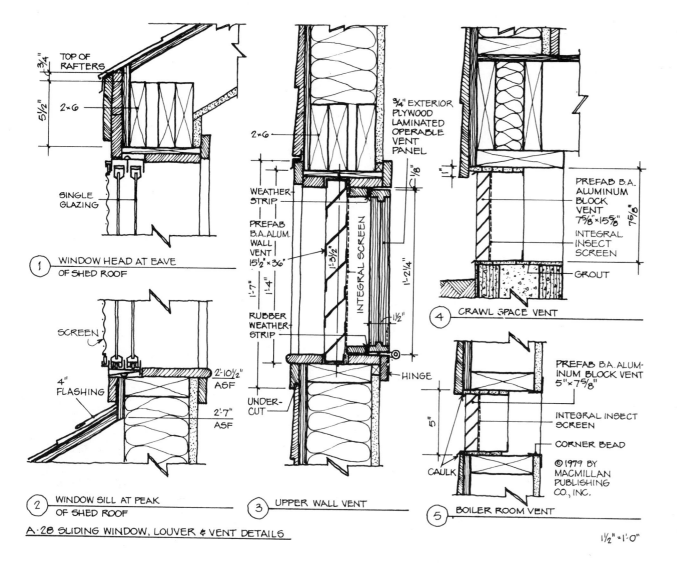

TOP OF RAFTERS

$\frac{3}{4}$"

$5\frac{1}{2}$"

2×6

SINGLE GLAZING

① WINDOW HEAD AT EAVE OF SHED ROOF

SCREEN

4" FLASHING

2'-10½" ASF

2'-7" ASF

② WINDOW SILL AT PEAK OF SHED ROOF

A-28 SLIDING WINDOW, LOUVER & VENT DETAILS

2×6

WEATHER STRIP

PREFAB B.A. ALUM. WALL VENT 15½"×36"

1'-7"

1'-4"

RUBBER WEATHER STRIP

UNDER-CUT

³⁄₄" EXTERIOR PLYWOOD LAMINATED OPERABLE VENT PANEL

2⅛"

INTEGRAL SCREEN

1'-3½"

1'-2¼"

1½"

HINGE

③ UPPER WALL VENT

PREFAB B.A. ALUMINUM BLOCK VENT 7⅝"×15⅝"

7⅝"

INTEGRAL INSECT SCREEN

GROUT

④ CRAWL SPACE VENT

PREFAB B.A. ALUM- INUM BLOCK VENT 5"×7⅝"

5"

INTEGRAL INSECT SCREEN

CORNER BEAD

© 1979 BY MACMILLAN PUBLISHING CO., INC.

CAULK

⑤ BOILER ROOM VENT

1½"=1'-0"

HEATILATOR FIREPLACE

Detailed instructions accompany this unit, and they should be followed religiously, as should details 4 and 5 on drawing A-30. You can use any number of materials for the hearth: the same ceramic tile you use in the bathroom in a dark color, which is what we show in detail 7 on drawing A-29, or a slab of the Johns-Manville Colorlith we suggested for the countertops in finish group 2. As this was developed to withstand the heat generated by a bunson burner which has fallen on its side, it would be more than appropriate.

In detail 5 on drawing A-30 we show an ordinary 7" stovepipe above the roof. Fit it in with stovepipe cement. If winds are high where you're building, run at least three guy wires to screw-eyes at the roof trim. Triangulate them for optimum bracing.

KITCHEN CABINETWORK

As we suggested at the beginning of this chapter, no building ever gets built in absolute accordance with the plans. Therefore, before you even begin thinking about the kitchen cabinetwork, measure the actual length and height of the entire east wall of the kitchen and living room, and the west wall, which will house the sink and major appliances. We can assure you that it won't conform to the exact dimensions we indicate. When you study the cabinetwork details on drawings A-31 through A-34, you will notice that many of the details anticipate that these differences will occur. You will notice a scribe strip for use at the end wall. This strip is of soft pine and has been routed out, so it's very easy to plane. Small errors in the length of the cabinets can be absorbed, and a perfect fit can be made. The scribe strip also accommodates the wall if it is slightly out of plumb.

Cabinetwork requires a greater degree of accuracy than anything you've done so far. You may prefer to subcontract your cabinets. In developed areas where there's a fair amount of building, there will also be a fair number of competent cabinetmakers. They are usually in the field more for the love of craft than the lure of money. Thus, more often than not, it is as inexpensive to have your cabinets custom built as to have store-bought cabinets fitted, especially if the detailing is simple. But if you are in a very rural or remote area, you may have no choice other than to buy them off the shelf or build them yourself.

A table saw, some C-clamps, and a few bar clamps are indispensable. Buy a dado blade set if you haven't already, and an accurate metal rule. For the dovetail joints in the drawers, you'll need a router, which you can rent.

Study the drawings carefully. The details are quite simple. We will start with the smallest, easiest cabinet: the short one between the range and the wall.

This cabinet is basically a plywood box with ¾" plywood sides and a ¼" plywood back. It sits on a 4" high base. A scribe strip spaces the cabinet out from the wall slightly. The countertop and backsplash are of plastic laminated onto ¾" plywood or particleboard, better known by the trademark "Formica." The door overlays the entire front of the box. There is one ad-

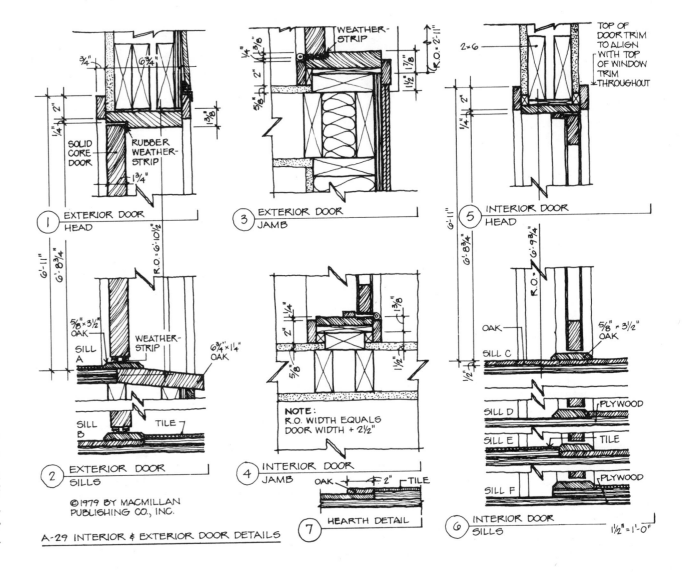

A-29 INTERIOR & EXTERIOR DOOR DETAILS

© 1979 BY MACMILLAN PUBLISHING CO., INC.

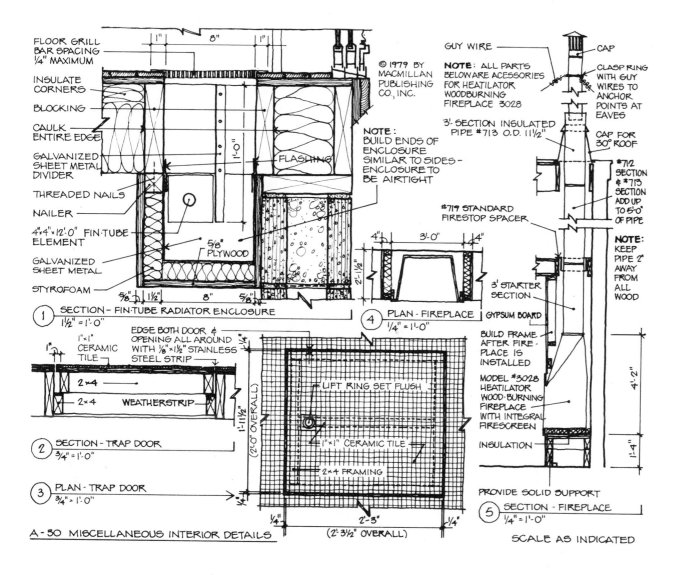

FLOOR GRILL BAR SPACING ¼" MAXIMUM

INSULATE CORNERS

BLOCKING

CAULK ENTIRE EDGE

GALVANIZED SHEET METAL DIVIDER

THREADED NAILS

NAILER

4"×4"×12'-0" FIN·TUBE ELEMENT

GALVANIZED SHEET METAL

STYROFOAM

5/8" PLYWOOD

1" 8" 1"

1'-0"

FLASHING

5/8" 1½" 8" 5/8"

NOTE: BUILD ENDS OF ENCLOSURE SIMILAR TO SIDES - ENCLOSURE TO BE AIRTIGHT

① SECTION - FIN·TUBE RADIATOR ENCLOSURE
1½" = 1'-0"

1" CERAMIC TILE

EDGE BOTH DOOR & OPENING ALL AROUND WITH 1/8"×1½" STAINLESS STEEL STRIP

1"×1" CERAMIC TILE

2×4

2×4   WEATHERSTRIP

② SECTION - TRAP DOOR
¾" = 1'-0"

③ PLAN - TRAP DOOR
¾" = 1'-0"

A-30 MISCELLANEOUS INTERIOR DETAILS

LIFT RING SET FLUSH

1"×1" CERAMIC TILE

2×4 FRAMING

2'-0" OVERALL

1'-11½"

¼" 2'-3" ¼"
(2'-3½" OVERALL)

GUY WIRE   CAP

CLASP RING WITH GUY WIRES TO ANCHOR POINTS AT EAVES

NOTE: ALL PARTS BELOW ARE ACESSORIES FOR HEATILATOR WOODBURNING FIREPLACE 3028

3'- SECTION INSULATED PIPE #713 O.D. 11½"

CAP FOR 30° ROOF

#712 SECTION & #713 SECTION ADD UP TO 5'-0" OF PIPE

#719 STANDARD FIRESTOP SPACER

NOTE: KEEP PIPE 2" AWAY FROM ALL WOOD

4" 3'-0" 4"

2'-½"

④ PLAN - FIREPLACE
¼" = 1'-0"

GYPSUM BOARD

3' STARTER SECTION

BUILD FRAME AFTER FIRE· PLACE IS INSTALLED

MODEL #3028 HEATILATOR WOOD·BURNING FIREPLACE WITH INTEGRAL FIRESCREEN

INSULATION

PROVIDE SOLID SUPPORT

4'-2"

1'-4"

⑤ SECTION - FIREPLACE
¼" = 1'-0"

SCALE AS INDICATED

---

justable shelf supported on tiny brackets which you buy at the hardware store. They are set into little holes. The door is ¾" finish birch plywood with 5/8" wide hardwood edge strips which you should order pre-milled from a cabinet supply shop.

Often cabinetmakers make up full-scale drawings of the cabinet details, known as shop drawings, by way of working out their approach to the fabrication, and confirming that their approach conforms to the designer's intent. We show only the principal details and joints. It will help you to think through the construction process to get some graph paper and draw up your own set of shop drawings based on what you learn from our drawings. The shop drawings and the templates will make it easy for you to calculate the exact size to which each piece must be cut. Pay close attention to the 1/16" spacing between door and drawer fronts, and the effect of the 5/8" edge strip on the plywood dimensions.

Cut the base pieces of the little cabinet first. Use the same ¾" by 4" stock you've been using for the base trim at walls. Cut the sides, notching back for the toe space. Cut them short to allow for the ¼" plywood back, and a minimum ¾" air space behind the cabinet. Using white glue, glue a strip of birch veneer over the rough edge and clamp it firmly in place. If edge stripping is called for, repeat the process. Sand the stripping flush with the plywood. Drill the holes in the sides for the adjustable shelf brackets.

Glue-nail the bottom to the sides and then the back in behind. Nail the base pieces and glue-nail in the 1 x 4 continuous blocking. Countersink and putty the nails and sand smooth. Start with medium sandpaper and progress to fine.

Cut the door and edge it all around. Hang it with a pair of Stanley flush overlay intermediate pivot hinges mortised into the sides of the door. Follow the manufacturer's instructions.

Rout out the pine scribe strip and nail it to the cabinet recessed ¾" from the face of the door. Set the nails so your plane won't nick them when it's time to do the actual installation. The cabinet should stand slightly free of the back wall.

Now remeasure your work and cut the ¾" particleboard and the 1/16" Formica for the countertop. This must be very precise. The Formica is applied to the particleboard with a highly flammable adhesive. Follow the directions on the can. Finally glue on the 1¼" deep hardwood edging. Be certain the top is flush with the adjacent Formica.

Fabricate the backsplash. Its height should correspond to the height of the backsplash of the range you've chosen. Consult the manufacturer's specifications to determine this dimension. Apply silicone caulk to the bottom edge and screw it to the countertop from below. Then attach the countertop with screws through the continuous blocking strip. Glue it down all around. A bead of silicone caulk applied all around the backsplash before pushing it into its final position will prevent water from seeping into the joint and swelling the wood.

Screw in the components for the magnetic catches, then the door pull, and your cabinet is complete but for the finishing, which could be three coats of matt

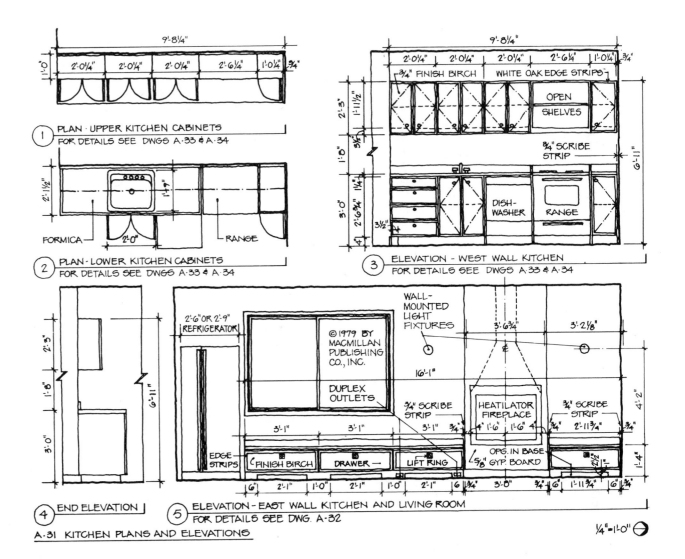

98

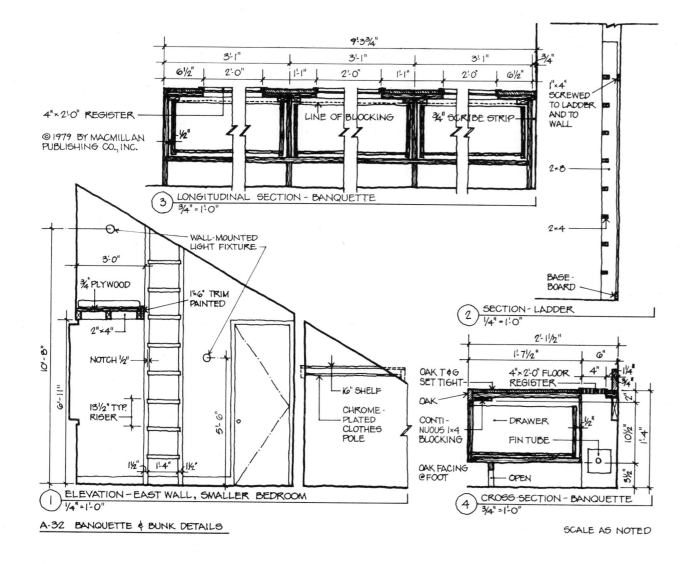

9'-3¾"
3'-1" 3'-1" 3'-1" ¾"
6½" 2'-0" 1'-1" 2'-0" 1'-1" 2'-0" 6½"

4"×2'-0" REGISTER

© 1979 BY MACMILLAN PUBLISHING CO., INC.

LINE OF BLOCKING   ¾" SCRIBE STRIP

½"

1"×4" SCREWED TO LADDER AND TO WALL

2×8

2×4

BASE-BOARD

③ LONGITUDINAL SECTION - BANQUETTE
¾" = 1'-0"

② SECTION - LADDER
¼" = 1'-0"

WALL-MOUNTED LIGHT FIXTURE

3'-0"

¾" PLYWOOD

1"×6" TRIM PAINTED

2"×4"

NOTCH ½"

13½" TYP. RISER

6" SHELF

CHROME-PLATED CLOTHES POLE

5'-6"

1½" 1'-4" 1½"

10'-8"   9'-1"

① ELEVATION - EAST WALL, SMALLER BEDROOM
¼" = 1'-0"

A-32 BANQUETTE & BUNK DETAILS

OAK T&G SET TIGHT

OAK

CONTI-NUOUS 1×4 BLOCKING

OAK FACING @ FOOT

2'-1½"
1'-7½"   6"   ¼"
4"×2'-0" FLOOR REGISTER   4"   ¾"

DRAWER   ½"   2"

FIN TUBE   10½" 1'-4"

OPEN   5½"

④ CROSS SECTION - BANQUETTE
¾" = 1'-0"

SCALE AS NOTED

polyurethane varnish, or linseed or lemon oil, depending on your preference.

If you've gotten this far, you'll know whether you want to continue or throw in the towel. In either case a few notes about the other units are in order.

The south edge of the large counter cabinet should be flush with the corner of the bathroom wall. You can either scribe the back of this side very carefully to fit the wall, or build it square and rely on a ¾" wide recessed scribe strip to take up any unevenness in the wall. However, the counter and backsplash must be scribed and fitted tight to all walls.

When constructing drawers, carefully note the joint details. Each drawer must clear its housing by ½" plus. This allows for the Grant full-extension metal drawer slides which come with instructions from the hardware store.

Install the kitchen sink in the precut hole after the cabinet is built and in place. It comes with little rim clips that screw the sink rim down tight to the counter from below. Part of the countertop cantilevers out over the dishwasher. The dishwasher has short adjustable legs; adjust them so the countertop rests directly on the dishwasher.

The overhead cabinets are similar in construction to those below. Note the bevel-cut hanging strip in detail 1 on drawing A-33. This is screwed to the wall. The other beveled piece is attached to the cabinet. This detail makes it relatively easy to hang the cabinet level.

MISCELLANEOUS CABINETWORK

The banquettes flanking the fireplace are fairly similar in construction. Build the top separately. It is covered with the same oak stripping we used for flooring. Before you join it to the top of the cabinet, cut the required openings in the top for the radiator grilles. Cut the long openings in the base, so air can circulate to the fin tubes behind. Use scribe strips in the locations indicated.

The bunkbed in the smaller bedroom is made of 2 x 4's, ¾" plywood, and the facing piece is pine. Make the ladder of clear fir. You can notch the treads into the sides and fasten them with lagbolts countersunk and dowelled. Or if you want a little glitter, cut the rungs from 1" diameter, chrome-plated stock for shower curtain rods. Rout slightly larger-diameter holes into the inside faces of the vertical pieces. Assemble the components on the floor, clamp it, raise it, and bolt it in place.

The shelving in the linen closet is made with paint grade plywood, edge-trimmed and supported on 1 x 2 pine strips or cleats nailed to the studding behind.

Constructing the stair would be a challenge for any carpenter or cabinetmaker. We will leave you to struggle with it on your own except for suggesting a possible building sequence: Install the newel post first, using temporary braces and blocking. Then build the winders, starting with the lowest and working up, screwing each riser to the newel post as shown. Then build the knee wall, then the straight run of steps. Finally, and of course this seems mysteriously backwards, set in place

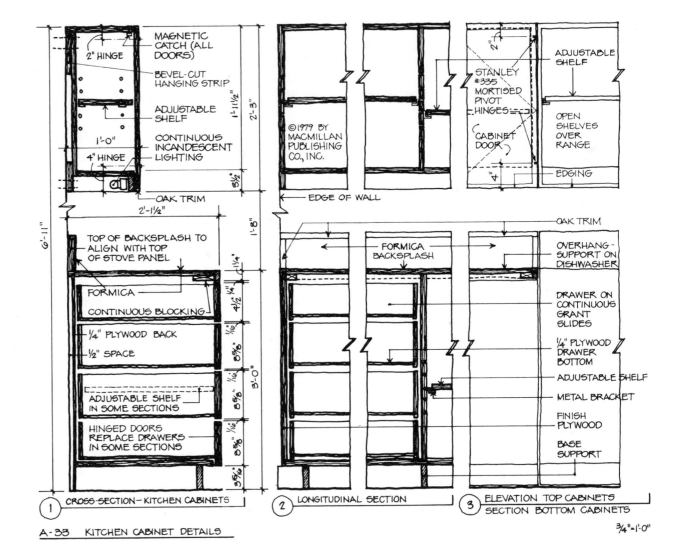

A-33   KITCHEN CABINET DETAILS

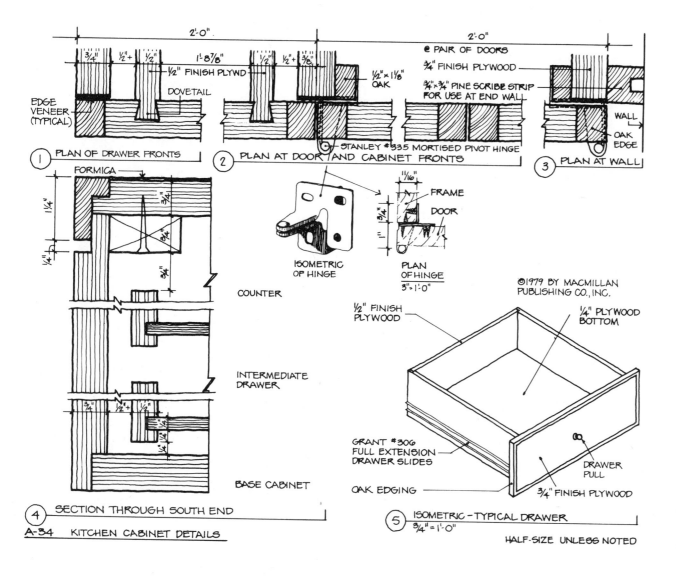

2'-0"

3/4" · 1/2" · 1/2"

EDGE VENEER (TYPICAL)

DOVETAIL

1/2" FINISH PLYWD

① PLAN OF DRAWER FRONTS

1'-8 5/8"

1/2" · 1/2" · 3/8"

1/2" × 1 1/8" OAK

STANLEY #335 MORTISED PIVOT HINGE

② PLAN AT DOOR AND CABINET FRONTS

2'-0"

@ PAIR OF DOORS

3/4" FINISH PLYWOOD

3/4" × 3/4" PINE SCRIBE STRIP FOR USE AT END WALL

WALL

OAK EDGE

③ PLAN AT WALL

FORMICA

1/4"

3/4"

3/4"

1/4"

3/4"

COUNTER

INTERMEDIATE DRAWER

3/4" · 1/2" · 1/2"

1/4"

3/4"

BASE CABINET

④ SECTION THROUGH SOUTH END

A-34   KITCHEN CABINET DETAILS

ISOMETRIC OF HINGE

11/16"

3/4"

1"

FRAME

DOOR

PLAN OF HINGE
3" = 1'-0"

©1979 BY MACMILLAN PUBLISHING CO., INC.

1/2" FINISH PLYWOOD

1/4" PLYWOOD BOTTOM

GRANT #306 FULL EXTENSION DRAWER SLIDES

OAK EDGING

DRAWER PULL

3/4" FINISH PLYWOOD

⑤ ISOMETRIC - TYPICAL DRAWER
3/4" = 1'-0"

HALF-SIZE UNLESS NOTED

one sheet of gypboard for the railing, then the gypboard framing, then the other sheet of gypboard. Trim and finish. The local carpenters will think you're a genius.

BATHROOM FINISHES

Be certain to use special waterproof gypsumboard on all four walls and the ceiling. Notice that the gypboard laps over the edge of the tub. Fill the crack all around with white caulk.

Study drawing A-36 showing the bathroom elevations and ceramic tile floor and base detail. Notice that a second subfloor of 5/8" exterior plywood must be nailed down first. Do not put in a single nail until the positions of all pipes underneath have been located on the existing subfloor. Then put down the layer of 5/8" exterior plywood, avoiding these pipes for your life. Use threaded nails located 8" apart over the entire plywood surface, not just at the edges. This provides an especially rigid base for the tile, so that its joints won't crack and admit water.

Directions for using ceramic tile adhesive are on the can. Use a sawtooth trowel as they recommend. Begin tiling along the west wall where the proper alignment of the floor tile joints and the wall tile joints will be most visible, and work east. This concentrates the accumulation of error behind the plumbing fixtures where it won't be seen. You will have to cut some tiles. This is easy to do with an inexpensive hand tool which you can get at any tile supply store.

Continue tiling up the walls as shown. Use bullnose, cove, and corner pieces where indicated. If your toilet accessories are ceramic, install them as you go. Use latex grout to finish, following the manufacturer's instructions.

Now do the floor of the shed. Pay attention to the sill details for the doors which open onto it. Tile the trapdoor to match the floor. Notice the metal strip around the rim, and the pullring. Then tile the hearth if this is the finish you've selected.

You're almost done. Now begins the endless anti-climax. Rent a floor-sanding machine and edge sander and enjoy the dubious pleasure of refilling your new house with sawdust. Sweep it clean, then vacuum all the walls and ceiling. Finish the floor with a minimum of three coats of matt polyurethane varnish, sanding between coats. Don't cheat on the number of coats or the sanding.

Install the rest of the base trim. The heating man will now install his floor grilles and fin-tube units so the banquette can be installed. The plumber will connect the kitchen sink, squash the toilet down on its gasket, hook up the lavatory, the clothes washer and dishwasher. Meanwhile plastic dropcloths are scattered about while the painting goes sporadically forward.

The Little House described in this chapter is what's called a one-of-a-kind house. This is one of the many qualities that makes the Little House special. The drawings which describe it or any other architectural design are one-of-a-kind as well. There will be an occasional minor discrepancy in dimensions and/or details. If ours were the conventional architect-builder relation-

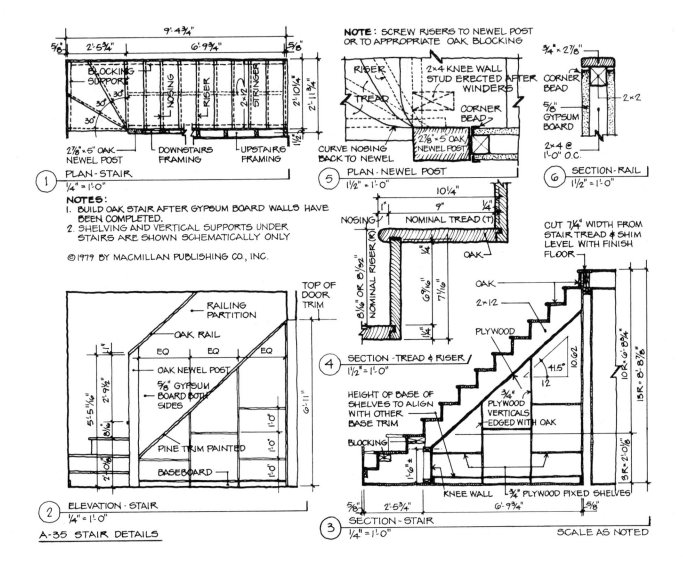

A-35 STAIR DETAILS

102

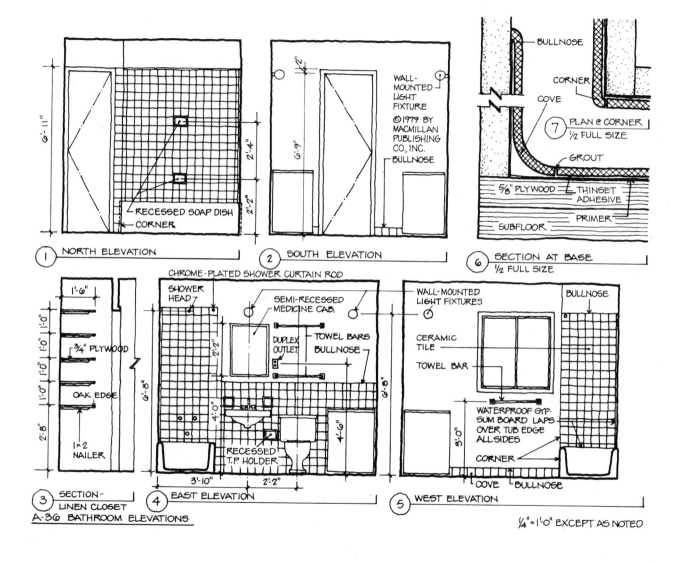

BULLNOSE

CORNER

COVE

⑦ PLAN @ CORNER
½ FULL SIZE

GROUT

5/8" PLYWOOD — THINSET
ADHESIVE

PRIMER

SUBFLOOR

⑥ SECTION AT BASE
½ FULL SIZE

WALL-MOUNTED
LIGHT
FIXTURE

© 1979 BY
MACMILLAN
PUBLISHING
CO., INC.

BULLNOSE

① NORTH ELEVATION

② SOUTH ELEVATION

6'-11"

2'-4"

2'-2"

RECESSED SOAP DISH

CORNER

6'-9"

3'-2"

CHROME-PLATED SHOWER CURTAIN ROD

SHOWER
HEAD

SEMI-RECESSED
MEDICINE CAB.

DUPLEX
OUTLET

TOWEL BARS

BULLNOSE

RECESSED
T.P. HOLDER

WALL-MOUNTED
LIGHT FIXTURES

BULLNOSE

CERAMIC
TILE

TOWEL BAR

WATERPROOF GYP-
SUM BOARD LAPS
OVER TUB EDGE
ALL SIDES

CORNER

COVE   BULLNOSE

1'-6"

1'-0"

1'-0"

1'-0"

1'-0"

2'-8"

3/4" PLYWOOD

OAK EDGE

1×2
NAILER

6'-8"

2'-2"

4'-0"

4'-6"

3'-10"   2'-2"

6'-0"

3'-0"

③ SECTION—
LINEN CLOSET

④ EAST ELEVATION

⑤ WEST ELEVATION

A-36 BATHROOM ELEVATIONS

¼"=1'-0" EXCEPT AS NOTED

ship, there would be a boiler-plate-type clause or note somewhere in the contract documents placing on you, as the builder, the responsibility of bringing these discrepancies to our attention, as the architects, so we can help you in making the appropriate adjustments. Unfortunately ours is not the conventional relationship, thus we can only suggest that you do your best to resolve these discrepancies when and if they occur. This is not an apology, it is a fact of life.

103

7

Alternate Construction Details

Having provided you with a complete set of drawings and details for the basic Little House, we intend now to look back at each of the Little House variations and combinations and pick out those details the design and execution of which are a little too complicated to extrapolate from the details of the basic Little House. While these details are all done for finish group 1 as they are in chapter 6, at the end of this chapter we also include details relating to the application of the finishes cited in the three alternate finish groups. The drawings are numbered AA-1 through AA-20—AA standing for alternate architectural.

UNOFFICIAL LITTLE HOUSE

As the whole point of presenting this unofficial variation is to persuade you that you're as free to break the rules governing the design of the Little House as you are to obey them, we don't want to take away all your fun by showing you how to do it. However, if you like our scheme and want something close to it, substitute 4" trim for the 2" trim of the basic Little House. Then scale off the widths of the window openings from the plans in the first chapter, and the heights from Section

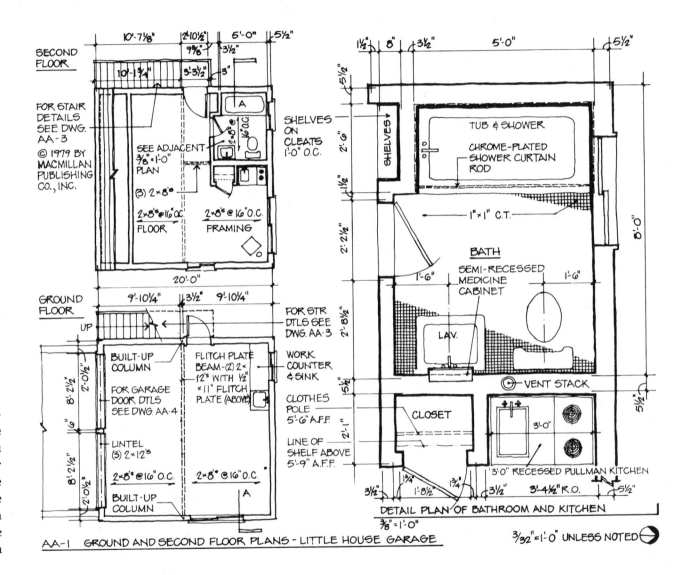

AA-1 GROUND AND SECOND FLOOR PLANS - LITTLE HOUSE GARAGE

DETAIL PLAN OF BATHROOM AND KITCHEN

3/32"=1'-0" UNLESS NOTED

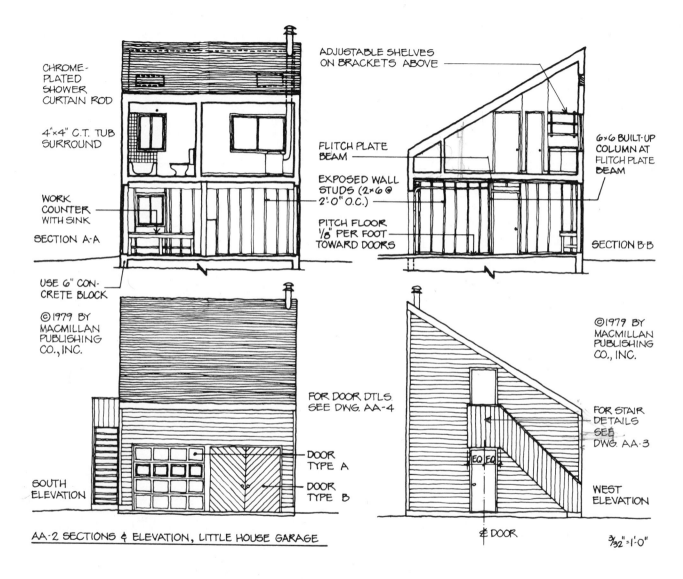

CHROME-
PLATED
SHOWER
CURTAIN ROD

4"×4" C.T. TUB
SURROUND

WORK
COUNTER
WITH SINK

SECTION A·A

USE 6" CON-
CRETE BLOCK

©1979 BY
MACMILLAN
PUBLISHING
CO., INC.

ADJUSTABLE SHELVES
ON BRACKETS ABOVE

FLITCH PLATE
BEAM

EXPOSED WALL
STUDS (2×6 @
2'-0" O.C.)

PITCH FLOOR
1/8 PER FOOT
TOWARD DOORS

6×6 BUILT-UP
COLUMN AT
FLITCH PLATE
BEAM

SECTION B·B

©1979 BY
MACMILLAN
PUBLISHING
CO., INC.

FOR DOOR DTLS.
SEE DWG. AA-4

DOOR
TYPE A

DOOR
TYPE B

SOUTH
ELEVATION

FOR STAIR
DETAILS
SEE
DWG. AA-3

WEST
ELEVATION

EQ EQ

AA-2 SECTIONS & ELEVATION, LITTLE HOUSE GARAGE

₵ DOOR

3/32" = 1'-0"

A-A and the smaller elevation drawings. An accurate translation of our design intent is not essential.

There are four different window sizes and they come right out of the Andersen catalogue of Permashield double-hung windows. These windows are quite expensive. On the exterior the wood is covered/protected by a coating of white plastic, hence the name Permashield. If you can get hold of an Andersen catalogue, install the windows as per their instructions. If you can't, or if you want a less expensive window, see what your lumberyard has in stock.

LITTLE HOUSE GARAGE

On drawing AA-1 we also show a detailed plan for the upstairs bathroom, kitchenette, and closet. You will find that the specifics of this plan can also be applied to the bathroom and downstairs kitchenette and closet of the Little House studio and also the second bathrooms where they appear in several of the combinations.

We are assuming that the floor of the garage is 4" slab on grade which is level with the foundation wall at the north end and slopes downward at 1/8" per foot toward the south wall. You will note on the elevation of the column between the two garage doors, detail on drawing AA-4, that we are assuming the foundation to be 6" wide concrete block as opposed to 8" wide, and that the trim does not stop at the top of the block but overlaps it to within 1/2" of finished grade. The garage doors butt right onto the sloping slab on the assumption that any rain driven under these doors will drain right back out.

On drawings AA-2 and AA-3 we show details for two types of garage doors. The details for the rolling overhead door shown in the section and elevations presented in chapter 3 come directly from the Overhead Door Company. The more cumbersome but also more attractive hinged doors that you saw in chapter 4 on the garage of Combination 6 are shown on the same drawing. These are made up of 1 x 6 tongue-and-groove planking nailed to a backing of ¾" exterior plywood with a layer of building paper between them. This is in turn nailed to a 2 x 4 frame. While the doors in Combination 6 are hung on strap hinges, detail 1, drawing AA-4, shows two pairs of extra heavy butt hinges instead. If you have your heart set on the strap hinges, widen the 2" trim pieces at the far sides so they cover the double 2 x 6 studs. This way you can screw the hinges directly into the 2 x 6's, assuring adequate support.

Our details on drawing AA-3 for the outside stairs show open risers so snow and other debris can easily be swept off the treads. There is only one tricky aspect to the framing of the stair but as it's repeated wherever we show a cantilevered deck, it's worth mentioning. The second-floor joists, which have been extended beyond the exterior of the building to support both the upper landing and the stair itself, have had their top section notched 2". The notching means that the top of the joist is 2" lower outside than inside, which in turn means that when rain or especially snow piles up on this deck it does not seep under the door to the inside. To reinforce these notched 2 x 8's, a 2 x 6 is nailed hard to

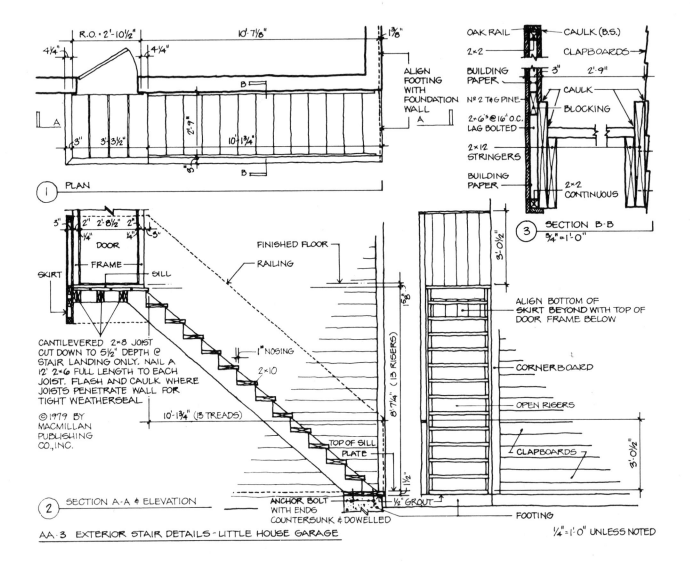

AA-3 EXTERIOR STAIR DETAILS - LITTLE HOUSE GARAGE

¼"=1'-0" UNLESS NOTED

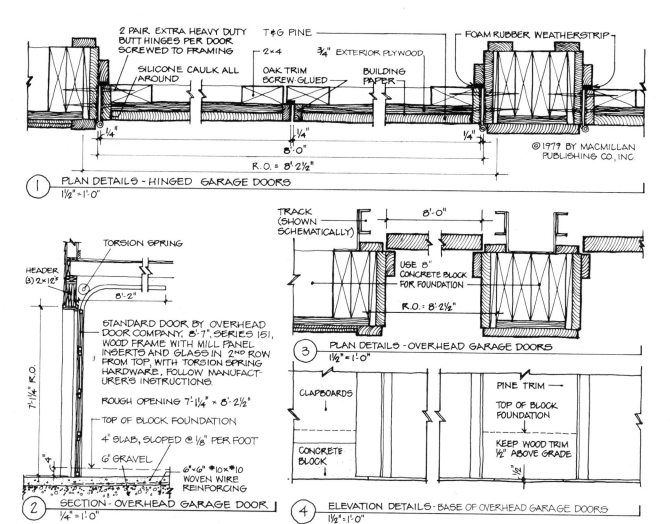

2 PAIR EXTRA HEAVY DUTY BUTT HINGES PER DOOR SCREWED TO FRAMING

T&G PINE

2×4

¾" EXTERIOR PLYWOOD

FOAM RUBBER WEATHERSTRIP

SILICONE CAULK ALL AROUND

OAK TRIM SCREW-GLUED

BUILDING PAPER

¼"

¼"

¼"

8'-0"

© 1979 BY MACMILLAN PUBLISHING CO., INC.

R.O. = 8'-2½"

① PLAN DETAILS - HINGED GARAGE DOORS
1½" = 1'-0"

TORSION SPRING

HEADER (3) 2×12's

8'-2"

TRACK (SHOWN SCHEMATICALLY)

8'-0"

USE 8" CONCRETE BLOCK FOR FOUNDATION

R.O. = 8'-2½"

STANDARD DOOR BY OVERHEAD DOOR COMPANY, 8'-7", SERIES 151, WOOD FRAME WITH MILL PANEL INSERTS AND GLASS IN 2ND ROW FROM TOP, WITH TORSION SPRING HARDWARE. FOLLOW MANUFACTURER'S INSTRUCTIONS.

ROUGH OPENING 7'-1¼" × 8'-2½"

7'-1¼" R.O.

TOP OF BLOCK FOUNDATION

4" SLAB, SLOPED @ ⅛" PER FOOT

6" GRAVEL

6"×6" #10×#10 WOVEN WIRE REINFORCING

③ PLAN DETAILS - OVERHEAD GARAGE DOORS
1½" = 1'-0"

CLAPBOARDS

CONCRETE BLOCK

PINE TRIM

TOP OF BLOCK FOUNDATION

KEEP WOOD TRIM ½" ABOVE GRADE

½"

② SECTION - OVERHEAD GARAGE DOOR
¼" = 1'-0"

④ ELEVATION DETAILS - BASE OF OVERHEAD GARAGE DOORS
1½" = 1'-0"

AA-4 ALTERNATE GARAGE DOOR DETAILS - LITTLE HOUSE GARAGE

SCALE AS NOTED

each one and run a long distance into the building. Caulking and flashing around these joists where they penetrate the exterior skin is tricky but essential if leaks aren't to develop.

The railing detail also appears elsewhere and deserves some comment. In order to obtain smooth exterior and interior faces, 2 x 6's 16" on center are lag-bolted to the face of the stringer, and blocking is set between them. Then 1 x 6 tongue-and-groove planks are nailed to both sides of the 2 x 6's and the intersticial blocking. They are then cut to follow the slope of the stair and capped with oak. Building paper is applied behind the boards to keep out moisture.

On the inside we show a simple work counter and sink in the uninsulated and unfinished downstairs. Upstairs the space is both insulated and finished. If you intend to use this space in winter, it should be heated either with electric baseboard heat, or have a small boiler installed next to the work counter below. However, you should be sure to separate the piping for the work sink from that serving the upstairs so it can be drained down during the winter.

For details relating to the 2 x 12 flitch plate beam required to span the entire floor space, refer to detail 2 for the railing in the Little House studio on drawing AA-6: they are very similar.

LITTLE HOUSE STUDIO

As suggested in chapter 3, the point and purpose of this variation is to have the downstairs wide open in both the horizontal and vertical dimensions. There are many different ways in which work surfaces, storage space, the components of a kitchen, furniture, and a fireplace can be disposed around its perimeter. The choice is yours. Should you wish to build what we show, trace the floor plans we show in chapter 3 and exclude the furniture. Do this freehand or with a straight edge, whichever you find most comfortable.

Using the working drawing plans for the basic Little House as a guide, lay in the dimensions for the location of window openings, adjusting the dimensions along the south wall to accommodate the single 8'0" sliding door rather than the two 6'0" doors shown elsewhere. Then get the manufacturer's specifications for the 5'0" kitchenette (Acme or Dwyer are the best-known manufacturers of these units). Using the detailed plan for the kitchenette, closet, and bath for the Little House garage, lay in and dimension your downstairs kitchenette and closet. Remember to size your rough opening in accordance with the rough opening recommended by the manufacturer and not in accordance with the nominal width of the unit you select. Then lay in your upstairs bath. It may take several tries before you get it right, and several more tries before you get it to look like anything approaching a legible working plan. Don't be discouraged. Each drawing in this book took us several tries, too.

On drawing AA-6 we show a large-scale section through the studio balcony, which in turn shows the dropped flitch plate beam and flitch plate required for the garage, studio, and any other Little House variation

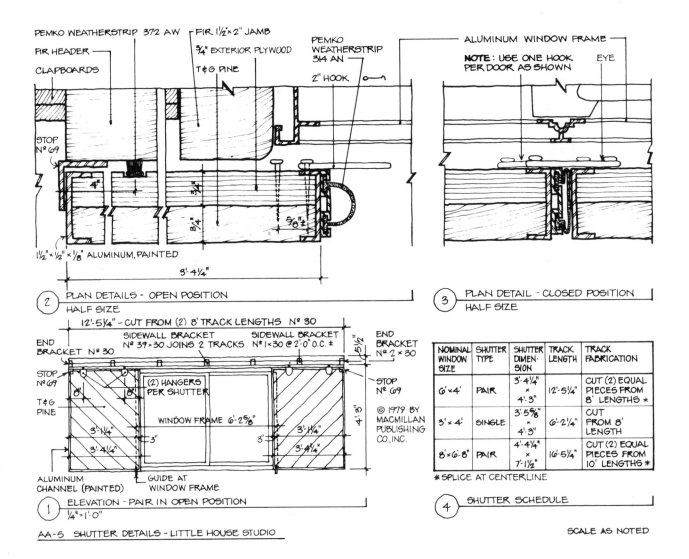

NOMINAL WINDOW SIZE	SHUTTER TYPE	SHUTTER DIMEN-SION	TRACK LENGTH	TRACK FABRICATION
6'×4'	PAIR	3'-4¼" × 4'-3"	12'-5¼"	CUT (2) EQUAL PIECES FROM 8' LENGTHS *
3'×4'	SINGLE	3'-5⅝" × 4'-3"	6'-2¼"	CUT FROM 8' LENGTH
8'×6'-8"	PAIR	4'-4¼" × 7'-1½"	16'-5¼"	CUT (2) EQUAL PIECES FROM 10' LENGTHS *

* SPLICE AT CENTERLINE

④ SHUTTER SCHEDULE

AA-5 SHUTTER DETAILS - LITTLE HOUSE STUDIO

SCALE AS NOTED

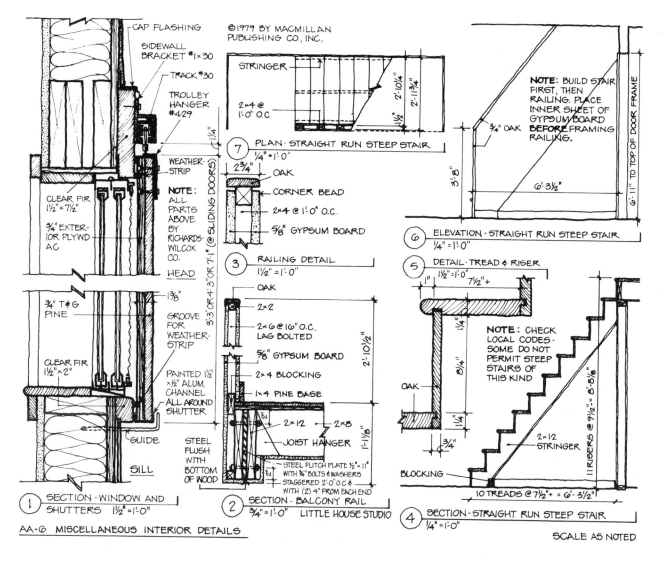

STRINGER

2×4 @ 1'-0" O.C.

(7) PLAN - STRAIGHT RUN STEEP STAIR
¼" = 1'-0"

OAK
CORNER BEAD
2×4 @ 1'-0" O.C.
⅝" GYPSUM BOARD

(3) RAILING DETAIL
1½" = 1'-0"

OAK
2×2
2×6 @ 16" O.C. LAG BOLTED
⅝" GYPSUM BOARD
2×4 BLOCKING
1×4 PINE BASE
2×12   2×8
JOIST HANGER
STEEL FLITCH PLATE ½" × 11" WITH ¾" BOLTS & WASHERS STAGGERED 2'-0" O.C. & WITH (2) 4" FROM EACH END

(2) SECTION - BALCONY RAIL
¾" = 1'-0"   LITTLE HOUSE STUDIO

CAP FLASHING
SIDEWALL BRACKET #1×30
TRACK #30
TROLLEY HANGER #429
WEATHER-STRIP
CLEAR FIR 1½" × 7½"
¾" EXTERIOR PLYWD AC
NOTE: ALL PARTS ABOVE BY RICHARDS-WILCOX CO.
HEAD
3'-3" OR 4'-3" OR 7'-1" (@ SLIDING DOORS)
¼"
1⅜"
¾" T&G PINE
GROOVE FOR WEATHER-STRIP
CLEAR FIR 1½" × 2"
PAINTED 1½" × ½" ALUM. CHANNEL ALL AROUND SHUTTER
GUIDE
STEEL FLUSH WITH BOTTOM OF WOOD
SILL

(1) SECTION - WINDOW AND SHUTTERS 1½" = 1'-0"

AA-6 MISCELLANEOUS INTERIOR DETAILS

NOTE: BUILD STAIR FIRST, THEN RAILING. PLACE INNER SHEET OF GYPSUM BOARD **BEFORE** FRAMING RAILING.

¾" OAK
3'-8"
6'-3½"
6'-11" TO TOP OF DOOR FRAME

(6) ELEVATION - STRAIGHT RUN STEEP STAIR
¼" = 1'-0"

(5) DETAIL - TREAD & RISER
1½" = 1'-0"
7½"+
1"
¼"
8¾"
¼"
OAK
¾"
NOTE: CHECK LOCAL CODES - SOME DO NOT PERMIT STEEP STAIRS OF THIS KIND

BLOCKING
2×12 STRINGER
11 RISERS @ 9½" = 8'-8⅝"
10 TREADS @ 7½"+ = 6'-3½"

(4) SECTION - STRAIGHT RUN STEEP STAIR
¼" = 1'-0"

SCALE AS NOTED

with an open ground-floor plan. You will note that the railing detail involves the same vertical cantilever that we saw in the stair railing in the garage, but here it is faced in gypboard rather than pine planking.

Drawing AA-5 is devoted to the sliding shutters, the use of which need not be confined solely to this variation. Using the schedule of sizes cited for the studio, you can make up your own depending on the size and number of openings in your version. The track is manufactured by the Richard Wilcox Company. It comes in specific lengths with hangers 2'0" on center. These lengths must be cut and the hangers adjusted to fit your building. Suspended from the track are trolley hangers, two of which are required per panel.

The panels themselves are similar to the hinged doors in the Little House garage. All four sides are edged in metal to protect the trim behind from being chewed up by the panels sliding back and forth. The trim itself is wider than the window trim for the basic Little House to insure that the sliding panels clear the slight projection of the window screens. Metal guides should be located as shown at the bottom to keep the panels from swinging out. These can be shudder nails or Z clips or whatever you can improvise.

LITTLE HOUSE REVERSED

If this is your choice, proceed to develop a set of working plans exactly as suggested above. Trace plans for the Little House reversed in chapter 3. Place the horizontal window and door openings on both floors of the south facade exactly as those on the north facade of the basic Little House. Lay in the dimensions for the windows on the east and west facades, again using the working plan of the basic Little House as a guide. Remember that while the precise locations differ substantially, the principle for their location is governed by the same design grid.

You won't need to lay out the downstairs kitchen, bath, and stair, since we have drawn these up in detail in drawing AA-7. But you will have to develop your own kitchen elevations, which you can do by working over the kitchen elevations for the basic Little House just as you have now learned to develop your own plans. Bathroom elevations are not essential as most of the information that we show in our basic Little House bathroom elevations can be indicated with notes on the plan. All you really need to convey is the height of the wainscoting, if any, and the mounting height of the lavatory, and the light fixtures.

In the next chapter, you will come upon our suggestions for lighting the basic Little House. There's a lot of thought behind these ideas. However, this scheme can't be applied to each variation and combination; you will have to revise it to suit your own plan, either accepting or rejecting the reasoning that determines the choice and location of each fixture. Don't leave these decisions to the end, when you're already under construction and the electrician is screaming at you about where you want your lights. This is no way to make a decision about something as important as lighting.

Drawing AA-8 indicates the framing and detailing for the semicircular balcony.

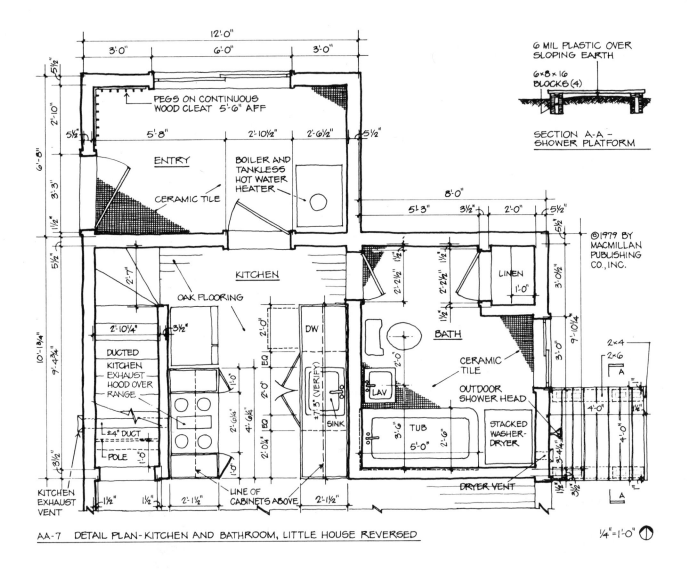

AA-7 DETAIL PLAN—KITCHEN AND BATHROOM, LITTLE HOUSE REVERSED

¼"=1'-0"

110

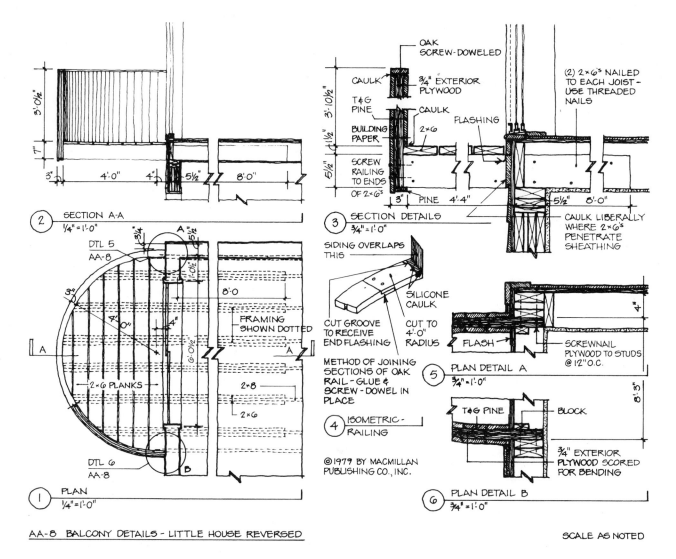

CAULK

OAK
SCREW-DOWELED

¾" EXTERIOR
PLYWOOD

T&G
PINE

CAULK

(2) 2×6'S NAILED
TO EACH JOIST -
USE THREADED
NAILS

BUILDING
PAPER

2×6

FLASHING

SCREW
RAILING
TO ENDS
OF 2×6'S

3"   PINE   4'-4"

5½"   8'-0"

CAULK LIBERALLY
WHERE 2×6'S
PENETRATE
SHEATHING

3'-10½"

1½"   3'-0½"

5½"

③ SECTION DETAILS
¾"=1'-0"

3'-0½"

SIDING OVERLAPS
THIS

SILICONE
CAULK

CUT GROOVE
TO RECEIVE
END FLASHING

CUT TO
4'-0"
RADIUS

FLASH

SCREWNAIL
PLYWOOD TO STUDS
@ 12" O.C.

METHOD OF JOINING
SECTIONS OF OAK
RAIL - GLUE &
SCREW - DOWEL IN
PLACE

⑤ PLAN DETAIL A
¾"=1'-0"

④ ISOMETRIC -
RAILING

© 1979 BY MACMILLAN
PUBLISHING CO., INC.

T&G PINE

BLOCK

¾" EXTERIOR
PLYWOOD SCORED
FOR BENDING

⑥ PLAN DETAIL B
¾"=1'-0"

SCALE AS NOTED

3'-0½"

7"

3"   4'-0"   4"   5½"   8'-0"

② SECTION A-A
¼"=1'-0"

¾"   5½"

DTL 5
AA-8

3"

A

A

8'-0

6'-0½"

4'-0"

4"

FRAMING
SHOWN DOTTED

2×6 PLANKS

2×8

2×6

DTL 6
AA-8

B

① PLAN
¼"=1'-0"

AA-8 BALCONY DETAILS - LITTLE HOUSE REVERSED

While you are encouraged to make the final balcony rectangular only as a last resort, you must start with something like a rectangle. Extend the pertinent floor joists 4'4" beyond the framing of the exterior wall (the joists on each side needn't project quite that far); notch them 2" as you would do the exterior stair landing for the Little House garage. Then nail 2 x 6's to both sides of the 2 x 8's and extend them back into the house at least 8'0". (We are overstructuring this cantilever somewhat as we want to be sure it will hold the crush of people that jam onto it during a party.) Lay the 2 x 6 planking across the beams, allowing the ends to overhang the beams somewhat. Space them no less than ⅛" apart to allow for swelling and no more than ¼" apart so high heels won't get stuck. From a point centered on the window opening but 4" away from the exterior wall framing, draw on the boards a semicircle with a radius of 4'0". Cut the planks along this arc with a jigsaw. Now you have a full-size template. Cut the built-up 2 x 8 joists below carefully, following the line of the curve.

Now for the construction of yet another variation on the vertically cantilevered railing, this time with a warped plywood core: Score two layers of ¾" exterior plywood, so they will wrap around the curved flooring. Place the end of the inside layer of plywood flush with the inside face of the studs and begin to nail it to the planking. When you get to the ends of the projecting joists nail it top and bottom. Repeat the process with the second layer, gluing it with exterior plywood glue to the first layer as well. Be certain to stagger the vertical

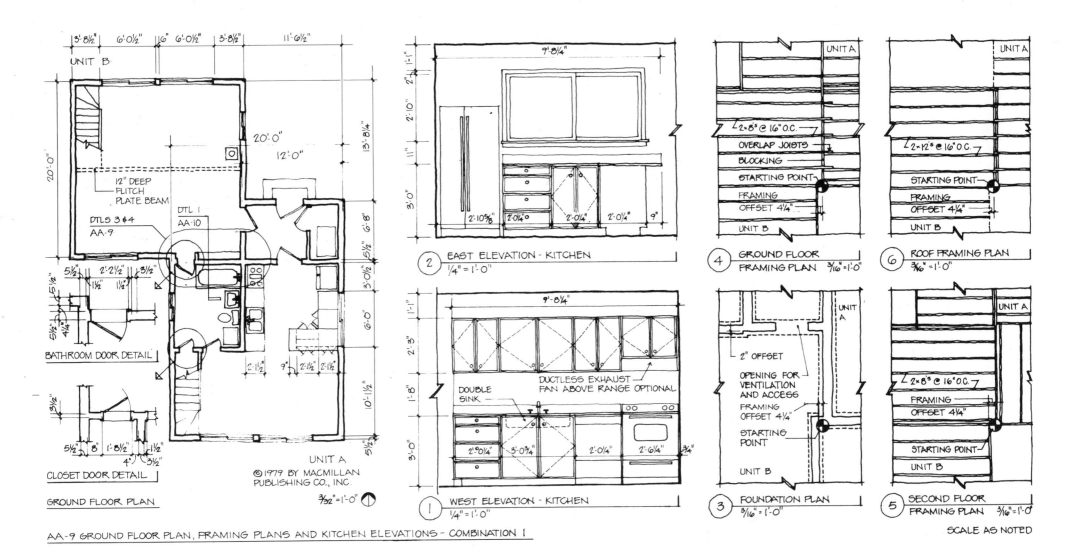

UNIT B

3'-8½" 6'-0½" 6" 6'-0½" 3'-8½" 11'-6½"

20'-0"
12'-0"

13'-8¾"

6'-8"

20'-0"

5½"

3'-0½"

6'-0"

10'-1½"

5½"

12" DEEP
FLITCH
PLATE BEAM

DTLS 3 & 4
AA-9

DTL 1
AA-10

BATHROOM DOOR DETAIL

5½" 2'-2½" 3½"
5½"
4¼" 1½" 1½"

CLOSET DOOR DETAIL

5½" 8" 1'-8½" 1½"
4" 3½"

GROUND FLOOR PLAN

2'-1½"
9" 2'-1½" 2'-1½"

UNIT A

© 1979 BY MACMILLAN
PUBLISHING CO., INC.

3/32" = 1'-0"

AA-9 GROUND FLOOR PLAN, FRAMING PLANS AND KITCHEN ELEVATIONS – COMBINATION 1

9'-8¼"

1'-1"
2'-0"
3'-0"

2'-10⅝" 2'-0¼" 2'-0¼" 9"

② EAST ELEVATION – KITCHEN
     ¼" = 1'-0"

9'-8¼"

1'-1"
2'-3"
1'-8"
3'-0"

DUCTLESS EXHAUST
FAN ABOVE RANGE OPTIONAL

DOUBLE
SINK

2'-0¼" 3'-0¾" 2'-0¼" 2'-6¼" ¾"

① WEST ELEVATION – KITCHEN
     ¼" = 1'-0"

UNIT A

2×8's @ 16" O.C.
OVERLAP JOISTS
BLOCKING
STARTING POINT
FRAMING
OFFSET 4¼"

UNIT B

④ GROUND FLOOR
     FRAMING PLAN   3/16" = 1'-0"

UNIT A

2" OFFSET

OPENING FOR
VENTILATION
AND ACCESS

FRAMING
OFFSET 4¼"

STARTING
POINT

UNIT B

③ FOUNDATION PLAN
     3/16" = 1'-0"

UNIT A

2×12's @ 16" O.C.

STARTING POINT
FRAMING
OFFSET 4¼"

UNIT B

⑥ ROOF FRAMING PLAN
     3/16" = 1'-0"

UNIT A

UNIT A

2×8's @ 16" O.C.
FRAMING
OFFSET 4¼"
STARTING POINT

UNIT B

⑤ SECOND FLOOR
     FRAMING PLAN   3/16" = 1'-0"

SCALE AS NOTED

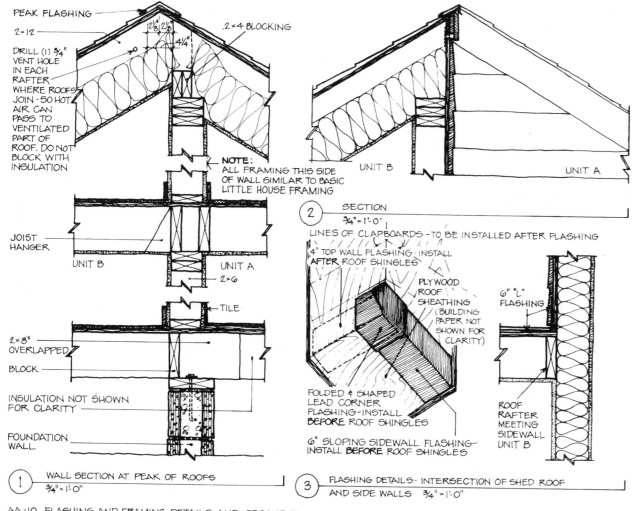

PEAK FLASHING

2 × 12

DRILL (1) ¾"
VENT HOLE
IN EACH
RAFTER
WHERE ROOFS
JOIN - SO HOT
AIR CAN
PASS TO
VENTILATED
PART OF
ROOF. DO NOT
BLOCK WITH
INSULATION

.2 × 4 BLOCKING

2⅛" 2⅛"

4¼"

NOTE:
ALL FRAMING THIS SIDE
OF WALL SIMILAR TO BASIC
LITTLE HOUSE FRAMING

JOIST
HANGER

UNIT B

UNIT A

2 × 6

TILE

2 × 8's
OVERLAPPED

BLOCK

INSULATION NOT SHOWN
FOR CLARITY

FOUNDATION
WALL

(1) WALL SECTION AT PEAK OF ROOFS
¾"=1'-0"

UNIT B

UNIT A

(2) SECTION
¾"=1'-0"

LINES OF CLAPBOARDS - TO BE INSTALLED AFTER FLASHING

4" TOP WALL FLASHING - INSTALL
AFTER ROOF SHINGLES

PLYWOOD
ROOF
SHEATHING
(BUILDING
PAPER NOT
SHOWN FOR
CLARITY)

6" "L"
FLASHING

FOLDED & SHAPED
LEAD CORNER
FLASHING - INSTALL
BEFORE ROOF SHINGLES

6" SLOPING SIDEWALL FLASHING -
INSTALL **BEFORE** ROOF SHINGLES

ROOF
RAFTER
MEETING
SIDEWALL
UNIT B

(3) FLASHING DETAILS - INTERSECTION OF SHED ROOF
AND SIDE WALLS ¾"=1'-0"

AA-10 FLASHING AND FRAMING DETAILS AND SECOND FLOOR PLAN - COMBINATION 1

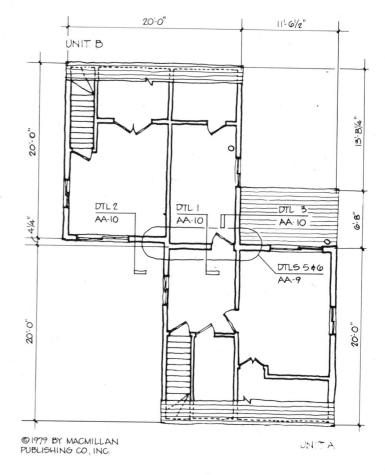

UNIT B

20'-0"

11'-6½"

13'-8¾"

4¼"

6'-8"

20'-0"

20'-0"

DTL 2
AA-10

DTL 1
AA-10

DTL 3
AA-10

DTLS 5&6
AA-9

UNIT A

SECOND FLOOR PLAN

³⁄₃₂"=1'-0"

SCALE AS NOTED

joints in the two layers. Sheath both sides of the rail with ¾″ tongue-and-groove pine. These boards must be no wider than 3″ or 4″ at the most else they won't follow the curve.

COMBINATION 1

In designing the framing for Combinations 1 through 5 we are assuming that units A and B will be built simultaneously. However, the foundation and framing plans shown on drawing AA-9 for Combination 1 are still valid if the units are built sequentially. In the presentation drawings in chapter 4 it would appear that in all the combinations (or at least 1 through 5 and 6B and C) the second unit is built right smack up against the first unit. But if you study the framing details on drawing AA-10, you will see that the element in unit A which must be built smack against the same element in unit B in order to convey this impression is the outermost edge of the roof trim. What with the sheathing, the siding, and the necessary overhangs, the outermost surface of this edge trim projects 2⅛″ beyond the exterior face of the studs. Thus in order to create the impression that two units are smoothly sliding past one another on the high, low, or sloping sides, there must be a 4¼″ space between the vertical framing of each unit. Understanding the necessity for this 4¼″ separation is critical to understanding the thinking behind all the framing plans and details we show.

The next assumption we have made is that where these two units meet, the vertical structure or stud wall of unit B is eliminated and the stud wall of unit A

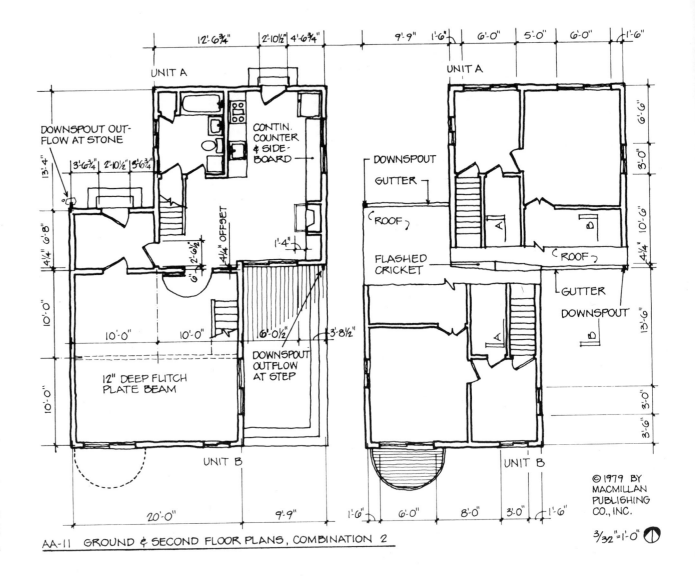

AA-11 GROUND & SECOND FLOOR PLANS, COMBINATION 2

3/32″=1'-0″

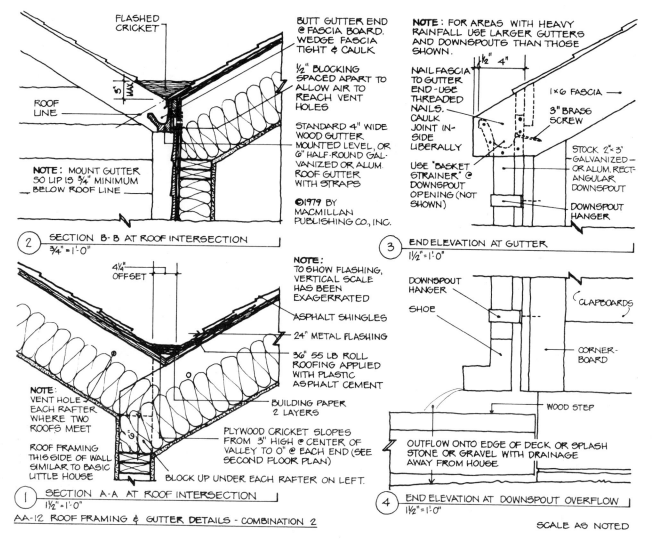

FLASHED CRICKET

ROOF LINE

5' MAX

NOTE: MOUNT GUTTER SO LIP IS ¾" MINIMUM BELOW ROOF LINE

BUTT GUTTER END @ FASCIA BOARD. WEDGE FASCIA TIGHT & CAULK

½" BLOCKING SPACED APART TO ALLOW AIR TO REACH VENT HOLES

STANDARD 4" WIDE WOOD GUTTER MOUNTED LEVEL, OR 6" HALF-ROUND GALVANIZED OR ALUM. ROOF GUTTER WITH STRAPS

©1979 BY MACMILLAN PUBLISHING CO., INC.

② SECTION B-B AT ROOF INTERSECTION
¾"=1'-0"

4¼" OFFSET

NOTE: VENT HOLE EACH RAFTER WHERE TWO ROOFS MEET

ROOF FRAMING THIS SIDE OF WALL SIMILAR TO BASIC LITTLE HOUSE

NOTE: TO SHOW FLASHING, VERTICAL SCALE HAS BEEN EXAGERRATED

ASPHALT SHINGLES

24" METAL FLASHING

36" 55 LB ROLL ROOFING APPLIED WITH PLASTIC ASPHALT CEMENT

BUILDING PAPER 2 LAYERS

PLYWOOD CRICKET SLOPES FROM 3" HIGH @ CENTER OF VALLEY TO 0" @ EACH END (SEE SECOND FLOOR PLAN)

BLOCK UP UNDER EACH RAFTER ON LEFT.

① SECTION A-A AT ROOF INTERSECTION
1½"=1'-0"

AA-12 ROOF FRAMING & GUTTER DETAILS - COMBINATION 2

NOTE: FOR AREAS WITH HEAVY RAINFALL USE LARGER GUTTERS AND DOWNSPOUTS THAN THOSE SHOWN.

½" 4"

NAIL FASCIA TO GUTTER END - USE THREADED NAILS. CAULK JOINT INSIDE LIBERALLY

USE "BASKET STRAINER" @ DOWNSPOUT OPENING (NOT SHOWN)

1×6 FASCIA

3" BRASS SCREW

STOCK 2"×3" GALVANIZED OR ALUM. RECTANGULAR DOWNSPOUT

DOWNSPOUT HANGER

③ END ELEVATION AT GUTTER
1½"=1'-0"

DOWNSPOUT HANGER

SHOE

CLAPBOARDS

CORNER-BOARD

WOOD STEP

OUTFLOW ONTO EDGE OF DECK OR SPLASH STONE OR GRAVEL WITH DRAINAGE AWAY FROM HOUSE

④ END ELEVATION AT DOWNSPOUT OVERFLOW
1½"=1'-0"

SCALE AS NOTED

carries the load imposed by the floor joists and roof rafters of both units A and B.

This means that at the common wall, the horizontal framing members of unit B must bridge the 4¼" gap and project at least 1'0" into unit A where they can be fastened securely to its framing members, as shown in the partial framing plans for Combination 1, drawing AA-9. The framing itself is very straightforward until you get to the common peak. You will notice that the ceiling of the smaller bedroom in unit B is higher at the top than that of unit A. Again this is because the underside of the rafter has to keep climbing as it reaches across the 4¼" to meet the wall of unit A. If you look at the top of the rafter, you will notice that before it reaches the vertical framing of unit A, its point is sliced off and it has already begun its descent down the other side of the roof even before it begins to overlap the rafters of unit A. The high point of the rafter is the magic line 2⅛" away from each unit at which they come together.

There is a comparable kink in the foundation plan. That both units share the foundation of unit A where they come together should not be surprising. However, you may be confused by the 2" offset of the foundation shared by the west wall of the shed of unit A and the east wall of unit B. Here's why it occurs: the actual width of the foundation we show for the basic Little House is 7½". The 2 x 6 framing that rests on it is 5½" wide. So the sheathing and siding can overlap the foundation, the 2" difference is placed under the house. While above the foundation the west wall of the shed

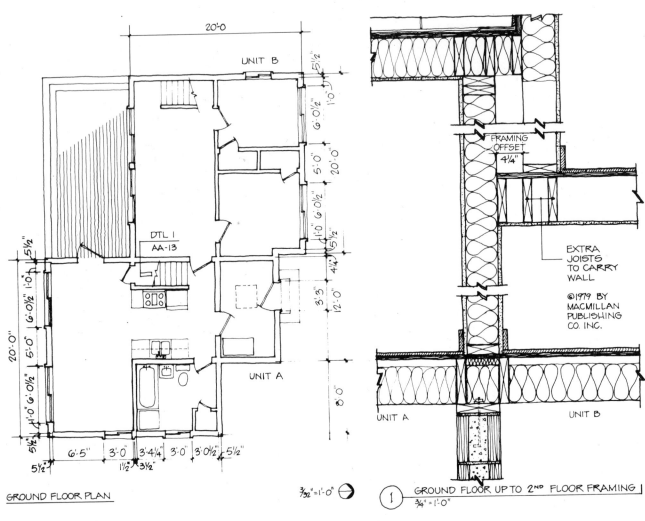

20'-0"

UNIT B

5½"

6'-0½" 1'-0"

5'-0" 20'-0"

6'-0½" 1'-0"

5½"

4¼" 5½"

DTL 1
AA-13

3'-3" 12'-0"

8'-0"

UNIT A

20'-0"

5'-0" 6'-0½" 1'-0"

1'-0" 6'-0½"

5½"

5½"

6'-5" 3'-0" 3'-4¼" 3'-0" 3'-0½" 5½"

1½" 3½"

5½"

GROUND FLOOR PLAN

3/32"=1'-0"

AA-13 GROUND FLOOR PLAN AND FRAMING DETAILS, COMBINATION 3

FRAMING
OFFSET
4¼"

EXTRA
JOISTS
TO CARRY
WALL

©1979 BY
MACMILLAN
PUBLISHING
CO. INC.

UNIT A   UNIT B

① GROUND FLOOR UP TO 2ND FLOOR FRAMING
¾"=1'-0"

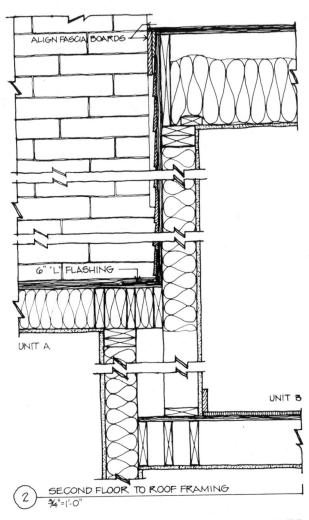

ALIGN FASCIA BOARDS

6" 'L' FLASHING

UNIT A

UNIT B

② SECOND FLOOR TO ROOF FRAMING
¾"=1'-0"

SCALE AS NOTED

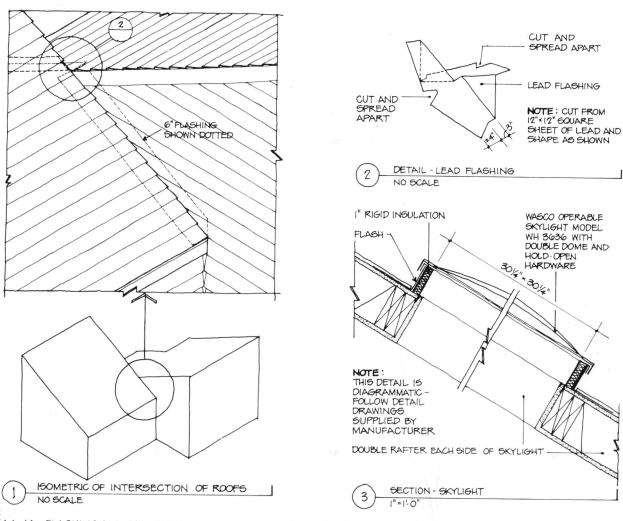

6" FLASHING
SHOWN DOTTED

② DETAIL - LEAD FLASHING
NO SCALE

CUT AND
SPREAD APART

LEAD FLASHING

CUT AND
SPREAD
APART

24"   3'

NOTE: CUT FROM
12"×12" SQUARE
SHEET OF LEAD AND
SHAPE AS SHOWN

① ISOMETRIC OF INTERSECTION OF ROOFS
NO SCALE

1" RIGID INSULATION

FLASH

WASCO OPERABLE
SKYLIGHT MODEL
WH 3636 WITH
DOUBLE DOME AND
HOLD-OPEN
HARDWARE

30¼" × 30¼"

NOTE:
THIS DETAIL IS
DIAGRAMMATIC -
FOLLOW DETAIL
DRAWINGS
SUPPLIED BY
MANUFACTURER

DOUBLE RAFTER EACH SIDE OF SKYLIGHT

③ SECTION - SKYLIGHT
1" = 1'-0"

AA-14   FLASHING AND SKYLIGHT DETAILS AND SECOND FLOOR PLAN - COMBINATION 3

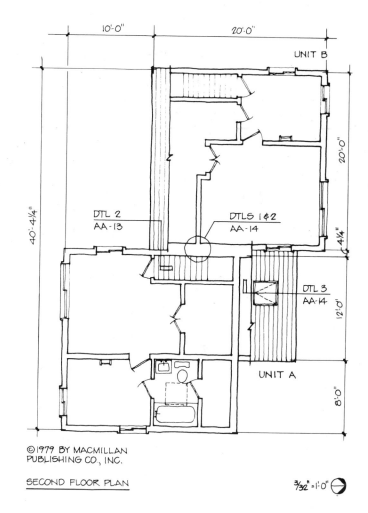

UNIT B

DTL 2
AA-13

DTLS 1&2
AA-14

DTL 3
AA-14

UNIT A

10'-0"   20'-0"

20'-0"

4¼"

12'-0"

8'-0"

40'-4¼"

© 1979 BY MACMILLAN
PUBLISHING CO., INC.

SECOND FLOOR PLAN

3/32" = 1'-0"

SCALE AS NOTED

117

and the east wall of unit B are one and the same, to be certain that the 2" step does not project on the exterior beyond this wall, it is placed inside. If both units are built simultaneously, this offset would not be required.

Also on drawing AA-9 we show detailed plans and elevations of the kitchen, as we think the projecting counter and seating make the most of unit A as a combination kitchen and dining room.

COMBINATION 2

We are showing working plans for Combinations 1 through 5 to get you off to a good start. But given that the thinking behind the framing of the common walls is virtually identical for all combinations, we show only framing details and no framing plans for Combination 2 and the subsequent combinations.

As you can see on drawing AA-12, what is new is the flashing of the valley where the low sides of the two roofs meet. Here you must install a flashed cricket, a sort of mini-roof made of metal which extends way under the shingles of the big roofs. It deflects the water from the big roofs to the east and west thus preventing it from collecting in the valley and causing leaks. Because in a heavy rain the volume of water shed by the cricket will be fairly substantial, we have detailed wood gutters to be installed along the fascia board on the low sides of units A and B with downspouts at the far end. A metal gutter would do just as well and is much cheaper. In either case, the gutter is terminated by extending the 1 x 6 sloping fascia trim. And in areas

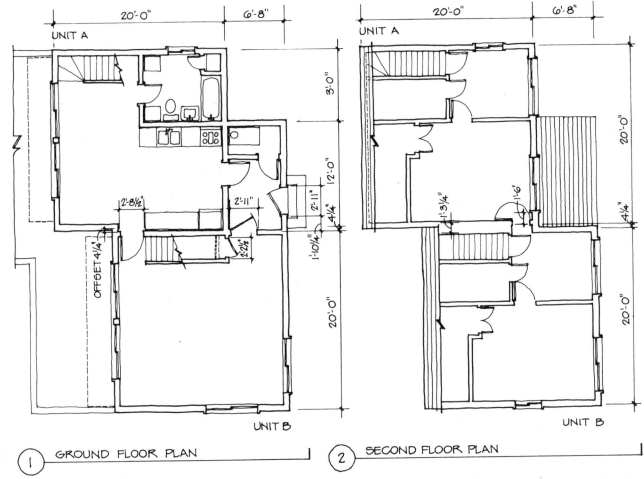

1 GROUND FLOOR PLAN

2 SECOND FLOOR PLAN

3/32" = 1'-0"

AA-15 FLOOR PLANS - COMBINATION 4

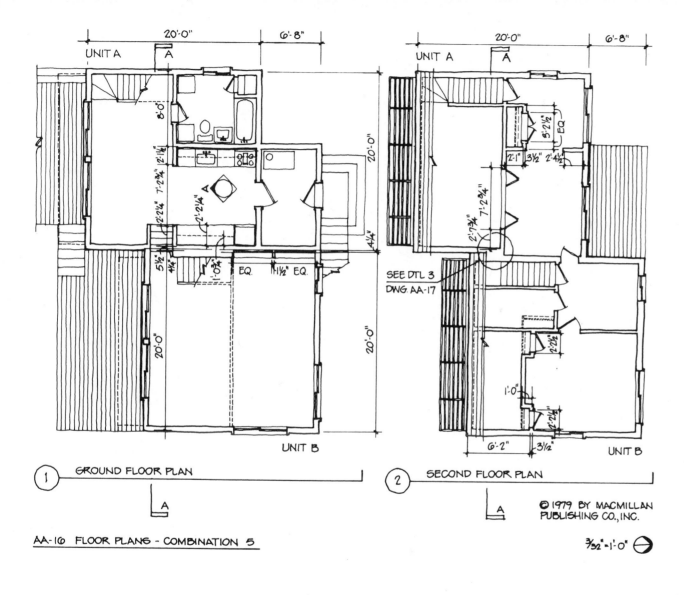

UNIT A

UNIT B

UNIT A

SEE DTL 3
DWG. AA-17

UNIT B

① GROUND FLOOR PLAN

② SECOND FLOOR PLAN

© 1979 BY MACMILLAN
PUBLISHING CO., INC.

AA-16 FLOOR PLANS - COMBINATION 5

3/32"=1'-0"

where there is snow, the lip of the gutter must be mounted below the projection of the roof to permit snow to slide off the roof without getting trapped by the gutter or, worse still, taking the gutter with it. The detail for gutter, downspout, and splashblock can be applied to any Little House variation or combination. Where a gutter is to run the full 20'0" across the low side, it should be set level with a downspout and some sort of splashblock at each end.

The final detail relating to Combination 3 is for the steeper stair with no winders. This appears with other miscellaneous details on drawing AA-6. If you want to use this stair rather than the other one, be certain there are no code restrictions relating to the slope of stairs where you're building.

COMBINATION 3

The two units of this combination can have a common wall only up to the second floor. Here, extra joists must be added to the second-floor framing of unit B to carry the upper portion of the exterior wall. Once again, these two stud walls must be $4\frac{1}{4}$" apart, so the fascia trim of unit A lies in the same plane as that of unit B. This should be clear from the detailed wall sections and isometric on drawings AA-13 and AA-14.

We call to your attention detail 3 on drawing AA-14 for the operable skylight. As mentioned in chapter 4, if you do not use a sliding door as the entrance to the shed, a similar fixed skylight should be set in its roof. In both cases, the opening for the skylight must be framed double all the way around much the way a window is framed.

COMBINATIONS 4 AND 5

While Combinations 4 and 5 look alike at first glance, there is little they share in common. Combination 4 is totally straightforward and easy to build, as both plans and section indicate. Framing the common wall between the two units is done much as it is for Combination 3, thus no specific details are included. Framing the common wall of the two units of Combination 5 is even simpler as their roofs are in the same plane, thus eliminating the necessity for fancy flashing details. However, Combination 5 is riddled with little things that must be adjusted to accommodate the level change between units A and B. Of these, we include on drawing AA-17 details of the connecting stair, and an elevation of the wall enclosing the upper level of unit A which, as you may recall, is a variation of a Little House studio. These come complete with details for trimming the large openings and the open railing at the second floor.

COMBINATION 6

The principal feature of this scheme is the greenhouse connector. All the other details have been covered elsewhere, including the plans for each unit, because Combination 6 is simply a composite of everything we have done so far. On drawing AA-18 we have provided you with details for a hypothetical greenhouse 6'8" wide by 8'3" long. It could just as easily be 9'0" by 12'0" or

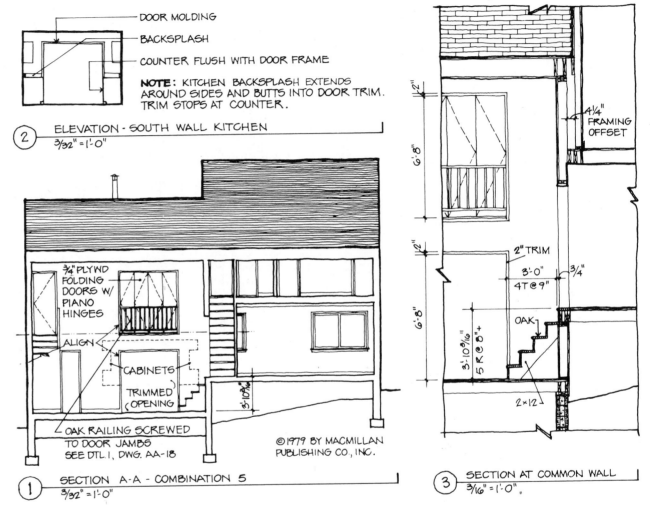

DOOR MOLDING
BACKSPLASH
COUNTER FLUSH WITH DOOR FRAME

NOTE: KITCHEN BACKSPLASH EXTENDS AROUND SIDES AND BUTTS INTO DOOR TRIM. TRIM STOPS AT COUNTER.

② ELEVATION - SOUTH WALL KITCHEN
3/32" = 1'-0"

¾" PLYWD FOLDING DOORS W/ PIANO HINGES

ALIGN

CABINETS

TRIMMED OPENING

OAK RAILING SCREWED TO DOOR JAMBS SEE DTL.1, DWG. AA-18

© 1979 BY MACMILLAN PUBLISHING CO., INC.

① SECTION A-A - COMBINATION 5
3/32" = 1'-0"

AA-17 DETAILS - COMBINATION 5

2"

6'-8"

2"

4¼" FRAMING OFFSET

2" TRIM

3'-0"
4T@9"

¾"

OAK

6'-8"

3'-10 3/16"
5R@8"+

2×12

③ SECTION AT COMMON WALL
3/16" = 1'-0"

SCALE AS NOTED

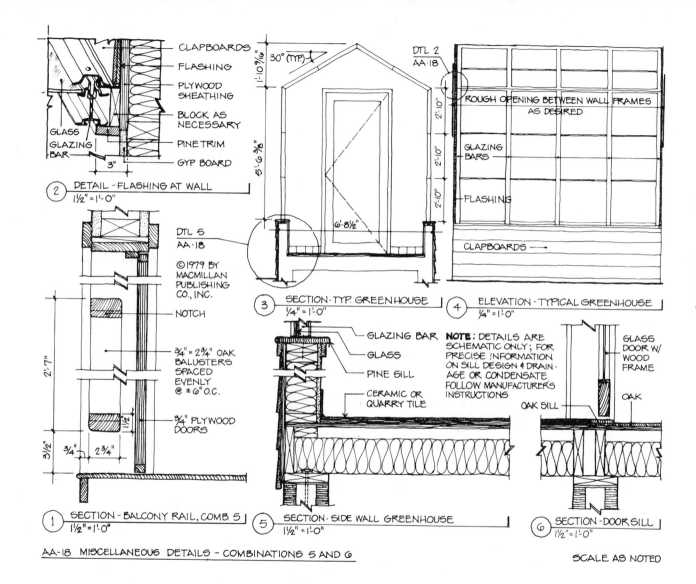

CLAPBOARDS
FLASHING
PLYWOOD SHEATHING
BLOCK AS NECESSARY
PINE TRIM
GYP BOARD

GLASS
GLAZING BAR

3"

② DETAIL - FLASHING AT WALL
1½" = 1'-0"

1'-10 9/16"

30° (TYP)

5'-6 3/8"

DTL 2
AA·18

ROUGH OPENING BETWEEN WALL FRAMES AS DESIRED

2'-10"

2'-10"

GLAZING BARS

2'-10"

FLASHING

CLAPBOARDS

DTL 5
AA·18

© 1979 BY MACMILLAN PUBLISHING CO., INC.

NOTCH

¾" × 2¾" OAK BALUSTERS SPACED EVENLY @ ±6" O.C.

2'-7"

6'-8½"

③ SECTION · TYP. GREENHOUSE
¼" = 1'-0"

④ ELEVATION · TYPICAL GREENHOUSE
¼" = 1'-0"

GLAZING BAR
GLASS
PINE SILL
CERAMIC OR QUARRY TILE

¾" PLYWOOD DOORS

1½"

3½"

¾" 2¾"

① SECTION · BALCONY RAIL, COMB. 5
1½" = 1'-0"

NOTE: DETAILS ARE SCHEMATIC ONLY; FOR PRECISE INFORMATION ON SILL DESIGN & DRAINAGE OR CONDENSATE FOLLOW MANUFACTURER'S INSTRUCTIONS

OAK SILL

⑤ SECTION · SIDE WALL GREENHOUSE
1½" = 1'-0"

GLASS DOOR W/ WOOD FRAME

OAK

⑥ SECTION · DOOR SILL
1½" = 1'-0"

AA·18 MISCELLANEOUS DETAILS - COMBINATIONS 5 AND 6

SCALE AS NOTED

any other dimension, so long as its overall width is no greater than 10'0" or half the width of the Little House. The most important dimension of whatever greenhouse you select is the outside dimension, as this will determine how far apart your Little House units should be. If you set the spacing of your Little House units first, you may get into having the components of your greenhouse connectors custom fabricated in order to fit in the space you've left between them, and this can be prohibitively expensive.

As promised, the final drawings in this chapter are large-scale sections and interior and exterior elevations which show how the materials in all four finish groups are applied to the basic framing and how they appear close at hand.

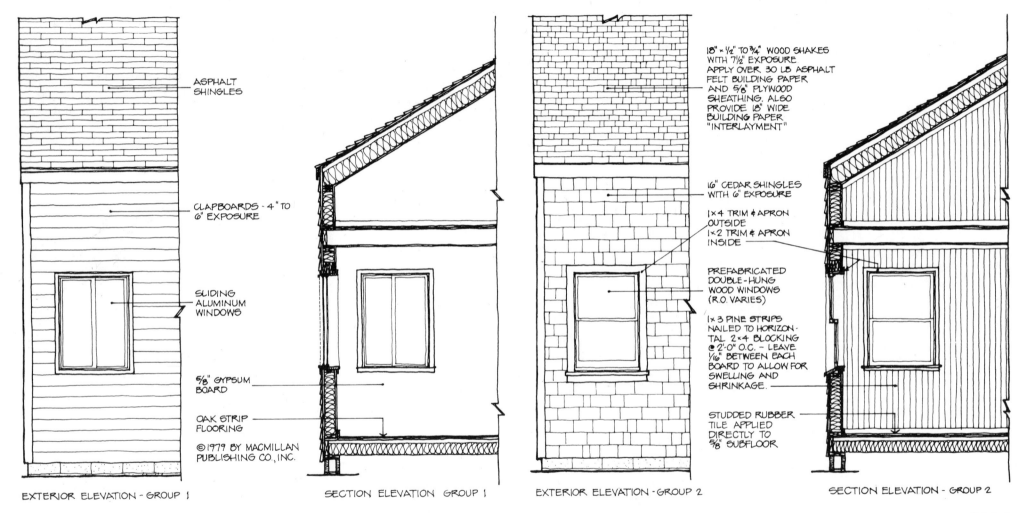

ASPHALT
SHINGLES

CLAPBOARDS - 4" TO
6" EXPOSURE

SLIDING
ALUMINUM
WINDOWS

5/8" GYPSUM
BOARD

OAK STRIP
FLOORING

© 1979 BY MACMILLAN
PUBLISHING CO., INC.

18" × 1/2" TO 3/4" WOOD SHAKES
WITH 7 1/2" EXPOSURE
APPLY OVER 30 LB ASPHALT
FELT BUILDING PAPER
AND 5/8" PLYWOOD
SHEATHING. ALSO
PROVIDE 18" WIDE
BUILDING PAPER
"INTERLAYMENT"

16" CEDAR SHINGLES
WITH 6" EXPOSURE

1 × 4 TRIM & APRON
OUTSIDE
1 × 2 TRIM & APRON
INSIDE

PREFABRICATED
DOUBLE-HUNG
WOOD WINDOWS
(R.O. VARIES)

1 × 3 PINE STRIPS
NAILED TO HORIZON-
TAL 2 × 4 BLOCKING
@ 2'-0" O.C. — LEAVE
1/16" BETWEEN EACH
BOARD TO ALLOW FOR
SWELLING AND
SHRINKAGE.

STUDDED RUBBER
TILE APPLIED
DIRECTLY TO
5/8" SUBFLOOR

EXTERIOR ELEVATION - GROUP 1

SECTION ELEVATION GROUP 1

EXTERIOR ELEVATION - GROUP 2

SECTION ELEVATION - GROUP 2

AA19   ELEVATIONS & SECTIONS, FINISH GROUPS 1 & 2

1/4" = 1'-0"

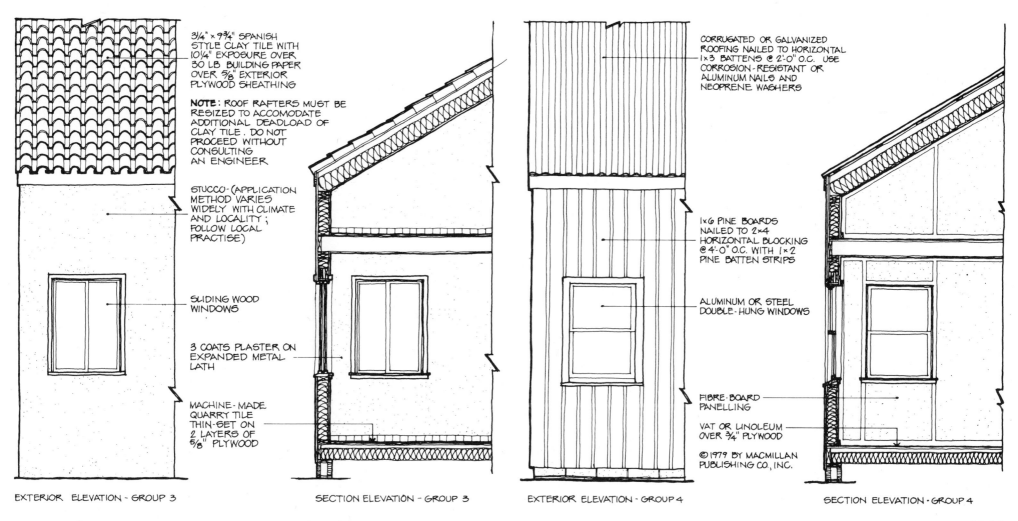

3¼" x 9¾" SPANISH STYLE CLAY TILE WITH 10¼" EXPOSURE OVER 30 LB BUILDING PAPER OVER ⅝" EXTERIOR PLYWOOD SHEATHING

NOTE: ROOF RAFTERS MUST BE RESIZED TO ACCOMODATE ADDITIONAL DEADLOAD OF CLAY TILE. DO NOT PROCEED WITHOUT CONSULTING AN ENGINEER

STUCCO - (APPLICATION METHOD VARIES WIDELY WITH CLIMATE AND LOCALITY; FOLLOW LOCAL PRACTISE)

SLIDING WOOD WINDOWS

3 COATS PLASTER ON EXPANDED METAL LATH

MACHINE-MADE QUARRY TILE THIN-SET ON 2 LAYERS OF ⅝" PLYWOOD

CORRUGATED OR GALVANIZED ROOFING NAILED TO HORIZONTAL 1x3 BATTENS @ 2'-0" O.C. USE CORROSION-RESISTANT OR ALUMINUM NAILS AND NEOPRENE WASHERS

1x6 PINE BOARDS NAILED TO 2x4 HORIZONTAL BLOCKING @ 4'-0" O.C. WITH 1x2 PINE BATTEN STRIPS

ALUMINUM OR STEEL DOUBLE-HUNG WINDOWS

FIBRE-BOARD PANELLING

VAT OR LINOLEUM OVER ¾" PLYWOOD

© 1979 BY MACMILLAN PUBLISHING CO., INC.

EXTERIOR ELEVATION - GROUP 3

SECTION ELEVATION - GROUP 3

EXTERIOR ELEVATION - GROUP 4

SECTION ELEVATION - GROUP 4

AA20   ELEVATIONS & SECTIONS, FINISH GROUPS 3 & 4

¼"=1'-0"

Mechanical Systems

There are three components to the mechanical systems for any building, whatever its size. The first is heating, ventilating, and air conditioning. The second is plumbing, and the third electrical. While there is basically only one way to plumb a house and one way to wire it, there are many more approaches to heating and ventilating a house than the hydronic system we have included in the working drawings of the basic Little House. If your Little House is only a weekend or a vacation house, you may choose simply to heat it with a fireplace or, better still, one of the Jotul or Franklin wood-burning stoves we discussed in chapter 5. For a year-round abode in regions where temperatures drop below freezing, this approach, although workable, is generally only for the hearty. For long-term comfort and convenience, you should consider an automatic heating system.

Most residential heating systems fall into three broad categories: water systems, all-electric systems, and air systems. Before reviewing each one, let us show you how to determine the amount of heat you will need to maintain the inside of your Little House at 65 to 70 degrees Fahrenheit during the winter. The amount of heat you need is measured in BTUs per hour of heat your Little House loses through its exterior envelope. A BTU, or British Thermal Unit, is the amount of heat

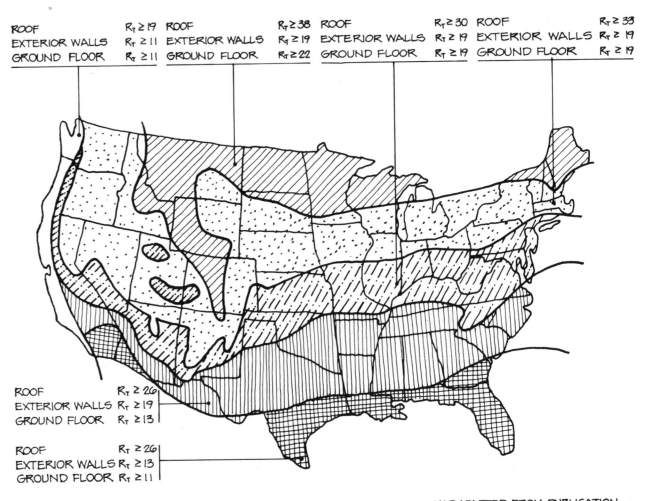

ROOF	$R_T \geq 19$	ROOF	$R_T \geq 38$	ROOF	$R_T \geq 30$	ROOF	$R_T \geq 33$
EXTERIOR WALLS	$R_T \geq 11$	EXTERIOR WALLS	$R_T \geq 19$	EXTERIOR WALLS	$R_T \geq 19$	EXTERIOR WALLS	$R_T \geq 19$
GROUND FLOOR	$R_T \geq 11$	GROUND FLOOR	$R_T \geq 22$	GROUND FLOOR	$R_T \geq 19$	GROUND FLOOR	$R_T \geq 19$

ROOF	$R_T \geq 26$
EXTERIOR WALLS	$R_T \geq 19$
GROUND FLOOR	$R_T \geq 13$

ROOF	$R_T \geq 26$
EXTERIOR WALLS	$R_T \geq 13$
GROUND FLOOR	$R_T \geq 11$

INSULATION MAP - UNITED STATES OF AMERICA

MAP ADAPTED FROM PUBLICATION NO. 5-BL 8096 "ENERGY EFFICIENT HOME." © OWENS-CORNING FIBERGLAS CORP. 1977 WITH THEIR PERMISSION.

1. NUMBERS ON INSULATION MAP REFER TO R_T OR THE TOTAL THERMAL RESISTANCE THAT MUST BE OFFERED BY THE COMPONENTS OF EACH EXTERIOR SECTION INCLUDING INSULATION AND AIR SPACE.

2. THE R_T-VALUES ON THE U & R-VALUE CHARTS IMMEDIATELY FOLLOWING RELATE TO HOW TO BUILD UP THIS RESISTANCE WITH INSULATION. THE U-VALUES REPRESENT THEIR RECIPROCALS: i.e. $U = 1/R_T$

3. IN THE ROOM-BY-ROOM HEAT LOSS CHARTS, YOU WILL MULTIPLY THESE U-VALUES BY THE DIFFERENCE BETWEEN THE INDOOR & OUTDOOR DESIGN TEMPERATURES IN YOUR AREA (T_D) TO DETERMINE THE AMOUNT OF BTU'S/HOUR OF HEAT LOST THROUGH EACH SQUARE FOOT OF SURFACE: i.e. $U \times T_D$ = BTU/HR/SQ.FT. OF HEAT LOSS.

4. IN THE ADJACENT CHART FOR WINDOW AND DOOR OPENINGS THIS HAS ALREADY BEEN DONE BECAUSE AIR INFILTRATION & TRANSMISS LOSSES AROUND & THROUGH THE FRAME ARE HARD TO COMPUTE & MUST BE INCLUDED. T_D IS ASSUMED TO BE 70° F.

HEAT LOSS FOR WINDOW AND DOOR OPENINGS
IN BTU'S/HR/SQ.FT. OF SASH AREA

FINISH GROUP	SINGLE PANE	INSUL.GLASS
ONE AND FOUR: METAL DOUBLE-HUNG AND/OR SLIDING WINDOWS & SLIDING DOORS; WEATHERSTRIPPED (NON-WEATHERSTRIPPED)	109 (148)	72 (112)
TWO AND THREE: WOOD DOUBLE-HUNG AND/OR SLIDING WINDOWS & SLIDING DOORS; WEATHERSTRIPPED (NON-WEATHERSTRIPPED)	103 (116)	65 (79)
ONE THROUGH FOUR: FIXED GLASS, e.g. SKYLIGHTS	79	42

ASSUME ALL EXTERIOR DOORS, SOLID CORE OR GLAZED, TO HAVE SAME HEAT LOSS AS SINGLE PANE WOOD WINDOWS

WHERE STORM WINDOWS OR DOORS WILL BE ADDED, ASSUME HEAT LOSS TO BE 50% OF NON-WEATHERSTRIPPED EQUIVALENT.

WINTER CLIMATE FACTOR	OUTSIDE DESIGN TEMPERATURES					
	+30° F	+20° F	+10° F	0	-10° F	-20° F
65° INSIDE DESIGN TEMP.	.60	.77	.95	1.11	1.29	1.45
70° INSIDE DESIGN TEMP.	.69	.85	1.03	1.20	1.37	1.54
75° INSIDE DESIGN TEMP.	.77	.95	1.12	1.28	1.45	1.63

HEAT LOSS THROUGH WINDOWS AND DOORS, WINTER CLIMATE FACTOR AND RELATED ASSUMPTIONS

energy required to raise the temperature of one pound of water one degree Fahrenheit. (The metric equivalent is the calorie/kilocalorie.)

One of the most important factors in determining heating requirements is insulation. In response to the current trend toward energy conservation, our drawings for the basic Little House show 6" of insulation in the walls and crawl space and 8" of insulation in the roof. To help you make the right choice for your Little House, we have included an insulation map. The three numbers shown in each zone indicate the thermal resistance to heat loss that must be offered by the materials which make up the roof, the exterior walls, and the ground floor—that is to say the envelope of the building. (These figures are recommended by the Owens Corning Fiberglass Corporation.) The total thermal resistance (R_T) is the sum of the thermal resistivity of each of the components of a section of a building including ¾" air space and insulation.

Identify the zone you are building in and the three numbers which apply to you. Then you must determine the thermal resistivity of your roof, exterior wall, and ground-floor sections. This is a function of the exterior cladding and sheathing and the interior finishes applied to the studs, roof, and floor joists. The double U and R value chart lists, among other things, the total thermal resistance of the roof, exterior walls, and ground floor for each of the four finish groups. Subtract the R_T values for your finish group from the R_Ts cited for your zone to find how much resistance must be supplied by the insulation. Given that the thermal resistance for blanket or batt insulation is 3.70 per inch of thickness, you can then determine the thickness you require.

The second set of numbers on this chart are the U values for each of the three exterior sections in each of the four finish groups. This value is simply the reciprocal of the total thermal resistance ($U = 1/R_T$) and expresses the heat transmission in BTUs per hour per square foot per degree Fahrenheit difference in temperature between inside air and outside air. This coefficient, rather than the total thermal resistance, will be used in subsequent calculations to determine the total heat loss on a room-by-room basis and ultimately the total amount of heat your system will have to generate.

Now you must determine the difference between inside and outside temperature. Inside temperature is customarily assumed to be 70 degrees Fahrenheit. But those of us who are more energy conscious work with 65 degrees. The outside temperature, known as the winter design temperature, can be obtained from your local weather bureau and is based on average winter temperatures taken over several years. With this figure in hand, compute the heat loss factor for each of your exterior sections by multiplying the U value (including insulation) by the temperature difference.

Now we must take into account the heat loss through the windows and exterior doors as they too are part of the Little House envelope. Our second chart lists all the window types we have considered so far, and their associated heat loss factors. Here you do not have to multiply the U value by the temperature difference;

BUILDING SECTION		FINISH GROUP 1		FINISH GROUP 2	
ROOF 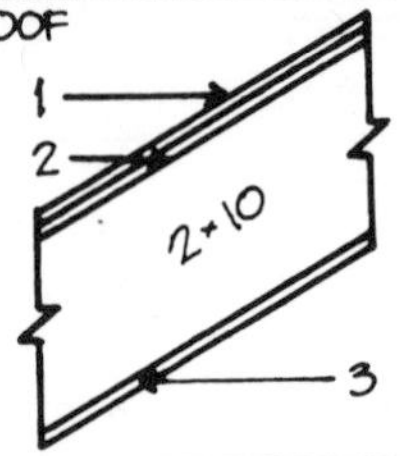 1 2 2×10 3	COMPONENTS: 1. ASPHALT SHINGLES 2. ¾" PLYWOOD 3. ⅝" GYPSUM BOARD			1. WOOD SHINGLES 2. ¾" PLYWOOD OR 1×6 ROOFERS 3. ½" × 3" PINE STRIPS	
	NO INSULATION	$R_T = 3.37$	$U = 0.30$	$R_T = 4.80$	$U = 0.20$
	4" INSULATION	$R_T = 18.17$	$U = 0.06$	$R_T = 19.60$	$U = 0.05$
	6" INSULATION	$R_T = 25.57$	$U = 0.04$	$R_T = 27.00$	$U = 0.04$
	8" INSULATION	$R_T = 32.97$	$U = 0.03$	$R_T = 34.40$	$U = 0.03$
EXTERIOR WALLS 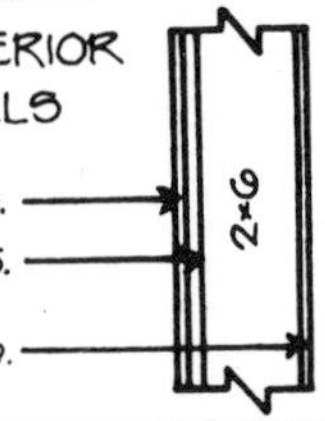 4. 5. 6. 2×6	COMPONENTS: 4. WOOD CLAPBOARDS 5. ¾" PLYWOOD 6. ⅝" GYPSUM BOARD			4. WOOD SHINGLES 5. ¾" PLYWOOD 6. ½" × 3" PINE STRIPS	
	NO INSULATION	$R_T = 4.16$	$U = 0.24$	$R_T = 4.98$	$U = 0.20$
	4" INSULATION	$R_T = 18.96$	$U = 0.05$	$R_T = 19.78$	$U = 0.05$
	6" INSULATION	$R_T = 25.39$	$U = 0.04$	$R_T = 26.21$	$U = 0.04$
GROUND FLOOR 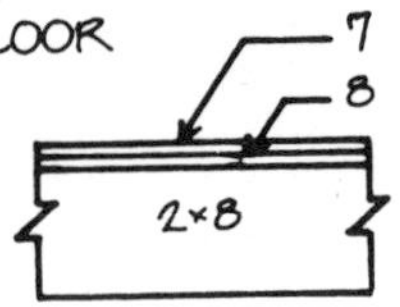 7 8 2×8	COMPONENTS: 7. 1¼" T & G OAK STRIP 8. ¾" PLYWOOD			7. RESILIENT RUBBER TILE 8. ¾" PLYWOOD	
	NO INSULATION	$R_T = 4.01$	$U = 0.25$	$R_T = 2.56$	$U = 0.39$
	4" INSULATION	$R_T = 18.81$	$U = 0.05$	$R_T = 17.36$	$U = 0.06$
	6" INSULATION	$R_T = 26.21$	$U = 0.04$	$R_T = 24.76$	$U = 0.04$
	8" INSULATION	$R_T = 33.61$	$U = 0.03$	$R_T = 32.16$	$U = 0.03$
BATHROOM FLOOR 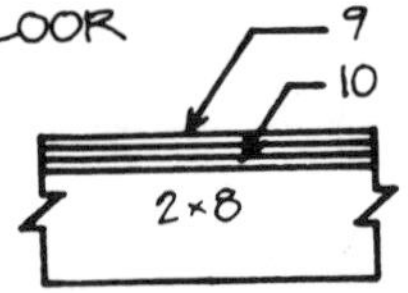 9 10 2×8	COMPONENTS: 9. CERAMIC TILE, THIN SET 10. 2 LAYERS ¾" PLYWOOD			9. RESILIENT RUBBER TILE 10. ¾" PLYWOOD	
	NO INSULATION	$R_T = 1.69$	$U = 1.59$	AS ABOVE	AS ABOVE
	4" INSULATION	$R_T = 16.49$	$U = 0.06$		
	6" INSULATION	$R_T = 23.89$	$U = 0.04$		
	8" INSULATION	$R_T = 31.29$	$U = 0.03$		

U AND R VALUES FOR EXTERIOR SECTIONS - FINISH GROUPS 1 AND 2   ½"=1'-0"

FINISH GROUP 3		FINISH GROUP 4		ENTER YOUR CHOICE HERE	
1. CLAY TILE 2. ¾" PLYWOOD 3. ¾" PLASTER		1. CORRUGATED METAL 2. 1×3 BATTENS @ ± 2'-0" O.C. 3. ± ½" FIBREBOARD		1. 2. 3.	
$R_T = 3.25$ $R_T = 18.05$ $R_T = 25.45$ $R_T = 32.85$	$U = 0.31$ $U = 0.06$ $U = 0.04$ $U = 0.03$	$R_T = 3.73$ $R_T = 18.53$ $R_T = 25.93$ $R_T = 33.53$	$U = 0.27$ $U = 0.05$ $U = 0.04$ $U = 0.03$		
4. STUCCO ON WIRE MESH * 5. PAPER BACKED REINFORCEMENT 6. ¾" PLASTER ON WIRE MESH		4. ROUGH CUT BOARD & BATTEN 5. BLOCKING & BUILDING PAPER 6. ± ½" FIBREBOARD		4. 5. 6.	
$R_T = 2.55$ $R_T = 17.35$ $R_T = 24.75$	$U = 0.39$ $U = 0.06$ $U = 0.04$	$R_T = 3.67$ $R_T = 18.47$ $R_T = 25.87$	$U = 0.27$ $U = 0.05$ $U = 0.04$		
7. QUARRY TILE - THIN SET 8. ¾" PLYWOOD		7. VAT OR LINOLEUM 8. ¾" PLYWOOD		7. 8.	
$R_T = 1.61$ $R_T = 16.41$ $R_T = 23.81$ $R_T = 31.21$	$U = 0.62$ $U = 0.06$ $U = 0.04$ $U = 0.03$	$R_T = 2.56$ $R_T = 17.36$ $R_T = 24.76$ $R_T = 32.16$	$U = 0.39$ $U = 0.06$ $U = 0.04$ $U = 0.03$		
9. QUARRY TILE - THINSET 10. ¾" PLYWOOD		9. VAT OR LINOLEUM 10. ¾" PLYWOOD		9. 10.	
AS ABOVE	AS ABOVE	AS ABOVE	AS ABOVE		

U AND R VALUES FOR EXTERIOR SECTIONS - FINISH GROUPS 3 & 4

* THICKNESS OF STUCCO AND TYPE OF BACKING WILL DIFFER FROM AREA TO AREA

these figures not only take into account transmission losses through the windows and frames, but also include an allowance for losses due to air infiltration through cracks around window and door frames.

Now you are ready to compute the amount of heat that will be lost to the outside through the exterior envelope on a room-by-room basis. In the next chart, list in the heat loss factor column the heat loss factors for the windows, roof, walls, and ground floor of your Little House. Then start with the living area—the south half of the ground floor: enter the square footage of the window area on the left and the product of the area and your heat loss factor for windows on the right. Enter the square footage of the *exterior walls only* less the window area below on the left and the product of this net area and the *U* factor for your exterior wall section on the right. Walls contiguous to unheated spaces such as the shed and upstairs storage areas should be counted as exterior walls. Finally, include the floor over the crawl space.

Do this for each room in your house until the chart is complete. Multiply the BTU/hour subtotals by the "winter climate factor" associated with your winter design temperature and you will come up with the total BTU/hour heat loss which your radiation or ductwork will have to make up. The winter climate factor is a sort of safety measure. For winter design temperatures under 10 degrees Fahrenheit it increases the total, and for those above it reduces it somewhat. We include a sheet of typical calculations to indicate how this is done and the sort of numbers you can expect to come up with.

Now you must calculate the amount of radiation required per room. The formulas for these calculations depend on the heating system which you have selected. For hydronic and all-electric systems you will need to know the number of linear feet of radiator required. Select a radiator, the same length or longer than what you determine to be the required length. Its slightly greater capacity will take up piping and/or wiring losses. If the length you come up with is greater than the length of exterior wall available, go to a unit with a higher BTU rating and repeat the calculations. In no event may you install lengths of radiators vertically or stacked one on top of the other.

Calculating the amount of radiation called for with forced air is similar except the results are in cubic feet of heated air to be delivered to the room per minute. The 1.08 in the formula is a design constant which must be multiplied by the difference between the supply air temperature and the indoor design temperature. You will use the results of this formula to size the ductwork and supply registers in each room.

Enter on the room-by-room radiation chart the actual length of radiator and the manufacturer's BTU rating for this length or, in the case of forced air, the cubic feet of heated air per minute required for each room. Add up the total number of BTUs per hour that you must supply to this radiation or through the ductwork, and this will give you the required capacity of your boiler or furnace, or by how much your electrical service will have to be increased to accommodate your electrical baseboard radiation.

BUILDING SECTION	ROOFS			EXTERIOR WALLS		
UNIT AND ROOM	AREA IN SQ. FT.	HEAT LOSS FACTOR $U \times T_D$	BTU/HR HEAT LOSS	AREA ALL WALLS	HEAT LOSS FACTOR $U \times T_D$	BTU/HR HEAT LOSS
UNIT A LIVING AREA *						
KITCHEN/DINING *						
BATHROOM						
SMALL BEDROOM						
LARGE BEDROOM						
OTHER						
SUB-TOTAL UNIT A						
UNIT B DOWNSTAIRS ROOM #1 *						
DOWNSTAIRS ROOM #2 *						
DOWNSTAIRS ROOM #3 *						
UPSTAIRS ROOM #4						
UPSTAIRS ROOM #5						
OTHER						
SUB-TOTAL UNIT B						
* THESE SPACES CAN BE COMPUTED SEPARATELY OR TOGETHER, DEPENDING ON HOW THEY'RE USED.	FOR SLOPED CEILING UNDER ROOF, USE ACTUAL ROOF AREA, NOT PROJECTION OF ROOF ON FLOOR PLAN.			WALLS ADJACENT TO UNHEATED SPACES COUNT AS EXTERIOR WALLS. SUBTRACT DOOR & WINDOW AREAS.		

ROOM BY ROOM HEAT LOSS IN BTU'S/HR

GROUND FLOOR			WINDOWS & DOORS			SUB-TOTAL	WINTER CLIMATE FACTOR	TOTAL
AREA IN SQ. FT.	HEAT LOSS FACTOR $U \times T_o$	BTU/HR HEAT LOSS	AREA IN SQ. FT.	HEAT LOSS FACTOR $U \times T_o$	BTU/HR HEAT LOSS			
FLOOR OVER UNHEATED BASEMENT COUNTS AS FLOOR ABOVE CRAWL SPACE. NO HEAT LOSS TO HEATED BASEMENT			* TRANSFER HEAT LOSS FIGURES DIRECTLY FROM CHART. ALLOWANCE OF $T_o = 70°F$ IS ALREADY BUILT-IN.			TOTAL HEAT LOSS FOR ENTIRE HOUSE :		

ROOM BY ROOM HEAT LOSS IN BTU'S/HOUR CONTINUED

While we have shown how to compute the total amount of heat you will need, plus the amount of heat to be supplied to each room, we have yet to present the pros and cons of each of the three systems.

HYDRONIC SYSTEM

For the basic Little House we chose a hydronic or hot-water system because it is an approach which we consider to be applicable under the greatest number of circumstances given the lower installation and operating costs generally associated with piped hot water, and because it offers the advantage of generating domestic hot water within the boiler itself. (Domestic hot water is the hot water circulated to the kitchen, bathroom, and the various appliances.) However, with this setup there is no storage capability and no recovery. To be certain there is enough hot water to draw from during peak periods—when people want to bathe and run the dish-washer and clothes washer simultaneously—you should provide a hot-water storage tank in addition to the boiler. Your options are set forth on the boiler and domestic hot-water charts. The capacities given for separate hot-water heater and storage tanks are applicable to all-electric and forced-air systems as well.

Determining the type of boiler to use also depends on the fuels available in your area and their relative costs both now and in the future. Assuming gas and oil are equally available, which is becoming less and less a fair assumption given the decreasing supply of natural gas, the normal procedure is to determine local costs of fuel per therm, which is to say per 100,000 BTU. There are elaborate methods for determining this, but a few inquiries as to what fuel your neighbors are using will get you the answer just as fast.

As the basic Little House has no specific site, we are arbitrarily assuming that oil is as available and less expensive than gas. Therefore, the boiler will be oil-fired.

A hydronic system of the type we show works in the following manner: a heating unit or boiler is fired by oil. An integral thermostat maintains the water in the boiler at a set temperature. A separate thermostat located in the living space serves to activate a circulating pump which moves hot water through the radiator units.

If you are not put off by the precision and detail associated with measuring and cutting piping, soldering joints, and installing fittings, you might wish to consider installing your own hydronic system. Otherwise, secure the services of a competent heating contractor.

To design the particular system we show we had to assume much more about the hypothetical location of the basic Little House than what fuel is most appropriate. We are not sharing our calculations with you because we want you to go through these steps either on your own or with your contractor, using our scheme as a guide only. However, for most of the main hot-water supply and return circuits, 1" piping will be required with ½" branches to the radiation elements. A brief check of the pipe sizing table will insure a proper selection.

In the process of designing your system take into

1. HYDRONIC SYSTEM

TO DETERMINE THE LENGTH OF RADIATION REQUIRED PER ROOM

DIVIDE — THE BTU/HR HEAT LOSS OF ROOM — AS DETERMINED IN THE PRECEDING CHART — BY THE RATING OF THE RADIATION ELEMENT IN BTU/HR PER LINEAR FOOT, AS SET FORTH IN THE MANUFACTURER'S CATALOG

EXAMPLE: $\dfrac{\text{BTU/HR HEAT LOSS OF ROOM}}{\text{MFG'S RATING OF ELEMENT}} = \dfrac{10,000 \text{ BTU/HR}}{500 \text{ BTU/HR/FT}} = \underline{20}$ FT. MINIMUM

2. FORCED AIR (ADDED CAPACITY FOR COOLING NOT INCLUDED)

TO DETERMINE THE CUBIC FEET PER MINUTE (CFM) OF HOT AIR REQUIRED PER ROOM:

DIVIDE — THE BTU/HR HEAT LOSS OF ROOM — AS DETERMINED IN THE PRECEDING CHART — BY THE CONSTANT $1.08 \times \Delta_T$ (HOT AIR SUPPLY TEMP. LESS INDOOR DESIGN TEMP.)

EXAMPLE: $\dfrac{\text{BTU/HR HEAT LOSS OF ROOM}}{\Delta_T = 40°} = \dfrac{10,000 \text{ BTU/HR}}{1.08 \times 40°} = \underline{231}$ CFM MINIMUM

3. ELECTRIC HEATING

TO DETERMINE THE LENGTH OF RADIATION REQUIRED PER ROOM:

FIRST DIVIDE — $\dfrac{\text{THE BTU/HR HEAT LOSS PER ROOM}}{\text{BY } 3.4 \text{ BTU/HR PER WATT}} = $ REQUIRED RADIATION IN WATTS

THEN DIVIDE — $\dfrac{\text{THE REQUIRED RADIATION IN WATTS}}{\text{THE MFG'S RATING OF THE RADIATION ELEMENT IN WATTS PER LINEAR FOOT}}$

EXAMPLE: $\dfrac{\text{BTU/HR HEAT LOSS OF ROOM}}{\text{CONVERSION FACTOR}} = \dfrac{10,000 \text{ BTU/HR}}{3.4 \text{ BTU/HR/WATT}} = \underline{2940}$ WATTS REQUIRED

$\dfrac{\text{REQUIRED WATTAGE}}{\text{MFG'S RATING OF ELEMENT}} = \dfrac{2940 \text{ WATTS}}{50 \text{ WATTS/FT.}} = \underline{11.75}$ FEET MINIMUM

RADIATION AND CFM FORMULAE

UNIT AND ROOM		MIN. LENGTH OF RADIATION OR CFM OF HOT AIR REQ'D/RM	LENGTH OF ELEMENTS OR CFM CAP. OF DUCT SELECTED TO MEET MIN.	MFR'S RATING OF SELECTED ELEMENTS OR DUCT WORK	TOTAL BTU/HR, CFM OR WATTAGE TO BE DELIVERED TO ROOM
UNIT A	LIVING AREA		1. 2.	1. 2.	
	KITCHEN/DINING		1. 2.	1. 2.	
	BATHROOM		1. 2.	1. 2.	
	SMALL BEDROOM		1. 2.	1. 2.	
	LARGE BEDROOM		1. 2.	1. 2.	
	OTHER		1. 2.	1. 2.	
SUB-TOTAL UNIT A					
	DOWNSTAIRS ROOM #1 #1		1. 2.	1. 2.	
	DOWNSTAIRS ROOM #2		1. 2.	1. 2.	
	DOWNSTAIRS ROOM #3		1. 2.	1. 2.	
	UPSTAIRS ROOM #4		1. 2.	1. 2.	
	UPSTAIRS ROOM #5		1. 2.	1. 2.	
	OTHER		1. 2.	1. 2.	
SUB-TOTAL UNIT B					
REQUIRED CAPACITY OF BOILER, FURNACE OR ADDITIONAL ELECTRIC SERVICE					

ROOM BY ROOM RADIATION AND CFM COUNT TO DETERMINE TOTAL CAPACITY OF SYSTEM

account the following considerations: since trapped air tends to accumulate at high points, try to arrange piping to avoid frequent ups and downs; remember to insulate piping that runs in spaces you do not wish to heat in areas where it may freeze; arrange the boiler flue to conform to local codes governing this type of installation; install the boiler in strict accordance with the manufacturer's recommendations and make sure that necessary safety devices and relief valves are installed; do not try to adjust the burner assembly of your boiler for proper combustion unless you are truly expert. It is very difficult to do, but most suppliers of fuel will adjust the burner for you as part of their normal service. Finally, if oil is your fuel, be certain you have provided adequate tank capacity.

ALL-ELECTRIC HEAT

There are a few parts of this country where electricity is actually the cheapest form of energy. Should you be building your Little House in one of these, you should consider all-electric heat. It's much lower in first cost, and permits individual control in each room, but its principal virtue is that it permits you to shut down your house during unoccupied winter periods without having to drain the piping for the heating system. If yours is to be a weekend or vacation house, this advantage might well prompt you to install electric heat even though oil or gas might be cheaper. You will still have to drain down or otherwise protect the plumbing piping if you wish to leave the house unheated during winter freeze conditions. But this needn't be a big production.

FORCED-AIR HEAT

An air system is worth considering if you have a special requirement for humidity control in winter, or if the cost of electricity is exorbitant in your area but you plan on winter weekend use and thus want to shut down the house during the week without draining the heating pipes. Another advantage of a forced-air system is that it allows for the addition of central air conditioning. An integrated heating and air-conditioning system is not only quiet, efficient, and aesthetically unobtrusive, it can often be less expensive to install and operate than the separate systems for heating and cooling.

Several supply outlets offer central conversion kits consisting of an outdoor compressor, a coil suitable for mounting in an all-air system discharge plenum, pre-charged interconnecting piping, and a control changer kit. If you understand this terminology, you are probably able to do the installation yourself. Thus you could end up buying the components required to provide central air conditioning for well under $1,000.00.

PLUMBING

The art of plumbing is quite technical but at the same time straightforward. Most localities have enacted a plumbing code, and the specifics of your installation will have to conform with its requirements as to materials, sizes, and piping techniques.

To start, you will need an adequate supply of water. This can come either from a public water main if one is close at hand, a well, or some other source such as

ASSUME: <u>BASIC LITTLE HOUSE IN FINISH GROUP 1</u> TO BE EQUIPPED WITH HYDRONIC SYSTEM IN VICINITY OF ST. LOUIS, MISSOURI :

FROM A.S.H.R.A.E. GUIDE : WINTER DESIGN TEMPERATURE $\quad$ +6° $\quad$ 97.5% OF TIME
ST. LOUIS, MISSOURI $\quad$ +2° $\quad$ 99.0% OF TIME
B.O.C.A. CODE USED IN MO. SAYS 97.5% FIGURE CAN BE USED AS WINTER DESIGN TEMP., ∴ FOR EASE OF ARITHMETIC ASSUME WINTER DESIGN TEMP. = +5° F.

ASSUME : INDOOR DESIGN TEMPERATURE = 70°F ∴ T_D = 65°
FROM 2ND CHART, WINTER CLIMATE FACTOR = $\dfrac{1.03\,(FOR\,+10°)+1.20\,(FOR\,0°)}{2}$ = 1.11

FROM INSULATION MAP : ROOF SECTION MUST HAVE TOTAL THERMAL RESISTANCE $\quad R_T \geq 30$
EXTERIOR WALL SECTION $\quad$ " $\quad$ " $\quad$ " $\quad R_T \geq 19$
GROUND FLOOR SECTION $\quad$ " $\quad$ " $\quad$ " $\quad R_T \geq 19$

FROM U AND R VALUE CHARTS : WITH 8" INSULATION R_T FOR THE ROOF = 32.97 $\quad$ U = 0.03
WITH 6" INSULATION R_T FOR EXT. WALLS = 25.57 $\quad$ U = 0.04
WITH 6" INSULATION R_T FOR GROUND FL. = 25.57 $\quad$ U = 0.04

LET US TAKE THE LARGE UPSTAIRS BEDROOM THROUGH ALL THE REQUISITE STEPS THAT LEAD TO THE DETERMINATION OF THE AMOUNT OF RADIATION PER ROOM & ULTIMATELY THE TOTAL CAPACITY OF THE BOILER. (ALL DIMENSIONS WILL BE ROUNDED OFF TO THE NEAREST HALF.)

<u>TOTAL HEAT LOSS THROUGH EXTERIOR SURFACES OF ROOM :</u>

<u>WINDOW AND DOOR OPENINGS :</u> NORTH WALL - LARGE WINDOW $\quad$ 6'-0" × 4'-0" = 24.0 SQ.FT. ⎫
LOUVERED VENT $\quad$ 3'-0" × 1'-6" = 4.5 SQ.FT. ⎬ 28.5 SQ.FT.
EAST WALL - SMALL WINDOW $\quad$ 3'-0" × 4'-0" = 12.0 SQ.FT.
SOUTH WALL - DOOR TO UNHEATED
STORAGE AREA $\quad$ 3'-0" × 4'-6" = 13.5 SQ.FT.
WEST WALL - NO HEAT LOSS AS WALL IS ADJACENT TO HEATED SPACE

ALSO FROM 2ND CHART : FOR WEATHERSTRIPPED WINDOWS IN FIN. GROUP 1 : HEAT LOSS = 72 BTU/HR/SQ.FT.
ASSUME : LOUVERED VENT = NON-WEATHERSTRIPPED WOOD DOUBLE-HUNG WINDOW WITH INSULATED GLASS : HEAT LOSS = 79 BTU/HR/SQ.FT.

<u>TYPICAL CALCULATIONS - HYDRONIC SYSTEM</u>

132

CLOSET DOOR TO UNHEATED STORAGE AREA = AN EXTERIOR DOOR WHICH IN TURN = A
SINGLE PANE WOOD WINDOW, WEATHERSTRIPPED : HEAT LOSS = 103 BTU'S/HR/SQ.FT.

TOTAL HEAT LOSS THROUGH WINDOWS AND OTHER OPENINGS :

24.0 SQ.FT	× 72 BTU/HR/SQ.FT. =	1728
12.0 "	× 72 "	864
4.5 "	× 79 "	355
13.5 "	× 103 "	1390
		4337 BTU/HR.

EXTERIOR WALLS : U = .04   NORTH WALL - 11'-0" WIDE × 12'-6" HIGH =   137.5 SQ.FT.
LESS AREA OF OPENING   28.5 "
109.0 NET AREA

EAST WALL - 14'-0" WIDE × $\dfrac{12'-6"+5'-0"}{2}$ =   122.5 SQ.FT.

LESS AREA OF OPENING   12.0 "
110.5 NET AREA

SOUTH WALL - 11'-0" WIDE × 5'-0" HIGH =   55 SQ.FT.
LESS AREA OF OPENING   13.5 "
41.5 NET AREA

WEST WALL -   NO HEAT LOSS AS WALL IS ADJACENT TO HEATED SPACE

TOTAL HEAT LOSS THROUGH EXTERIOR WALLS :   AREA × U FACTOR (.04) × T_D (65°)

109.0 SQ.FT. × .04 × 65° =   283.4
110.5 " × .04 × 65° =   287.3
41.5 " × .04 × 65° =   107.9
678.6 ≈ 679 BTU/HR.

ROOF : U = .03   11'-0" WIDE × 15'-0" (ACTUAL LENGTH SLOPING EDGE) = 165.0 SQ.FT.
165 SQ.FT. × .03 × 65 = 322 BTU/HR

FLOOR :   NO HEAT LOSS AS BEDROOM FLOOR IS ABOVE HEATED SPACE (KITCHEN)

TYPICAL CALCULATIONS CONTINUED - HYDRONIC SYSTEM

a spring, or a dammed stream.

If you're lucky enough to have a natural source, you must have the water checked early on by your local health department to insure that its bacterial and chemical quality meet the minimum standards of the American Water Works Association. Your source may require some kind of treatment system to bring the water up to these standards.

You may have the option of sharing a water source, be it a spring, stream, or well, with your neighbors. If you do, be certain to have a lawyer draw up a document spelling out in full detail the terms and costs of your sharing and have it signed by all parties concerned.

If you are going to dig a well, you are also going to have to buy a pump to deliver the well water to your house. For a shallow well a surface pump is adequate. But for a well deeper than 65 to 75 feet you will need a submersible pump.

The next step is to check on the water pressure. For most plumbing fixtures, the minimum recommended pressure is 20 psi (pounds per square inch, or 138 kilopascals for the metric minded). In addition, as a building increases in height, the pressure goes down. Friction also has the effect of reducing pressure. This means that if you build the Little House garage or studio, both of which have the bathroom on the second floor, or if you install an upstairs bath in the basic Little House, you will probably need 30 psi of water pressure to make the fixtures in this bathroom function properly. If the pressure is less than 30 psi, you will either have inadequate flows or malfunctioning equipment. These low pressures must be corrected by a booster pump.

If you are tapping into a public water main which can deliver no more than 25 psi, or if you are relying on well water or some other natural source, in addition to requiring some kind of a pump to bring the water from the source to your house, you will also require a small (approximately 30-gallon capacity) hydropneumatic tank. This tank has an air cushion on top which maintains the water pressure in your system. When the water level in the tank drops, the pressure also drops and activates the pump to build it up again. This tank can be either adjacent to the water source or installed within the house itself. It is not shown on our drawings because whether or not it is required and how it should be located depend on your specific source of supply.

With adequate flow and pressure assured, we continue. Cold water is then distributed to each fixture. Hot water from the boiler is then fed to the required fixtures. Hot- and cold-water pipes generally run adjacent to each other and are provided with control valves positioned to facilitate maintenance.

The warnings given regarding the routing of piping for heating apply here as well: avoid high points in hot-water piping as these trap air and restrict flow; insulate piping which runs in cold spaces when freezing temperatures may occur; and also insulate cold-water piping within ceilings and walls where "sweating"—the formation of condensate on the exterior of the pipe—may occur and damage interior finishes. Finally, if you plan to vacate your Little House for part of the year, be certain to arrange the piping so it is easy to drain.

TOTAL HEAT LOSS FOR ROOM:

WINDOWS AND OPENINGS	4337	BTU/HR
EXTERIOR WALLS	+ 679	
ROOF	+ 322	
	= 5338	
MULTIPLIED BY WINTER CLIMATE FACTOR	× 1.10	
TOTAL	= 5872	BTU/HR

ENTER THESE FIGURES OR YOUR EQUIVALENT ON THE ROOM-BY-ROOM HEAT LOSS CHART & REPEAT THE PROCESS FOR EACH ROOM IN YOUR LITTLE HOUSE OR LITTLE HOUSE COMBINATION.

NOW SELECT A MANUFACTURER OF FINNED-TUBE RADIATION ELEMENTS, AND - MORE OR LESS ARBITRARILY - SELECT A SPECIFIC ELEMENT. PLUG ITS RATING PER LINEAR FOOT INTO RADIATION FORMULA NO. 1 FOR HYDRONIC SYSTEMS

ASSUME RATING OF 500 BTU/LIN. FT: $\dfrac{5872 \text{ BTU/HR TOTAL HEAT LOSS}}{500 \text{ BTU/HR/LINEAR FOOT}} = 11.7 \text{ FT. MIN.} \approx 12 \text{ FT.}$

AS THE LONGEST WALL IN THIS ROOM IS ONLY 11'-0", WE CAN EITHER GO TO 2 RADIATION ELEMENTS - A LARGE ONE ON THE NORTH WALL AND A SMALL ONE ON THE EAST WALL - WHICH TAKES UP MORE SPACE, INVOLVES ADDITIONAL PIPING AND RADIATOR ENCLOSURES AND THUS EXPENSE - OR WE CAN SELECT AN ELEMENT WITH A HIGHER RATING.

ASSUME RATING OF 600 BTU/LIN. FT: $\dfrac{5872 \text{ BTU/HR TOTAL HEAT LOSS}}{600 \text{ BTU/HR/LINEAR FOOT}} = 9.8 \text{ FT. MIN.} \approx 10 \text{ FT.}$

THIS WILL FIT ALONG THE NORTH WALL. THEREFORE, IN THE LAST COLUMN OF THE ROOM-BY-ROOM RADIATION CHART, ENTER THE PRODUCT OF THE LENGTH OF THE UNIT SELECTED TIMES ITS RATING, WHICH IN THIS CASE IS 6000 BTU/HR. REPEAT FOR EACH ROOM. THE SUM OF THE FIGURES IN THE LAST COLUMN WILL GIVE YOU THE REQUIRED CAPACITY OF YOUR BOILER.

TYPICAL CALCULATIONS CONTINUED - HYDRONIC SYSTEM

SUGGESTED PIPE SIZING FOR HYDRONIC SYSTEM

PIPE SIZE	FLOW IN G.P.M GALLONS PER MINUTE	APPROXIMATE HEATING CAPACITY (@ 20° ΔT)*
1½" & ½	2 GPM	20,000 BTU
¾"	4 GPM	40,000 BTU
1"	9 GPM	90,000 BTU
1¼"	15 GPM	150,000 BTU

* ΔT = TEMPERATURE DIFFERENTIAL BETWEEN SUPPLY AND RETURN HOT WATER

OPTIONS FOR DOMESTIC HOT WATER

| ONE BATHROOM

LITTLE HOUSE OR LITTLE HOUSE COMBINATION

INCLUDING DISHWASHER & CLOTHES WASHER | 1. 30-GALLON HOT-WATER HEATER, STORAGE TANK AND CIRCULATING PUMP

IN ADDITION TO OIL OR GAS-FIRED BOILER, FURNACE OR ELECTRIC HEAT.

2. HYDRONIC SYSTEM ONLY: 4-GALLON-PER-MINUTE HOT-WATER TANKLESS HEATING COIL INTEGRAL WITH BOILER.

NOTE: BOILER CAPACITY MUST BE INCREASED SLIGHTLY FOR ADDITION OF DOMESTIC HOT-WATER HEATING LOAD | TWO BATHROOM

LITTLE HOUSE OR LITTLE HOUSE COMBINATION

INCLUDING DISHWASHER & CLOTHESWASHER | 1. 50-GALLON HOT-WATER HEATER, STORAGE TANK AND AND CIRCULATING PUMP

IN ADDITION TO OIL OR GAS-FIRED BOILER, FURNACE OR ELECTRIC HEAT.

2. HYDRONIC SYSTEM ONLY: 4-GALLON-PER-MINUTE HOT-WATER TANKLESS HEATING COIL WITH DOMESTIC HOT-WATER CIRCULATING PUMP PIPED TO SEPARATE 50-GALLON VERTICAL STORAGE TANK. |

SUGGESTED PIPE SIZING - HYDRONIC SYSTEM AND DOMESTIC HOT-WATER OPTIONS

What is considered acceptable material for piping varies from area to area. Copper pipe is the most costly but gives the best performance and has the longest life. Galvanized steel costs less and is particularly subject to corrosion where the quality of water is poor—the quality being a function of the chemical constituents of the water and not environmental pollution. Furthermore, threaded joints are more difficult to fabricate in steel piping. Plastic pipe, better known as PVC (polyvinyl chloride), is very low in cost, extremely easy to install but in many areas it is not permitted. Furthermore, it is never suitable for hot water. We recommend that first you find out what is permitted by local plumbing codes, then consult with the local water authorities regarding the relationship between water quality and pipe life before making your decision.

The second component of the plumbing system is drainage, i.e., the removal of waste. This is accomplished by a series of waste and soil pipes connected to each of the fixtures. It is important to note that each fixture must be separated from the drainage system proper by a "trap." In bathtubs, the trap is concealed as it is installed under the drain. It is built into the body of a water closet. But the trap is clearly visible under sinks and lavatories. The purpose of the trap is to prevent objectionable sewer gases from seeping into occupied spaces. It accomplishes its purpose by providing a water seal in the loop of the trap. Thus we have not only waste liquid but also trapped gas in the drainage system. This means that together with the drainage piping we need a secondary system of vent piping which permits air to circulate in the network of pipes, protects the water seal in the traps, and reduces noise in the drainage system.

The final question is what to do with the waste once it is collected in the drainage system. If you can't tie into a local city sewer, you must build a septic tank or cesspool. A septic tank is a sealed, underground dual-chamber holding tank that separates waste material into solids and liquids. The liquids leach or drain out into the earth through perforated tile drains, and the solids sink to the bottom and must be removed periodically by a tank-pumping truck. In areas where the soil is coarse and sandy you can build a cesspool instead. This is also an underground tank but instead of being sealed, it has perforated sides and an open bottom through which wastes leach out into the soil. Thus the dual processes of sewage treatment and disposal are accomplished in a single step and no pumping truck is required. Do not install a cesspool based on your own appraisal of the coarseness of your soil. Be certain to have its percolation tested beforehand.

Again, local authorities will let you know the limitations on both cesspool and septic tank construction in your area, particularly with regard to its distance from your water supply (usually 100 feet minimum), your house, and your lot lines.

ELECTRICAL

Of all the building services, the electrical system is perhaps the most difficult. Unless you understand elec-

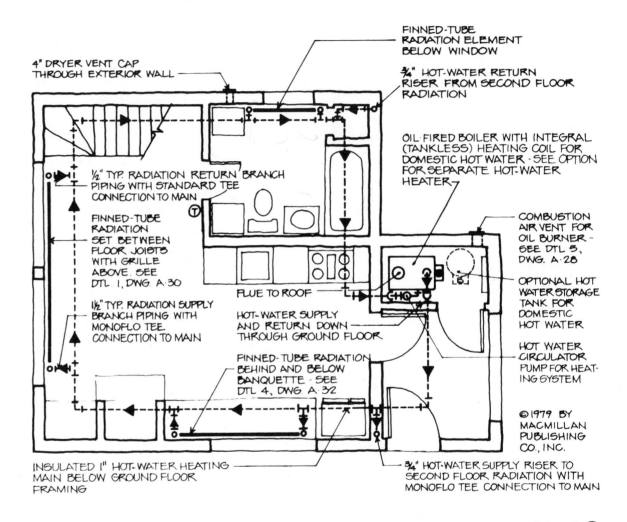

4" DRYER VENT CAP THROUGH EXTERIOR WALL

FINNED-TUBE RADIATION ELEMENT BELOW WINDOW

¾" HOT-WATER RETURN RISER FROM SECOND FLOOR RADIATION

½" TYP. RADIATION RETURN BRANCH PIPING WITH STANDARD TEE CONNECTION TO MAIN

OIL-FIRED BOILER WITH INTEGRAL (TANKLESS) HEATING COIL FOR DOMESTIC HOT WATER - SEE OPTION FOR SEPARATE HOT-WATER HEATER

FINNED-TUBE RADIATION SET BETWEEN FLOOR JOISTS WITH GRILLE ABOVE. SEE DTL. 1, DWG. A-30

COMBUSTION AIR VENT FOR OIL BURNER - SEE DTL 5, DWG. A-28

OPTIONAL HOT WATER STORAGE TANK FOR DOMESTIC HOT WATER

½" TYP. RADIATION SUPPLY BRANCH PIPING WITH MONOFLO TEE CONNECTION TO MAIN

FLUE TO ROOF

HOT-WATER SUPPLY AND RETURN DOWN THROUGH GROUND FLOOR

HOT WATER CIRCULATOR PUMP FOR HEATING SYSTEM

FINNED-TUBE RADIATION BEHIND AND BELOW BANQUETTE - SEE DTL 4, DWG. A-32

© 1979 BY MACMILLAN PUBLISHING CO., INC.

INSULATED 1" HOT-WATER HEATING MAIN BELOW GROUND FLOOR FRAMING

¾" HOT-WATER SUPPLY RISER TO SECOND FLOOR RADIATION WITH MONOFLO TEE CONNECTION TO MAIN

M-1   HYDRONIC HEATING SYSTEM - GROUND FLOOR PLAN

³⁄₁₆" = 1'-0"

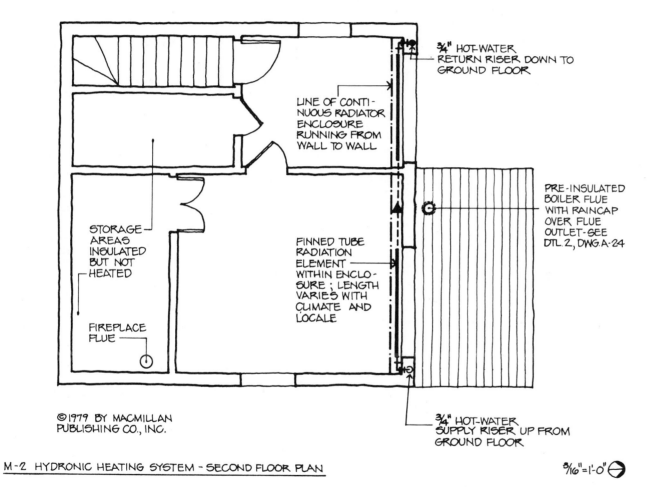

¾" HOT-WATER
RETURN RISER DOWN TO
GROUND FLOOR

LINE OF CONTI-
NUOUS RADIATOR
ENCLOSURE
RUNNING FROM
WALL TO WALL

PRE-INSULATED
BOILER FLUE
WITH RAINCAP
OVER FLUE
OUTLET - SEE
DTL. 2, DWG. A-24

STORAGE
AREAS
INSULATED
BUT NOT
HEATED

FINNED TUBE
RADIATION
ELEMENT
WITHIN ENCLO-
SURE ; LENGTH
VARIES WITH
CLIMATE AND
LOCALE

FIREPLACE
FLUE

M-2 HYDRONIC HEATING SYSTEM - SECOND FLOOR PLAN

¾" HOT-WATER
SUPPLY RISER UP FROM
GROUND FLOOR

³⁄₁₆"=1'-0"

tricity and have had experience with the components of an electrical system, and unless you have fully read and understood the detailed and stringent requirements of the National Electrical Code and any supplementary local codes, *do not* attempt to install your own wiring. In addition to running the risk of ultimately killing yourself and your neighbors, you will also have your efforts scrutinized by the local electrical inspector as part of the process of securing an Underwriters Certificate attesting to the acceptability of the installation. If you are not experienced, chances are you will end up redoing much of your work. Rather than subjecting yourself to this painful process, we suggest that you contact a qualified, locally licensed electrician and let him do the house wiring.

Regardless of how you proceed, you should understand the principles of an electrical installation. Power is generally supplied by a local utility company which will bring necessary wiring above ground from the road to your house. In more remote areas they may insist on cutting a 30' swath through any woods between your house and the road so trees don't blow against their wires. This swath can destroy the appearance of your land unless you plan an unobtrusive route for it. As shown in drawings A-7 and A-10 in chapter 6, the overhead service feeder, as it is called, comes into the house at the service entry weatherhead mounted at the peak of the north facade, whence it runs down the wall to the meter pan, essentially the junction box of the service feeder and a surface-mounted electrical meter used for billing. A far more attractive route is to run the service feeder from the road to the meter below ground even if it is not required by local code. However, no utility company will pick up the tab for the trenching, and it is costly in the extreme.

Beyond the meter, the electrical work is your responsibility and not that of the utility company. The heart of the system is the main panel, which we have located on the north wall of the shed. The panel receives the service, or power, from the meter and distributes it in a series of circuits throughout the house.

In this part of the world, most electrical devices use power at 110 volts, with some heavy-duty equipment (stoves, air conditioners, electrical clothes dryers) requiring 220 volts. Thus, the normal utility service will be rated at 220/110 volts. That is, you will be able to have both voltages available for your needs. The standard house service is also rated at 100 amps (amps or amperes, referring to the amount of current flowing through the wires), and this should be more than adequate for all requirements of the basic Little House. An all-electric heating installation or special equipment may dictate larger service, but these are special conditions.

Most circuits feeding receptacles, lighting, and equipment with small power requirements will be fed by 15-amp and 20-amp circuits. Large power consumers such as ovens, stoves, dryers, etc., will have larger wiring and circuit breakers, and, as mentioned before, may require 220-volt power. Do not be concerned if the sum of the amperage rating for all circuits in the house exceeds the 100-amp supply. Since not all devices are on at the same time, and since it is rare that each circuit

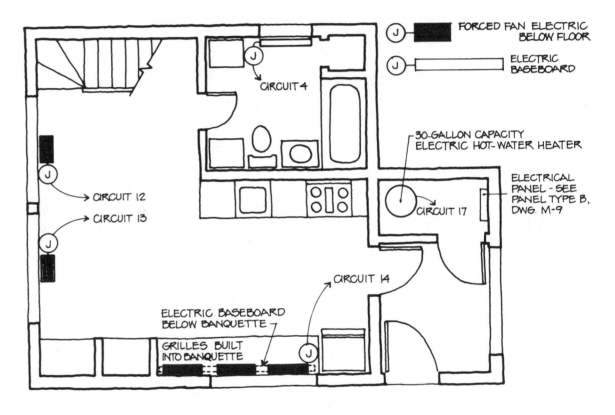

FORCED FAN ELECTRIC BELOW FLOOR

ELECTRIC BASEBOARD

CIRCUIT 4

30-GALLON CAPACITY ELECTRIC HOT-WATER HEATER

ELECTRICAL PANEL - SEE PANEL TYPE B, DWG. M-9

CIRCUIT 12

CIRCUIT 13

CIRCUIT 17

CIRCUIT 14

ELECTRIC BASEBOARD BELOW BANQUETTE

GRILLES BUILT INTO BANQUETTE

ALL OTHER ELECTRICAL WORK AS PER DWG. M-10

M-2   ELECTRIC HEAT- GROUND FLOOR PLAN

3/16"=1'-0"

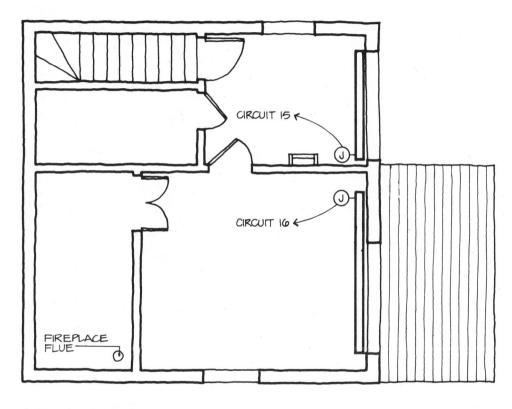

CIRCUIT 15

CIRCUIT 16

FIREPLACE
FLUE

ALL OTHER ELECTRICAL
WORK AS PER DWG. M-11

M-3 ELECTRIC HEAT - SECOND FLOOR PLAN

3/16" = 1'-0"

uses its full rated capacity, diversity will act to keep totals within the limits of the service capacity.

The main panel also contains circuit breakers which serve as switch and overload protection. These are intended to open circuits when excessive current flows occur, as during short circuits. They are rated to protect the circuit wiring from overheating and must be matched to the wire size. For example, No. 14 AWG wire is rated at 15 amps and must be protected by a 15-amp circuit breaker. No. 12 AWG wire can safely carry 20 amps.

The latest edition of the National Electric Code also requires certain circuits (such as those feeding exterior outlets) to be protected by ground fault interrupters. These devices can sense very small flows of current which go other than through the actual electrical circuit. Thus, in a situation where someone standing in water touches a live wire, the GFI senses the situation and breaks the circuit so quickly that a person does not even sense electrical flow or shock.

Let us now look at the actual electrical layout shown on the electrical plans. The National Electrical Code sets certain standards for the number of outlet receptacles, their positions and circuiting, as well as details on switching and lighting. These must be complied with in general, but there is wide latitude as to the exact location of these devices. As only you know how you will use your Little House, you shouldn't hesitate to adjust this layout to meet your requirements; there's nothing so annoying as long extension cords to forgotten electrical devices. But before you get creative with what may appear to be an overly elaborate scheme for built-in lighting, hear out its raison d'être.

The task of lighting is not only to provide the requisite number of foot candles to illuminate given activities, but also to light the space itself. The way light falls on the surface of a room and the location and type of source are absolutely critical to how big or small, alien or intimate, cluttered or sparse it feels. When you are building something as small as the Little House, you have to be very respectful of the space you have, whatever your budget. You cannot afford a lot of clutter, so we are suggesting that most of the lighting be built in. This does not mean that the light is indirect or that there's less of it.

Starting on the outside, you can light your paths and walkways with low-voltage or line-voltage lighting with GFI (ground fault interrupter) protection. We show only three surface-mounted fixtures on the east and south facades. These can be bracketed cylindrical fixtures, known as cans, if you want a few pools of light in a small area, or floodlights if you want a greater spread.

In the shed we show a wall-mounted fixture by the door. The alternative is to hang a fixture from the ceiling, but that's a bit fancy for so utilitarian a space. Furthermore, there's not enough headroom.

The kitchen with its two rows of overhead lights plus the undercabinet lighting may seem elaborately lit but in fact it is not. We returned to our design grid and centered two fixtures 4'6" apart in each of the three kitchen bays. These provide even light in the entire space and focus light on the table which, whatever its size, will invariably be centered on the window. Further-

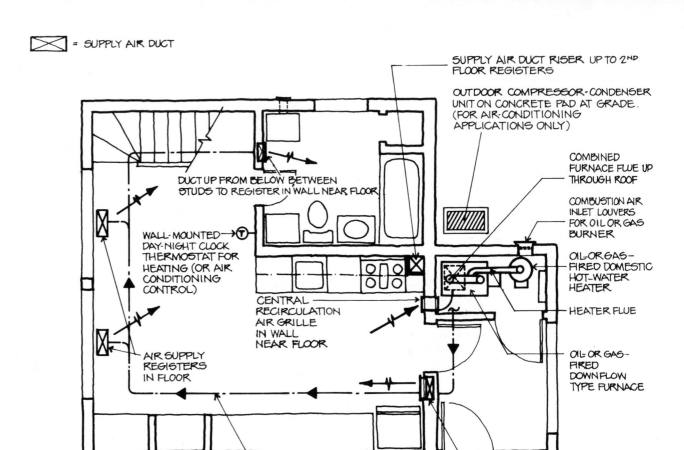

= SUPPLY AIR DUCT

SUPPLY AIR DUCT RISER UP TO 2ND FLOOR REGISTERS

OUTDOOR COMPRESSOR-CONDENSER UNIT ON CONCRETE PAD AT GRADE. (FOR AIR-CONDITIONING APPLICATIONS ONLY)

COMBINED FURNACE FLUE UP THROUGH ROOF

COMBUSTION AIR INLET LOUVERS FOR OIL OR GAS BURNER

OIL-OR-GAS-FIRED DOMESTIC HOT-WATER HEATER

HEATER FLUE

OIL-OR-GAS-FIRED DOWNFLOW TYPE FURNACE

DUCT UP FROM BELOW BETWEEN STUDS TO REGISTER IN WALL NEAR FLOOR

WALL-MOUNTED DAY-NIGHT CLOCK THERMOSTAT FOR HEATING (OR AIR CONDITIONING CONTROL)

CENTRAL RECIRCULATION AIR GRILLE IN WALL NEAR FLOOR

AIR SUPPLY REGISTERS IN FLOOR

©1979 BY MACMILLAN PUBLISHING CO., INC.

SUPPLY AIR TRUNK DUCT BELOW GROUND FLOOR FRAMING WITH 1" EXTERNAL INSULATION

DUCT UP FROM BELOW BETWEEN STUDS TO REGISTER IN WALL NEAR FLOOR

M-4 FORCED AIR HEATING SYSTEM WITH OPTIONAL COOLING - GROUND FLOOR PLAN

3/16 = 1'-0"

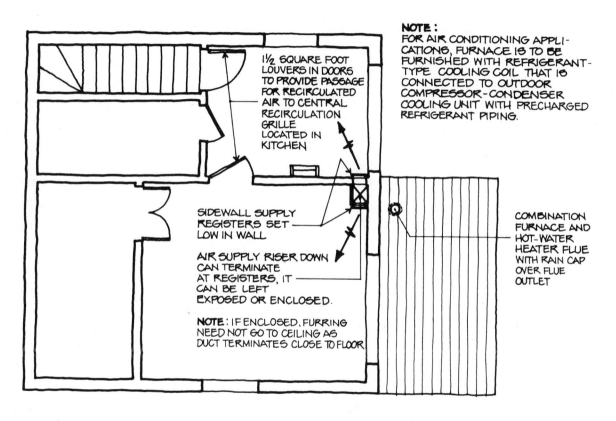

NOTE :
FOR AIR CONDITIONING APPLI-
CATIONS, FURNACE IS TO BE
FURNISHED WITH REFRIGERANT-
TYPE COOLING COIL THAT IS
CONNECTED TO OUTDOOR
COMPRESSOR-CONDENSER
COOLING UNIT WITH PRECHARGED
REFRIGERANT PIPING.

1½ SQUARE FOOT
LOUVERS IN DOORS
TO PROVIDE PASSAGE
FOR RECIRCULATED
AIR TO CENTRAL
RECIRCULATION
GRILLE
LOCATED IN
KITCHEN

SIDEWALL SUPPLY
REGISTERS SET
LOW IN WALL

AIR SUPPLY RISER DOWN
CAN TERMINATE
AT REGISTERS, IT
CAN BE LEFT
EXPOSED OR ENCLOSED.

NOTE: IF ENCLOSED, FURRING
NEED NOT GO TO CEILING AS
DUCT TERMINATES CLOSE TO FLOOR

COMBINATION
FURNACE AND
HOT-WATER
HEATER FLUE
WITH RAIN CAP
OVER FLUE
OUTLET

© 1979 BY MACMILLAN
PUBLISHING CO., INC.

M-5   FORCED AIR HEATING SYSTEM WITH OPTIONAL COOLING - SECOND FLOOR PLAN   3/16"=1'-0"

more, the six fixtures make an attractive pattern on the ceiling which seems to articulate gently the different areas designated for cooking and eating and for general living.

The fixtures themselves need not be elaborate. They can be surface-mounted cans or better still (and cheaper) porcelain sockets with clear round bulbs (G-40 or equivalent). For a few extra dollars you can put these on a dimmer switch. Don't be tempted to save money by settling for the traditional single ceiling fixture. It's the curse of any kitchen trying to live side by side with a living area. The quality of light given off is usually harsh, and the location of the fixture, while central enough, generally relates to nothing else in the room.

A word about the undercabinet lighting above the kitchen counter: for years we have been specifying continuous incandescent light strips in this particular application, in spite of the cost of the bulbs, because the quality of light is the best for cooking. If you object to the cost of these fixtures or the bulbs, we would rather see you eliminate the undercabinet lighting altogether than substitute less expensive fluorescent fixtures and bulbs, as fluorescent light tends to give food an unappetizing greenish tinge.

In the living room we show only two wall-mounted fixtures flanking the fireplace. These could either read as part of the building or they could be wall fixtures in the same genre as whatever floor or table lamps you use for reading light.

We are as offended by the central ceiling fixture in the bathroom as we are by its presence in the kitchen;

however, the traditional fixture over the sink doesn't provide enough light for the entire room. Thus we suggest using three such fixtures and centering the other two over the clothes washer and dryer respectively, as shown in the elevations of the bathroom, drawing A-36, chapter 6. The same porcelain sockets with G-40 bulbs suggested for the ceiling of the kitchen can be used on the walls of the bathroom as well.

Having made the decision not to use a ceiling fixture on the sloping ceiling of the shed, we carry the decision through to the stairwell and the smaller bedroom, both of which also have sloping ceilings and are lit by the same kind of wall-mounted fixture.

Ideally, the wall-mounted fixture at the level of the upper bunk should be the same kind as the lower fixture, providing general lighting for the room and switching at the door. However, the upper fixture should not be wired to this switch but should have its own switch for the use of whoever is occupying the upper bunk. A freestanding table lamp is intended to provide bedside light for the lower bunk.

In the master bedroom we have shown two wall-mounted fixtures with integral switches on the south wall. These are for night-lights which are to be mounted over the bed. If you think you will want your bed(s) elsewhere, such as we show in the cut-away isometric at the beginning of the book, be sure to move these junction boxes accordingly. General lighting in this room is provided by one or two floor and/or table lamps. So one of these lamps can be switched on from the door, one of the room's duplex outlets should be

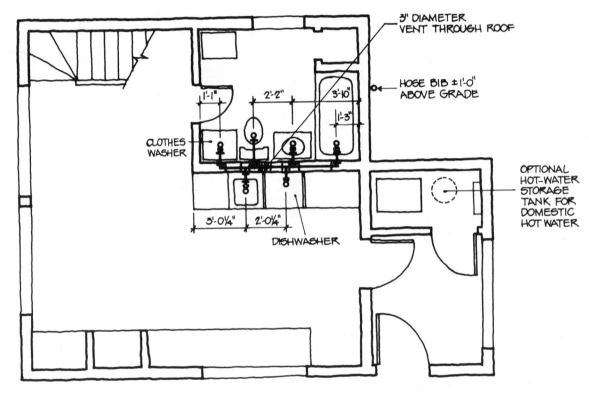

M-6 PLUMBING - GROUND FLOOR PLAN

3/16" = 1'-0"

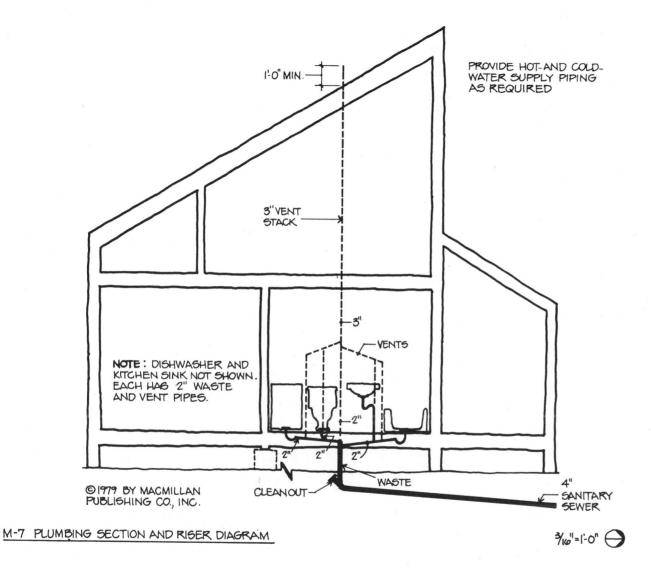

1'-0" MIN.

PROVIDE HOT-AND COLD-
WATER SUPPLY PIPING
AS REQUIRED

3" VENT
STACK

3"

VENTS

NOTE: DISHWASHER AND
KITCHEN SINK NOT SHOWN.
EACH HAS 2" WASTE
AND VENT PIPES.

2"

2" 2" 2"

© 1979 BY MACMILLAN
PUBLISHING CO., INC.

CLEANOUT

WASTE

4"
SANITARY
SEWER

M-7 PLUMBING SECTION AND RISER DIAGRAM

3/16" = 1'-0"

wired to a switch by the door.

There is no question that the number of built-in fixtures we suggest will add dollars to the electrical work not because the fixtures are expensive—they're not—but because whether you have built-in fixtures or not the code requires you to have a certain number of duplex outlets per running foot of wall; thus the wiring for the fixtures becomes an extra. However, we urge you to consider something like this if you want to get the most out of the space your Little House encloses.

Other things you should consider but which we don't show: a door bell, which may be a real convenience depending on where you are and how you plan to use the house; fire and/or smoke detection devices, which in many areas are required by code; other alarms relating to burglary, entry, high water, and the like; locations for hi-fi stereo equipment and speakers; and where you most want to watch television, if at all. Even if you can't afford or don't want to install this equipment now, thinking about it will afford you the pleasure of concealed wiring when you do.

If you contact the telephone company during the early stages of construction, they will usually install all telephone wiring within the partitions to outlet points which you specify. These need not conform to the locations we indicate. Getting the telephone company on the job this early in the game is no mean feat. But in the end, anything resulting in concealed wiring in a house this size is well worth the effort.

If, for whatever reason, you require air conditioning in the bedrooms, locate through-wall units in place of louvered vents high on the north facade. Here they will operate most efficiently and do the least damage to the exterior appearance. Frame the opening to accommodate the sleeve size of whatever unit you select. If you are installing only one unit and are leaving the other opening as a louver, adjust the size of the louver to correspond to the size of the air-conditioning sleeve. Be sure to install a 20-amp air-conditioning receptacle beside each sleeve. This should be wired to a switch accessible below so the unit(s) can be turned on and off from the floor.

So far we have assumed that you have access to electric power utility lines in your part of the country. However, some of you may not be so fortunate. Thus if you want electricity, you will have to purchase an electrical generator. But you may also want your own generator because the public utility in your area has a history of long outages at inconvenient times, or, because of the intended limited use you will make of the Little House, the economics favor a self-owned generator due to a high utility extension/connection charge.

In either case, you must make the distinction between an emergency generator and a permanent power-supply unit. Emergency generators are designed to handle only the critical loads in your house, such as the heating system (including the oil burner), the circulating pumps and the controls, plus the refrigerator and a few critical lights. Because of the high power requirements of electric cooking (and their brief periods of usage), connection of electric stoves and ovens to emergency generators

ELECTRICAL SYMBOLS AND ABBREVIATIONS

Symbol	Description	Symbol	Description
O	OUTLET FOR CEILING FIXTURE, REMOTE SWITCH	⊢O	DUPLEX RECEPTACLE 1'-8" A.F.F.
⊢O	OUTLET FOR WALL-MOUNTED FIXTURE, REMOTE SWITCH	⊢O$_{UC}$	UNDERCOUNTER RECEPTACLE
⊢O$_S$	OUTLET FOR WALL-MOUNTED FIXTURE WITH INTEGRAL SWITCH	⊢O$_C$	COUNTER RECEPTACLE 3'-8" A.F.F.
⊢O$_{PC}$	OUTLET FOR PULL CHAIN FIXTURE	⊢O$_{WP}$	WEATHERPROOF DUPLEX RECEPTACLE
—·—	CONTINUOUS UNDERCABINET LIGHTING	⊢O$_A$	APPLIANCE RECEPTACLE
⊢A	SINGLE POLE LIGHT SWITCH 4'-0" A.F.F.	⊢O	DUPLEX RECEPTACLE HALF ON SWITCH CONTROL
⊢A$_3$	3-WAY LIGHT SWITCH 4'-0"	⊢O	50-AMP 220-VOLT ELECTRIC RANGE RECEPTACLE
⊢A$_P$	SWITCH WITH PILOT LIGHT 4'-0" A.F.F.	⊢O	20-AMP AIR CONDITIONING RECEPTACLE
⊢O$_T$	WALL-MOUNTED DAY-NIGHT CLOCK THERMOSTAT	J	JUNCTION BOX
◁	TELEPHONE OUTLET	CB	CIRCUIT BREAKER
		WP	WEATHERPROOF

©1979 BY MACMILLAN PUBLISHING CO, INC.

LIGHT FIXTURE SCHEDULE FOR BASIC LITTLE HOUSE AS SHOWN ON ELECTRICAL DRAWINGS M-10 & M-11

NO.	LOCAT'N	TYPE	MFR & MODEL NO.	NO	LOCAT'N	TYPE	MFR & MODEL NO.
3	OUTSIDE	WP WALL MOUNTED		1	STAIR	WALL MOUNTED	
1	SHED	WALL MOUNTED		1	SM BR	WALL MOUNTED	
6	KITCHEN	CEILING MOUNTED		1	SM BR	WALL MNTD W/ SWITCH	
1	KITCHEN	CONTIN. UNDER CAB.		2	LG BR	WALL MNTD W/ SWITCH	
2	LIV. AREA	WALL MOUNTED		2	STORAGE	PULL CHAIN P.C.	
3	BATH	WALL MOUNTED		1	BOILER	PULL CHAIN P.C.	

NOTE: ALL RECEPTACLES SHLD BE GROUNDED TYPE

M-8 ELECTRICAL SYMBOLS AND ABBREVIATIONS AND LIGHT FIXTURE SCHEDULE

A. TYPICAL PANEL

A. TYPICAL PANEL

NO.	AMPS	CB	POLE	CIRCUIT LOAD
1	20A	CB	1P	GENERAL LIGHTING
2	20A	CB	1P	GENERAL LIGHTING
3	20A	CB	1P	GENERAL LIGHTING
4	20A	CB	1P	BOILER/FURNACE AND CIRCULATING PUMP
5	20A	CB	1P	CLOTHES WASHER WITH G.F.I.
6	20A 30A	CB CB	1P OR 2P	DRYER WITH G.F.I. (GAS) DRYER WITH G.F.I. (ELECTRIC)
7	20A	CB	1P	} REFRIGERATOR, DISH-WASHER & MISC. PLUG-IN APPLIANCES
8	20A	CB	1P	
9	50A	CB	2P	ELECTRIC RANGE (NOT REQ'D IF GAS IS USED)
10	20A	CB	1P	GENERAL LIGHTING
11	20A	CB	1P	GENERAL LIGHTING
12	20A	CB	1P	SPARE
13	20A	CB	1P	SPARE
14	40A	CB	2P	DOMESTIC HOT-WATER HEATER IF NOT GAS- OR OIL-FIRED OR INTEGRAL WITH BOILER
15	40A	CB	2P	OUTDOOR COMPRESSOR (FOR FORCED AIR WITH COOLING ONLY)

M-9 TYPICAL ELECTRICAL PANELS AND CIRCUIT LOADING

B. TYP. ELECTRICAL PANEL INCL. ELECTRIC HEAT

NO	AMPS	CB	POLE	CIRCUIT LOAD
1	20A	CB	1P	} SAME AS PANEL A
2	20A	CB	1P	
3	20A	CB	1P	
4				ELECTRIC BASEBOARD, BATHROOM
5	20A	CB	1P	} SAME AS PANEL A
6	20A 30A	CB CB	1P OR 2P	
7	20A	CB	1P	
8	20A	CB	1P	} SAME AS PANEL A
9	50A	CB	2P	
10	20A	CB	1P	
11	20A	CB	1P	©1979 BY MACMILLAN PUBLISHING CO., INC.
12	25A	CB	2P	FAN-FORCED ELECTRIC BASEBOARD LIV. AREA
13	25A	CB	2P	SAME AS 12
14	25A	CB	2P	ELECTRIC BASEBOARD, KITCHEN
15	25A	CB	2P	ELECTRIC BASEBOARD, SMALL BEDROOM
16	25A	CB	2P	ELECTRIC BASEBOARD, LARGE BEDROOM
17	40A	CB	2P	DOMESTIC HOT WATER
18 TO 22	20A	CB	1P	SPARE

NOTE: CIRCUITRY FOR BUILT-IN LIGHT FIXTURES AND DUPLEX RECEPTACLES SHOULD BE SEPARATED.

is normally discouraged.

For these purposes a gasoline-fueled 2.0- or 2.5-kilowatt generator is normally adequate. It should be provided with a transfer switch capable of switching predetermined "critical" loads from the normal power supply to the emergency generator.

Permanent power-supply units tend to be much larger and, for reasons of safety, reliability, and operating costs, they tend to be diesel units. Such generators would normally need to be 8 to 12 kilowatts in size depending on the specific electrical devices which will be fed and allowances for future needs, all of which should be checked by a knowledgeable professional before you proceed with this sizeable investment.

FUTURE EXPANSION

Many of you will wish to build only one Little House, knowing that it will now and forever meet your special requirements, but if you have the slightest inclination that you may want to build a second unit, plan for it now. You will probably wish to heat your second unit, and this will require a larger boiler and probably a larger flue (or larger electrical service, if you're going all-electric, or a larger furnace if you're using forced air). You will ultimately require additional piping (wiring or ductwork for the alternates) and, given that the system is larger, you may wish to arrange the heating in two zones.

Normally, bedroom areas are on one zone, with living areas on the second. You might prefer to zone each unit separately. In either case this modification permits maintaining different temperatures in these different living areas and achieves energy savings by permitting lower temperatures in unoccupied portions of the house.

While the plumbing requirements of the kitchen are not likely to change with the addition of a second unit, you might want to consider a second bathroom, either in the first unit above the original bath, or either up- or downstairs in the second unit. While this second bath will not have a major impact on your water pipe sizing, and the 4″ sanitary sewer provided is large enough to handle the additional fixtures, you will want to make certain that the basic water supply and pressure are sufficient and that the capacity of your hot-water heater is adequate. Be certain that the second unit does not block access to the drainage piping of the first unit.

As for the electrical system, the basic 100-amp service should be more than sufficient for any two-unit Little House combination. However, a second unit will necessitate additional branch circuits; thus, in most cases, the panel size will also be larger.

The incremental cost of expanding the mechanical systems to accommodate two Little House units is quite minimal since many of the basic elements are already sized to tolerate the additional load. Those that cannot should be resized at the outset in anticipation of the second unit. The importance of this cannot be overemphasized. For example, the cost of an oversized flue probably couldn't be recognized at the outset, but removing an old flue and replacing it later is a major (and costly) undertaking. The same is true for a slightly larger

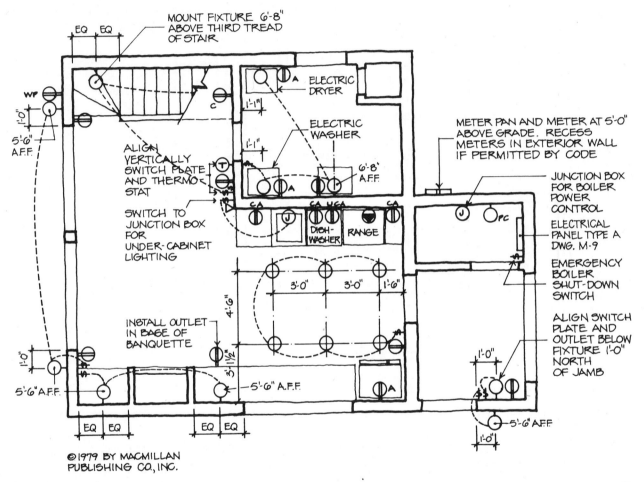

MOUNT FIXTURE 6'-8" ABOVE THIRD TREAD OF STAIR

ELECTRIC DRYER

ELECTRIC WASHER

METER PAN AND METER AT 5'-0" ABOVE GRADE. RECESS METERS IN EXTERIOR WALL IF PERMITTED BY CODE

JUNCTION BOX FOR BOILER POWER CONTROL

ELECTRICAL PANEL TYPE A DWG. M-9

EMERGENCY BOILER SHUT-DOWN SWITCH

ALIGN SWITCH PLATE AND OUTLET BELOW FIXTURE 1'-0" NORTH OF JAMB

ALIGN VERTICALLY SWITCH PLATE AND THERMOSTAT

SWITCH TO JUNCTION BOX FOR UNDER-CABINET LIGHTING

INSTALL OUTLET IN BASE OF BANQUETTE

DISH-WASHER   RANGE

5'-6" A.F.F.

5'-6" A.F.F.

5'-6" A.F.F.

© 1979 BY MACMILLAN PUBLISHING CO, INC.

M-10 ELECTRICAL PLAN - GROUND FLOOR

3/16"=1'-0"

146

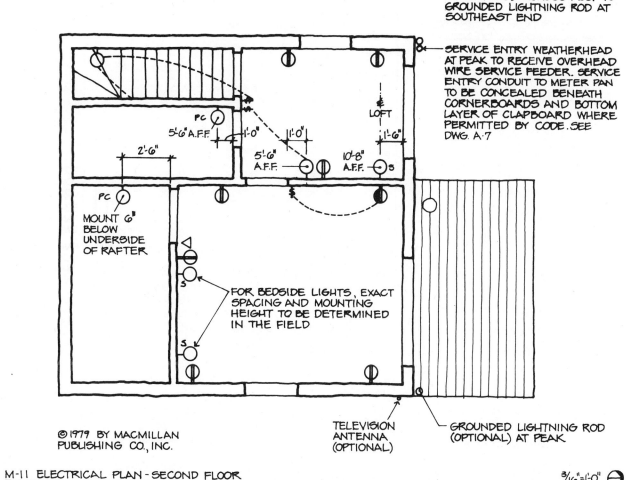

LIGHTNING ROD (OPTIONAL)
AT PEAK TIED ACROSS ROOF TO
GROUNDED LIGHTNING ROD AT
SOUTHEAST END

SERVICE ENTRY WEATHERHEAD
AT PEAK TO RECEIVE OVERHEAD
WIRE SERVICE FEEDER. SERVICE
ENTRY CONDUIT TO METER PAN
TO BE CONCEALED BENEATH
CORNERBOARDS AND BOTTOM
LAYER OF CLAPBOARD WHERE
PERMITTED BY CODE. SEE
DWG. A-7

LOFT

PC
5'-6" A.F.F.   1'-0"   1'-0"   1'-6"

2'-6"

5'-6"   10'-8"
A.F.F.   A.F.F.   S

PC

MOUNT 6"
BELOW
UNDERSIDE
OF RAFTER

FOR BEDSIDE LIGHTS, EXACT
SPACING AND MOUNTING
HEIGHT TO BE DETERMINED
IN THE FIELD

TELEVISION
ANTENNA
(OPTIONAL)

GROUNDED LIGHTNING ROD
(OPTIONAL) AT PEAK

M-11 ELECTRICAL PLAN - SECOND FLOOR

3/16" = 1'-0"

main electrical panel or larger water service. Depending
on the immediacy of any proposed expansion, you may
want to install a larger boiler or furnace or water heater
now. Further, you may wish to install some piping for
heating and domestic hot and cold water, conveniently
positioned to ease later construction and avoid ripping
up finished first-stage work. Expansion is easy if it has
been thought out in advance.

Costs, Quantities, and Contracts

The process of putting a price tag on a building is almost as complicated as the erection process itself. For your purpose it may seem less relevant than a discourse on how to obtain the money to pay the price, i.e., how to take out a loan, what is the best source, what tactics to use when approaching the bank, your father-in-law, or your employer; whether or not it is feasible to do the construction in stages, or to buy and store materials now and do the construction later when you can afford it. While financing is not our field of expertise, we feel that the more you know of how prices are gathered, the more control you will have over what it will cost you to build your Little House, given your means. And the more you know and the better organized you are, the easier it will be for you to obtain financing from the sources available to you.

To establish a price for a building, the first step is to measure the quantities, or ingredients, as they are set forth on the drawings and described in the specifications, if there are any. Thus we have developed a list of quantities for the basic Little House in each of the four finish groups. Our approach to such a "take-off," as it's called, is to separate the exterior walls from the interior walls, the roof construction from the floor construction and so forth, measuring all components—

FOUNDATION WORK		
STRIP AN AVERAGE OF 9" TOP SOIL (SAVE FOR FUTURE USE)	1000	SQ. FT.
EXCAVATE TRENCH FOR STRIP FOOTING (DEPENDING ON SOIL CONDITIONS)	± 25	CU. YDS.
ISOLATE CUT FOR PIER FOOTING	1	CU. YD.
BACKFILL EARTH AROUND FOUNDATIONS (DEPENDING ON SOIL CONDITIONS)	± 10	CU. YDS.
CONCRETE STRIP FOOTING	4	CU. YDS
CONCRETE PIER FOOTING	3.5	CU. FT
4" CONCRETE PAD AT ENTRY STEPS	15	SQ. FT.
FORMWORK TO SIDES OF STRIP FOOTING	170	SQ. FT.
FORMWORK TO SIDES OF PIER FOOTING	10	SQ. FT.
FORMWORK TO SIDES OF CONCRETE PAD	5	SQ. FT.
4" DRAIN TILE AROUND FOUNDATION	100	LIN. FT.
9" × 12" GRAVEL AROUND 4" DRAIN TILE	100	LIN. FT.
4" GRAVEL BED UNDER DECK	180	SQ. FT.
8" BLOCK FOUNDATION WALL - BASED ON 4'-0" FROST LINE	400	SQ. FT.
8" × 16" × 16" BLOCKS AT PIER	6	EACH
8" × 16" × 16" BLOCKS AT DECK FOOTINGS	9	EACH
DAMPPROOFING TO BLOCK FOUNDATION WALL	390	SQ. FT.
PARGE COAT TO BLOCK FOUNDATION WALL	85	SQ. FT.
MORTAR - INCLUDING FILL FOR CONCRETE BLOCKS WHERE CALLED FOR	2.5	CU. YD.

EXTERIOR STEP AND DECKING		
2×6 FRAMING	50	LIN. FT.
2×4 JOISTS	30	LIN. FT.
2×8 JOISTS	120	LIN. FT.
2×10 FRAMING	45	LIN. FT.
GALVANIZED METAL JOIST HANGERS	24	EACH
5" EXPANSION BOLTS	20	EACH
6" ANCHOR STRAPS	12	EACH
2×6 FLOOR BOARDS	420	LIN. FT.
6" × 3/4" TRIM	20	LIN. FT.
STEEL & MISCELLANEOUS METAL		
STEEL FLITCH PLATE 7" × 3/8"	12	LIN. FT.
3/4" BOLTS W/ WASHERS AT 2'-0" O.C., STAGGERED TOP & BOT, W/ 2 @ EA. END	9	EACH
INSECT SCREEN - 4" STRIP CUT IN SQUARES	12	LIN. FT.
PRE-FAB ALUMINUM BLOCK VENTS W/ INTEGRAL INSECT SCREEN		
BLOCK VENT - FOUNDATION	3	EACH
WALL VENT - BOILER RM 5" × 7 5/8"	1	EACH
WALL VENT - BED RM 15 1/2" × 36"	2	EACH
CLOTHES DRYER VENT (INCL. W/ DRYER)	1	EACH
FOR FINNED-TUBE RADIATOR ENCLOSURE:		
GALVANIZED METAL U-SHAPED GIRTH	26	SQ. FT.
GALVANIZED SHEET METAL DIVIDER	12	SQ. FT.
1/8" × 1 1/2" STAINLESS STEEL EDGING FOR TRAP DOOR	18	LIN. FT.

LIST OF QUANTITIES - FOUNDATION WORK, EXTERIOR STEPS AND DECKING

WOOD FRAMING - FLOOR

2 × 8 JOISTS AT GROUND FLOOR	560	LIN. FT.
2 × 8 JOISTS AT SECOND FLOOR	600	LIN. FT.
2 × 8 SILL PLATE - TOP OF FOUND-ATION WALL	105	LIN. FT.
8" ANCHOR BOLTS	27	EACH
8" WIDE SCREEN STOP	100	LIN. FT.
2 LAYERS 5/8" PLYWOOD @ TOP OF PIER	4	SQ. FT.
2 × 4 LEDGER AT GROUND FLOOR	5	LIN. FT.
2 × 12 JOISTS AT GROUND FLOOR	60	LIN. FT.
GALVANIZED METAL JOIST HANGERS	62	EACH
2 × 6 BLOCKING	12	LIN. FT.
1 × 8 FASCIA AT BRISE SOLEIL	26	LIN. FT.
2 × 5 BLOCKING AT BRISE SOLEIL	20	LIN. FT.
1½" × ¾" LEDGER STRIPS AT BRISE SOLEIL	20	LIN. FT.
5/8" PLYWOOD AT FINNED-TUBE ENCLOSURE	32	SQ. FT.

WOOD FRAMING - EXTERIOR WALLS

2 × 6 WOOD STUDS - INCLUDING SILLS AND HEAD PLATES	1640	LIN. FT.
2 × 6 LINTELS	80	LIN. FT.
2 × 8 LINTELS	60	LIN. FT.
2 × 10 LINTELS	40	LIN. FT.

WOOD FRAMING - INTERIOR WALLS

2 × 6 WOOD STUDS - WET WALL	185	LIN. FT.
2 × 10 WOOD LINTEL - DOORS	20	LIN. FT.
2 × 4 WOOD STUDS	610	LIN. FT.
2 × 4 WOOD STUDS AT STAIR RAIL	35	LIN. FT.
1½ × 1½ WOOD STUD AT STAIR RAIL	20	LIN. FT.

WOOD FRAMING - ROOF

2 × 12 ROOF JOISTS	410	LIN. FT.
2 × 8 BLOCKING (SEE ROOF FRAMING PLAN DWG. A-17)	20	LIN. FT.
1 × 6 TRIM AT MAIN ROOF	90	LIN. FT.
1 × 3 BLOCKING UNDER TRIM	90	LIN. FT.
2 × 6 ROOF JOISTS - SHED	80	LIN. FT.
1 × 6 TRIM AT SHED ROOF	30	LIN. FT.
1 × 3 BLOCKING UNDER TRIM	30	LIN. FT.
LEDGER CUT FROM 2 × 4	12	LIN. FT.
2 × 6 BLOCKING	12	LIN. FT.

PLYWOOD SHEATHING & DECKING

BUILDING PAPER & 5/8" PLYWOOD TO

FLOOR DECK AT GROUND FLOOR	480	SQ. FT.
FLOOR DECK AT SECOND FLOOR	375	SQ. FT.
ROOF DECK	560	SQ. FT.
EXTERIOR WALLS	1270	SQ. FT.

LIST OF QUANTITIES - FRAMING, SHEATHING AND DECKING

studding, sheathing, cladding, flashing—at one time. This method of measurement and the subsequent apportionment of costs permits you to focus on what aspect of the house is particularly costly or what changes and/or substitutions of materials or methods can be made without drastically compromising the overall intent of the design.

Those of you who plan to do much of the work yourself will find this list very useful. However, even if you plan to build the basic Little House in one of the four finish groups without a single deviation, you *must* not use this as a literal shopping list because it makes no provision for waste. We considered adding a multiplier for waste for each category but rejected it, as the percentage which must be added for loss by waste varies greatly, and to some extent also depends upon the skill of the individual worker. If you are a novice but want to do your own interior finishing, feel free. But you will have to buy enough material to afford a few mistakes. Furthermore, if you take the section on lumber directly to a lumberyard for pricing, they may insist you reorganize the format to make it easier for them, e.g., they may want the precise number of 2 × 6 studs that are 7'8¼" long, and so forth, before they are willing to start pricing.

Excluded from the list are the number and types of nails and screws required, as well as the number of pounds of taping compound and yards of tape required to conceal the gypboard joints, and the number of gallons of paint required to cover the inside and/or outside of the house. You will have to develop these quantities yourself. The quantities for mechanical, plumbing, and electrical services delineate the principal items only. Piping and wiring have not been measured in detail, as the requirements of each will vary with each individual installation. While this isn't a shopping list, it will be useful as a check against which to evaluate your builder's quantities, not to mention the advice of well-meaning friends.

In order to give you some guidelines as to what part of the total price you might anticipate the framing to cost as opposed to the roofing or the finish flooring, our final chart lists the percentage of the total cost represented by each component, in each of the four finish groups. These percentages are based on a take-off we did using union labor and suppliers in the vicinity of St. Louis, Missouri. We used union sources to insure consistent data for the percentages we cite, and we cite the specific location because certain items are more expensive in some parts of the country than in others. If you're building somewhere other than the environs of St. Louis and if you're using nonunion labor and suppliers, don't be surprised if your percentages differ from ours.

Needless to say, we don't expect you to use union labor and suppliers because the size of a construction contract for even a combination of two Little House units in the most expensive finish groups is too small to warrant the attention of a union builder. Chances are you'll be dealing with small-scale nonunion contractors and subcontractors who will be intrigued by the Little House, the quality of its materials and detailing, and

EXTERIOR WALL FINISHES

FINISH GROUP 1: CLAPBOARDS	1200	SQ. FT.
FINISH GROUP 2: WOOD SHINGLES	1200	SQ. FT.
FINISH GROUP 3: STUCCO	1200	SQ. FT.
FINISH GROUP 4: ROUGH-CUT BOARD AND BATTEN	1200	SQ. FT.

ROOFING

FINISH GROUP 1: ASPHALT SHINGLES	560	SQ. FT.
FINISH GROUP 2: WOOD SHINGLES	560	SQ. FT.
FINISH GROUP 3: CLAY TILE	560	SQ. FT.
FINISH GROUP 4: CORRUGATED GALVANIZED METAL	560	SQ. FT.

FLASHING, LEADERS & GUTTERS

6" WIDE PERFORATED PEAK FLASHING, MAIN ROOF	20	LIN. FT.
8" WIDE PEAK FLASHING, SHED ROOF	12	LIN. FT.
EAVE FLASHING	32	LIN. FT.
FLASHING AT DECK	20	LIN. FT.
6" CAP FLASHING AT BRISE SOLEIL	20	LIN. FT.
CAP FLASHING ABOVE SLIDING DOORS AND WINDOWS, ENTRY DOOR & VENTS	55	LIN. FT.
2½" WIDE FLASHING @ FINNED-TUBE ENCL.	25	LIN. FT.
6" HALF-ROUND GALVANIZED METAL ROOF GUTTER & STRAPS FIXED TO FASCIA	32	LIN. FT.

2×3 GALVANIZED METAL RECTANGULAR ROOF LEADER & TIES FIXED TO EXTERIOR WALL - OPTIONAL	20	LIN. FT.
2×2×4 PRECAST SPLASH BLOCKS AT BASE OF LEADERS - OPTIONAL	2	EACH

INSULATION

8" BATT INSULATION AT ROOF	465	SQ. FT.
6" BATT INSULATION AT GROUND FLOOR	480	SQ. FT.
6" BATT INSULATION AT EXTERIOR WALLS	1240	SQ. FT.
ALUMINUM FOIL AT ROOF	465	SQ. FT.
ALUMINUM FOIL AT EXTERIOR WALL	1240	SQ. FT.
1½" STYROFOAM INSULATION AT FINNED-TUBE ENCLOSURE	20	SQ. FT.

CAULKING AND SEALANTS

CAULKING AT FASCIA AND AT 2"×8" BLOCKING AT OVERHANG	30	LIN. FT.
CAULKING AT BOILER & B.R. VENTS	20	LIN. FT.
CAULKING AT ALUMINUM DOORS AND WINDOWS	175	LIN. FT.
WEATHERSTRIPPING FOR VENTS	20	LIN. FT.

EXTERIOR TRIM   (FIN. GROUPS 1 & 2 SPECIFICALLY)

1×6 FASCIA BOARD - ROOF	105	LIN. FT.
¾" × 3½" CORNER BOARDS	145	LIN. FT.
¾" × 2" WINDOW, DOOR & VENT TRIM	186	LIN. FT.
¾" × 6" TRIM BETW'N SLIDING DOORS	7	LIN. FT.

LIST OF QUANTITIES - EXTERIOR FINISHES, FLASHING, INSULATION, CAULKING AND SEALANTS

WINDOWS, GLAZING & HARDWARE

FINISH GROUP 1: ALCOA B.A. ALUM.
SLIDING WINDOWS INCLUDING
INSULATED GLASS, HARDWARE &
INSECT SCREENS

2'-11½" H × 2'-11⅞" W #3030	1	EACH
3'-11½" H × 2'-11⅞" W #3040	2	EACH
3'-11½" H × 5'-11⅞" W #6040	3	EACH
3'-11½" H × 5'-11⅞" W WITH SINGLE GLAZING #6040	1	EACH

FINISH GROUP 2: WOOD DOUBLE-HUNG
WINDOWS INCLUDING INSULATED
GLASS, HARDWARE AND INSECT
SCREENS.

± 3'-0" H × 3'-0" W	1	EACH
± 4'-0" H × 3'-0" W	2	EACH
± 4'-0" H × 3'-0" W	3	PAIRS
± 4'-0" H × 3'-0" W WITH SINGLE GLAZING	1	PAIR

FINISH GROUP 3: WOOD SLIDING
WINDOWS INCLUDING INSULATED
GLASS, HARDWARE & INSECT
SCREENS – APPROXIMATELY SAME
SIZES AS FINISH GROUP ONE.

SAME QUANTITIES AS FINISH GROUP ONE

FINISH GROUP 4: SLIDING OR DOUBLE-
HUNG STEEL WINDOWS, INCLUDING
HARDWARE & INSECT SCREENS –
DOUBLE GLAZING OPTIONAL
APPROXIMATELY SAME SIZES AS
FINISH GROUP ONE

SAME QUANTITIES AS FINISH GROUP ONE

ALL FINISH GROUPS - ¾" EXTERIOR PLYWOOD LAMINATED VENT PANELS	2	EACH

LIST OF QUANTITIES - WINDOWS AND DOORS

SLIDING DOORS

FINISH GROUP 1 - ALCOA B.A. ALUM SLIDING DOOR INCL. INSULATED GLASS, HARDWARE & SLIDING SCREEN 6'-8¼" H × 6'-0⅛" W	2	EACH
FINISH GROUPS 2 & 3: WOOD SLIDING INCL. INSULATED GLASS, HARDWARE & SLIDING SCREEN APPROX 6'-8" H × 6'-0" W	2	EACH
FINISH GROUP 4: STEEL SLIDING DOOR HARDWARE & SLIDING SCREEN. INSULATED GLASS OPTIONAL APPROX. 6'-8" H × 6'-0" W	2	EACH

WOOD DOORS (INCLUDING FRAMES)

S.C. ENTRY DOOR 1¾" × 2'-8" × 6'-8"	2	EACH
H.C. INT. DOOR 1⅜" × 2'-8" × 6'-8"	1	EACH
S.C. BATHRM DOOR 1⅜" × 2'-0" × 6'-8"	1	EACH
H.C. CLOSET DOOR 1⅜" × 2'-0" × 6'-8"	1	EACH
H.C. BEDRM DOOR 1⅜" × 2'-4" × 6'-8"	2	EACH
PLYWD CLOS. DOOR ¾" × 1'-6" × 6'-8"	1	EACH
PLYWD CLOS. DOOR ¾" × 5'-0" × 6'-8"	1	PAIR

SILLS AND SADDLES

TYPE A: 6¾" × 1¼" OAK SADDLE	3	LIN. FT
3½" × ⅝" OAK SILL	3	LIN. FT
TYPES B, C, D, E, & F: 3½" × ⅝" OAK SADDLE	18	LIN. FT.
TYPE G: 6¾" × 1¼" OAK SADDLE	12	LIN. FT.
⅝" × 3½" OAK SADDLE	12	LIN. FT.
VENT SILL: 3½" × ¾"	7	LIN. FT.

who will thus give you the most for your money.

However, before blindly accepting a price for your Little House, obtain references and check out examples of work previously completed by any builder from whom you are soliciting prices. Ask for a financial statement for his company (or for his personal worth) to be certain that he can sustain a loss should something unforeseen go wrong during the construction of your project. You can also get a bonding company to put up a performance bond. Thus should your builder go bankrupt during construction the bonding company pays off his debts, as they relate to your project, and takes over the execution of the construction contract. This kind of protection is excellent but the premiums can be prohibitively expensive, especially if the builder's assets are inconsequential.

A more practical way to protect yourself is to sign a contract whereby you are obliged only to pay for materials already purchased and labor already completed. Your builder may be small and may have a legitimate cash flow problem. He may have to submit applications for payment as often as every two weeks. But he must have enough cash or credit to float two weeks' worth of labor and materials. If not, you are completely vulnerable and you are proceeding at your own risk.

Another protective device is to require certification that the last payment you made was distributed to the subcontractors and suppliers involved. In addition, to insure that the general contractor doesn't walk off the job at the end when everyone is tired of picking up loose ends, it is customary to deduct 10% from each application for payment as work progresses. When the work is deemed complete by both you and your builder, the 10% deducted from each application is paid in full and the job is "signed off."

If after wading through the technicalities of chapters 6, 7, and 8 you are persuaded that you don't want to do much of the actual work yourself but you don't have the funds to hire a general contractor either, you might want to consider being your own general contractor. While this means that you will be able to plow the general contractor's 5 to 25 percent surcharge for profit and overhead back into the house, it also means that it will be almost impossible for you to hold down your own job and do this work as well, especially if your Little House is to be a weekend or vacation house and it's located far from where you live and work during the week. But if there's more than one of you involved, and the one of you who has time to spare has a head for business and scheduling, plus the capacity for quick decisions in times of crisis, by all means be your own general contractor. You will have to get the plans approved by local authorities and obtain the required building permit(s). You will have to take out worker's compensation insurance, which will cover your employees; public liability insurance, which covers anyone who breaks a leg on your property, whether an illegal trespasser or an invited guest; property damage insurance, which covers your concrete truck going out of control and mowing down your neighbor's prize Japanese maple. You will have to arrange for temporary power and sanitary facilities, and adequate vehicular

WINDOW AND VENT TRIM

5" x ¾" PINE TRIM SLIDING WINDOWS	80	LIN. FT.
6½" x ¾" PINE SILL - WINDOWS	35	LIN. FT.
2" x ¾" PINE TRIM - WINDOWS	140	LIN. FT.
3" x ¾" PINE TRIM INSIDE VENT OP'NGS	18	LIN. FT.
1" x ¾" PINE STOP - VENT		

NOTE: IF B.A. ALUM. WINDOWS OF FIN. GROUP ONE ARE TO BE USED, EXTERIOR TRIM CAN BE ELIMINATED IN INTERESTS OF ECONOMY

DOOR TRIM

3" x ¾" PINE TRIM - SLIDING DOORS	40	LIN. FT.
7" x ¾" TRIM BETWEEN SLIDING DOORS	7	LIN. FT.
2" x ¾" PINE TRIM ALL DOORS	260	LIN. FT.

BASEBOARD

1 x 4 PINE	210	LIN. FT.

WALL AND CEILING FINISHES

FINISH GROUP ONE:		
WALLS - ⅝" GYPSUM BOARD	2100	SQ. FT.
CLG. - ½" GYPSUM BOARD	825	SQ. FT.
FINISH GROUP TWO:		
WALLS - ½" x 3" PINE STRIPS	2100	SQ. FT.
CLG. - ½" x 3" PINE STRIPS	825	SQ. FT.
FINISH GROUP THREE:		
WALLS - 3 COATS PLASTER ± ¾"	2100	SQ. FT.
CLG. - 3 COATS PLASTER ± ¾"	825	SQ. FT.

FINISH GROUP FOUR:		
WALLS - FIBREBOARD	2100	SQ. FT.
CLG. - FIBREBOARD	825	SQ. FT.

NOTE: IN ALL FINISH GROUPS, WALL & CEILING FINISHES CAN BE ELIMINATED IN UPSTAIRS STORAGE AREAS IN INTERESTS OF ECONOMY, BUT NOT INSULATION.

FLOOR FINISHES

FINISH GROUP ONE:		
OAK STRIP	515	SQ. FT.
CERAMIC TILE AT ENTRY & HEARTH	50	SQ. FT.
2ND LAYER OF PLYWOOD BENEATH ENTRY AND HEARTH	50	SQ. FT.
PLYWOOD SUBFLOOR EXPOSED: BOILER AND UPSTAIRS STORAGE AREAS.	115	SQ. FT.
FINISH GROUP TWO:		
STUDDED RESILIENT RUBBER TILE	560	SQ. FT.
HEARTH - COLORLITH	5	SQ. FT.
PLYWOOD SUBFLOOR EXPOSED IN BOILER & STORAGE AREAS	115	SQ. FT.
FINISH GROUP THREE:		
QUARRY TILE (INCL. HEARTH)	565	SQ. FT.
PLYWOOD SUBFLOOR EXPOSED IN BOILER & STORAGE AREAS	115	SQ. FT.
FINISH GROUP FOUR:		
VINYL-ASBESTOS TILE OR LINOLEUM	560	SQ. FT.
CERAMIC TILE OR COLORLITH HEARTH	5	SQ. FT.
PLYWOOD SUBFLOOR EXPOSED IN BOILER & STORAGE AREAS	115	SQ. FT.

LIST OF QUANTITIES - INTERIOR TRIM AND FINISHES

BATHROOM WALL & CEILING FINISHES

FINISH GROUP ONE :

WALLS - ⅝" WATERPROOF GYP. BD.	275	SQ. FT.
CLG - ½" WATERPROOF GYP. BD	70	SQ. FT.
WAINSCOTING TO 3'-10" A.F.F. & TUB	95	SQ. FT.
SURROUND - 4"×4" CERAMIC TILE		

FINISH GROUP TWO :

WALLS- PLYWOOD/GYP UNDERLAYMENT	275	SQ. FT.
½"×3" PINE STRIPS	220	SQ. FT.
CLG- PLYWOOD/GYP UNDERLAYMENT	70	SQ. FT.
½"×3" PINE STRIPS	70	SQ. FT.
TUB SURROUND 2"×2" CERAMIC TILE	55	SQ. FT.

FINISH GROUP THREE :

WALLS- KEENE'S PLASTER	275	SQ.FT.
CLG. - KEENE'S PLASTER	70	SQ.FT.
TUB SURROUND 2"×2" CERAMIC TILE	55	SQ.FT.

FINISH GROUP FOUR :

WALLS ⅝" WATERPROOF GYP. BD.	275	SQ.FT.
CLG.- ½" WATERPROOF GYP. BD.	70	SQ.FT.
TUB SURROUND- PLAST. LAM. OR FIBREGLASS	55	SQ.FT.

BATHROOM FLOOR & BASE FINISHES

FINISH GROUP ONE :

FLOOR- 1"×1" CERAMIC TILE	50	SQ. FT.
BASE- 4"×4" C.T. S&W WALLS & CLOSET	20	LIN. FT.

FINISH GROUP TWO :

FLOOR- STUDDED RESIL. RUBBER TILE	50	SQ. FT.
BASE- 4" RUBBER OR VINYL	25	LIN. FT.

FINISH GROUP THREE :

FLOOR- 6"×6" QUARRY TILE	50	SQ. FT.
BASE- 3" OR 4" HIGH QUARRY TILE	25	LIN. FT.

FINISH GROUP FOUR :

FLOOR- VINYL ASB. TILE OR LINOLEUM	50	SQ. FT.
BASE - 4" RUBBER	25	LIN. FT.

STAIR

OAK STAIR WITH 13 RISERS @ 8¹⁄₁₆". 9 STRAIGHT TREADS @ 10¼" & 3 WINDERS. TOTAL RISE 8'-8⅞". TOTAL RUN = 9'-4¾". TO INCLUDE OAK POSTS, STRINGERS, WOOD FRAMING & GYP. BD RAILING & PARTITION AS PER DTLS 1-6, DWG. A-35	1	EACH
GYP. BD. AT SLOPING SOFFIT OF STAIR	30	SQ. FT.
GYPSUM BOARD AT RAILING	50	SQ. FT.

MISC. CABINETWORK AND SHELVING

BANQUETTE WITH 3 STORAGE DRAWERS± BELOW 9'-3" × 2'-1½" × 1'-4" AS PER DWGS A-31 AND A-32	10	LIN. FT.
BANQUETTE WITH 1 STORAGE DRAWER± BELOW 2'-11¾" × 2'-1½" × 1'-4"	3	LIN. FT.
CHROME-PLATED CLOTHES POLES @ 3'-6" LONG, 1 WITH SHELF ABOVE	2	EACH
¾" PLYWOOD SHELVES ON CLEATS IN LINEN CLOS. 1'-10½" W × 1'-6" DEEP	5	EACH
LOFT BED 3'-0" WIDE × 7'-6" LONG INCL. 2×4 FRAMING, ¾" PLYWD. DECK & 1×6 EDGE TRIM AS PER DWG. A-32	1	EACH
LOFT BED LADDER 1'-7" WIDE × 10'-9" HIGH WITH 8 WOOD OR CHROME RUNGS	1	EACH
¾" PLYWOOD SHELVING UNDER STAIR CONFIGURED AS DESIRED- OPTIONAL	1	EACH
TRAP DOOR 2'-0" × 2'-3" INCL. 2×4 FRAMING & RING PULL HANDLE	1	EACH

LIST OF QUANTITIES - BATHROOM FINISHES AND MISCELLANEOUS CABINETWORK

access for work trucks. You will have to order materials, coordinate deliveries, arrange for storage, coordinate trades and the like.

Whether you have a general contractor or are your own, the first thing you must do is assemble from the pages of this book a set of working drawings for your Little House, be it one of the given variations or combinations or your own version, that is to say dimensioned plans, sections and elevations, then details of the component parts—something resembling the set of drawings we presented in chapter 6 for the basic Little House. Have the pages in this book which show drawings relevant to your version photocopied. Please note that you need to get written permission from the Macmillan Publishing Co., Inc., to reproduce this material, but there's no fee involved. Photocopy only the drawings in chapters 6, 7, 8, and the Appendix for the purpose of studying and assembling working drawings for your own Little House. If your floor plans differ from those we show, develop your own plan using the technique we suggested in chapter 7. Lay a sheet of tracing paper over the one nearest to yours that we show. Trace the elements the two plans share, then add your own variations. What is most critical is to keep to the same format we use, complete with dimension strings, numbered window and door openings and the like, because this is the language of construction drawings whether they are done freehand or with a straight edge. Do the same for the sections and elevations. Be sure your choice of finishes is clearly indicated. Use the same graphic technique for designating these materials that we use in chapters 6 and 7.

Do not include the foundation drawings shown in chapter 6. In fact, insofar as we can, we prohibit their inclusion in your set. At the risk of repeating ourselves, we insist that you have the bearing capacity and drainage of your soil tested and your foundations designed accordingly by a locally licensed architect or engineer. To do this properly he or she will need the plans, sections, elevations, and framing information which you have assembled so far. Be certain to incorporate into your drawings any structural adjustments he or she considers necessary. You should be forewarned that many engineers and builders will consider the Little House overstructured and will suggest using fewer and/or lighter framing members which will result in considerable savings to you. For the record, we will stand by only what is shown on our drawings.

At the same time, go through the steps outlined in chapter 8 with regard to water and electrical supply, sewage treatment and disposal, availability of fuel and type of heating system to be employed. From this information develop an overall site plan using the survey of your land or a portion thereof as a base. Identify your water supply, be it a spring, well, creek, or city water main; the cesspool, septic tank, leaching field or sewer line; the nearest electrical pole and the proposed route of access to your house for the wires. Show a location for an oil storage tank if that is to be your fuel, a generous and practical route for vehicular access and of course show the house itself. Be certain this drawing shows any lot or property line setbacks, rights of way,

KITCHEN CABINETS

FINISH GROUP ONE - NATURAL FINISH BIRCH PLYWOOD WITH OAK EDGING, HARDWARE, ETC. OIL OR CLEAR LACQUER FINISH

LOWER UNIT 6'-0¾"x 2'-1½"x 3'-0"	6	LIN. FT.
SM LOWER UNIT 1'-0¼"x 2'-1½"x 3'-0"	1	LIN. FT.
UPPER UNIT 9'-7¾"x1'-0"x 2'-3"	10	LIN. FT.

FINISH GROUP TWO - ½"x 3" VERTICAL PINE STRIPS — AS ABOVE
SAME UNITS AS FIN. GROUP ONE

FINISH GROUP THREE - VENEERED PLYWOOD W/ VENEERED EDGES OAK ASH OR SPRAY LACQUER FINISH — AS ABOVE
SAME UNITS AS FIN. GROUP ONE

FINISH GROUP FOUR - STORE BOUGHT ACTUAL SIZE OF UNITS WILL BE DETERMINED BY AVAILABILITY — SIMILAR TO FINISH GROUP ONE

KITCHEN COUNTERS & BACKSPLASH

FINISH GROUP ONE - PLASTIC LAMINATE WITH OAK EDGING

COUNTERTOP - 2'-0½" DEEP CUT-OUT FOR SINK NOT EDUCTED	15	SQ. FT.
BACKSPLASH- HEIGHT DEPENDS ON BACKSPLASH OF RANGE	10	LIN. FT.

FINISH GROUP TWO - JOHNS-MANVILLE "COLORLITH" - SAME AS FIN GROUP ONE — AS ABOVE

FINISH GROUP THREE - BUTCHERBLOCK 1¼" FOR COUNTERTOP ¾" FOR BACKSPLASH — AS ABOVE

FINISH GROUP FOUR - STOREBOUGHT SIZE DETERMINED BY AVAILABILITY — SIMILAR TO GROUP ONE

APPLIANCES

2'-6" WIDE RANGE, GAS OR ELECTRIC RANGE/EXHAUST HOOD OPTIONAL	1	EACH
UNDER-COUNTER DISHWASHER	1	EACH
2'-6" OR 2'-9" 2-DR REFRIGERATOR	1	EACH
PORTABLE TYPE CLOTHES WASHER	1	EACH
PORTABLE TYPE CLOTHES DRYER WITH VENT TO OUTSIDE	1	EACH

FIREPLACE AND ENCLOSURE

PRE-FABRICATED FIREPLACE &/OR NON-COMBUSTIBLE FLOOR PAD	1	EACH
FLUE-CHIMNEY & CHIMNEY CAP	1	EACH

HARDWARE

ALLOW FOR SUFFICIENT FINISH HARDWARE FOR DOORS & BUILT- IN KITCHEN & MISC. CABINETWORK	ITEM

PAINTING

EXTERIOR

STEPS AND DECK	250	SQ. FT.
EAVES, FASCIA, DOOR & VENT TRIM	120	SQ. FT.
BRISE SOLEIL	175	SQ. FT.
EXTERIOR WALL FINISH	1200	SQ. FT.

INTERIOR

WALLS AND CEILINGS	3275	SQ. FT.
DOORS - BOTH SIDES	270	SQ. FT.
DOOR, WINDOW & BASE TRIM	790	LIN. FT.
MISC. CABINETWORK & SHELVING		ITEM
KITCH. CABINETWORK IF REQ'D		ITEM

LIST OF QUANTITIES - KITCHEN CABINETWORK, APPLIANCES AND EQUIPMENT, PAINTING

154

TOILET ACCESSORIES

CHROME-PLATED OR STAINLESS STEEL TOWEL BARS 2'-0" LONG	3	EACH
CHROME-PLATED SHOWER CURTAIN ROD 5'-0" LONG	1	EACH
SEMI-RECESSED MEDICINE CABINET W/ MIRRORED DOOR	1	EACH
RECESSED SOAP DISH	3	EACH
RECESSED TOOTHBRUSH & GLASS HOLDER	1	EACH
TOILET PAPER HOLDER	1	EACH
ROBE HOOKS	2	EACH

PLUMBING & HEATING (HYDRONIC)

FIXTURES - INCLUDING TRIM		
LAVATORY	1	EACH
BATHTUB AND SHOWER	1	EACH
WATER CLOSET	1	EACH
KITCHEN SINK	1	EACH
WASTE AND VENT PIPING - INSTALLED AS DIRECTED IN CHAPTER 8		
2" SEWER PIPE		ITEM
3" VENT PIPE		ITEM
4" SEWER PIPE		ITEM
4" CLEAN-OUT FITTING		ITEM
HOT & COLD WATER SUPPLY PIPING - INSTALLED AS DIRECTED IN CHAP. 8		
½" PIPE		ITEM
¾" PIPE		ITEM
1" PIPE		ITEM
EQUIPMENT - HYDRONIC SYSTEM ONLY OIL-FIRED HOT WATER HEATER W/ 4 GPM HEATING COIL FOR DOMESTIC HOT WATER PLUS FLUE STACK	1	EACH

LIST OF QUANTITIES - PLUMBING, HEATING AND ELECTRICAL

HOT WATER CIRCULATING PUMP	1	EACH
DAY-NIGHT CLOCK THERMOSTAT	1	EACH
4"×4" FIN. - TUBE RADIATION ELEMENT, FLOOR GRILLE AND/OR COVER - EXACT LENGTH DEPENDS ON LOCATION OF HOUSE		ITEM

ELECTRICAL

LIGHT FIXTURE OUTLETS		
INTERIOR	21	EACH
EXTERIOR	3	EACH
RECEPTACLES - GROUNDED TYPE		
CONVENIENCE/DUPLEX C, UC ETC	16	EACH
WEATHERPROOF	1	EACH
APPLIANCE - ABOVE & UNDER COUNTER	7	EACH
50 AMP 220V FOR ELECT. RANGE	1	EACH
20 AMP AIR COND. - OPTIONAL		ITEM
LIGHT SWITCHES		
SINGLE POLE	10	EACH
3-WAY	2	EACH
METER PANEL AND METER TO EXTERNAL WALL	1	EACH
ELECTRIC PANEL BOARD - TYPE A	1	EACH
SERVICE ENTRY WEATHERHEAD AT ROOF PEAK TO RECEIVE OVERHEAD WIRE SERVICE FEEDER	1	EACH
JUNCTION BOX FOR SWITCH CONTROL	2	EACH
ALLOWANCE FOR WIRING TO ALL FIXTURE OUTLETS, RECEPTACLES AND SWITCHES		ITEM
TELEPHONE OUTLETS	2	EACH
T.V. & HI-FI OUTLETS/JACKS - OPTIONAL		ITEM
LIGHTNING PROTECTION - 2 RODS W/ CABLE CONNECTION TO & INCLUDING ELECTRODE AT GRADE		ITEM

easements, and the like. For your own sake you should also locate all large trees, major rock outcroppings and other natural landmarks. Then take this site plan together with your floor plans and foundation plans to the local authorities and have them approved. This can be a very constructive process as they may suggest valuable changes based on their knowledge of problems specific to the area, or simply local building traditions—all of which you should incorporate into the drawings.

Now that you know you're legal, extrapolate from chapters 6 and 7 all details relating to the windows, doors and vents, interior finishes, door and window trim, cabinetwork and shelving, etc., of your choice. Again have the relevant pages photocopied and put a large X through those details not pertinent to your version; then include the sheet in your set. For easy reference, you should renumber the drawings.

When you have the drawings from this book photocopied have everything else on the page, i.e., the text, blocked out with white paper overlays. Position each drawing in a consistent place on each 8½" by 11" sheet. Position the drawings you do yourself in similar fashion. In the lower right-hand corner, number the sheets consecutively starting with A-1—the A standing for architectural. In the lower left corner of each, identify the project, as different drawings will be sent out to different subcontractors.

Following these drawings should be the heating, plumbing, and electrical drawings adjusted to reflect what you want to have happen in your version of the Little House. These can be numbered from M-1—M standing for mechanical.

The final section should include typed or legibly handwritten schedules covering your choice of kitchen appliances, toilet fixtures, and accessories. It should include any written specifications or manufacturers' instructions regarding the application of a particular finish or installation of special equipment. The schedules can be specific with regard to manufacturers or generic, thereby allowing a subcontractor to do some shopping for you.

The importance of beginning this process with a proper set of drawings cannot be overemphasized. Whether the drawings are 8½" by 11" or 24" by 36", they are called contract documents because they are all you and a contractor or subcontractor have to define what he is going to do for the price he quotes. Like the local authorities, he may suggest changes to save money, and you in turn may make changes for other reasons. All of these must be documented on the drawings, however informally, because they will affect the final price quoted by the particular subcontractor and the final sum you will actually pay him.

Keeping track of the changes is tedious but it saves a lot of aggravation on all sides when it comes to paying the bills. Furthermore, the annoyance of documenting changes will make you think twice before you make them. The expense in time and money of making changes during construction cannot be overemphasized. Recalling the right workers to the job can be very difficult. In the more remote areas where labor is scarce, the right man may be unable to come when you need him,

FINISH GROUP / ITEM		ONE – BASE PRICE	TWO – 8% MORE $ THAN GROUP I	THREE – 10% MORE $ THAN GROUP I	FOUR – 6% LESS $ THAN GROUP I
		ITEM PERCENT OF TOTAL CONSTRUCTION COST			
THE ENCLOSURE	FOUNDATION WORK	9.5%	8.5%	8.5%	9.5%
	EXTERIOR STEPS & DECKING	2.0	2.0	2.0	2.0
	STEEL & MISCELLANEOUS METAL	1.0	1.0	1.0	1.5
	WOOD FRAMING	16.0	15.0	15.0	17.0
	PLYWOOD, SHEATHING & DECKING	5.0	5.0	5.0	5.5
	EXTERIOR WALL FINISH	CLAP-BOARDS 3.5	WOOD SHINGLES 5.0	STUCCO 4.5	BOARD & BATTEN 4.0
	ROOFING	ASPHALT SHINGLES .5	WOOD SHINGLES 2.0	CLAY TILE 2.0	CORRUGATED METAL 1.0
	FLASHING, LEADERS & GUTTERS	.5	.5	.5	.5
	CAULKING & SEALANTS	.5	.5	.5	.5
	ROOFING & BUILDING INSULATION	3.0	2.5	2.5	3.0
	WINDOWS	SLIDING B.A. ALUM. 4.5	DBL-HUNG WOOD 5.0	SLIDING WOOD 4.5	DBL.-HUNG STEEL 4.5
	SLIDING DOORS	B.A. ALUMINUM 2.0	WOOD 2.0	WOOD 2.0	STEEL 2.0
	INTERIOR & EXTERIOR DOORS	3.5	3.0	3.0	3.5
	EXTERIOR PAINTING ALLOWANCE	1.5	1.0	1.0	1.5
PLUMBING & HEATING	PLUMBING FIXTURES & FITTINGS	1.5	1.5	1.5	1.5
	PLUMBING PIPING & ROUGHING	5.0	4.5	4.5	5.0
	BOILER & RADIATORS	5.5	5.0	5.0	5.5

PERCENTAGE COST BREAKDOWN · THE ENCLOSURE, BASIC LITTLE HOUSE

FINISH GROUP/ITEM	ONE - BASE PRICE	TWO - 8% MORE $ THAN GROUP 1	THREE - 10% MORE $ THAN GROUP 1	FOUR - 6% LESS $ THAN GROUP 1
	ITEM PERCENTAGE OF TOTAL CONSTRUCTION COST			
THE ENCLOSED				
WALL & CEILING FINISH	GYPSUM BOARD 3.5	½×3 PINE 8.5	PLASTER 8.0	FIBRE-BOARD 2.5
FLOORING	OAK 5.0	RUBBER TILE 2.5	QUARRY TILE 4.0	VAT/LINOLEUM 2.5
BASEBOARD, DOOR & WINDOW TRIM	3.0%	2.5%	2.5%	3.0
BATHROOM WALL & CEILING FINISHES	GYP. BD & 4×4 C.T. 1.0	½×3 PINE 1.0	KEENE'S PLASTER 1.5	GYPSUM BOARD .5
BATHRM FLOOR, BASE & WAINSCOTING	1×1 C.T. .5	RUBBER TILE .5	QUARRY TILE .5	VAT/LINOLEUM —
INTERIOR STAIR	2.5	2.5	2.5	3.0
MISC. CABINETS & SHELVING	2.0	2.0	2.0	2.0
KITCHEN CABINETS & HARDWARE	BIRCH PLYWOOD 2.5	½×3 PINE 3.0	VENEERED PLYWOOD 2.0	STOREBOUGHT 2.0
KITCHEN COUNTER & BACKSPLASH	PLASTIC LAMINATE .5	"COLORLITH" .5	BUTCHER BLOCK .5	STOREBOUGHT 1.5
KITCHEN/LAUNDRY APPLIANCES	4.0	3.5	3.5	4.0
FIREPLACE	HEATILATOR 2.5	JOTUL 2.0	HEATILATOR 2.5	FRANKLIN STOVE 1.5
HARDWARE ALLOWANCE	1.0	1.0	1.0	1.5
TOILET ACCESSORIES	—	—	—	.5
INTERIOR PAINTING ALLOWANCE	2.0	1.5	1.5	2.0
ELECTRICAL & MISC.				
ELECTRICAL PANEL & WIRING	1.0	1.0	1.0	1.0
SWITCHES, OUTLETS & LIGHTING	3.5	3.5	3.5	4.0
MISC: TV, PHONE, LIGHTNING RODS	.5	.5	.5	.5

PERCENTAGE COST BREAKDOWN - THE ENCLOSED, BASIC LITTLE HOUSE

and the job will drag on unfinished.

You will always find building prices absolutely staggering. You will be outraged. However hard we work to prepare you for this experience, there are also factors for which we cannot account. First the quotes that you will obtain will vary depending on the total amount of construction going on in your area as this will affect the number of subcontractors interested in estimating, much less bidding on a job as small as yours. If the building business is booming, it may well be in your interests to postpone your construction until things calm down and the available work force gets a little hungry. In more remote areas you may have to postpone your construction because there's only one man available to pour concrete and he's busy for the next three months. The quotes you receive will depend on the ever-changing costs of materials, which are in turn affected by supply and demand in the market, labor strikes, and the like. Finally, the quotes will depend on the degree to which you impress the bidders that you know what you want, that you have some understanding of the construction process and some humility about what you don't understand, and last but far from least, that you are likely to pay your bills promptly.

We should mention inflation, in that it will very much affect your decision whether to build your second Little House unit together with the first, a few years later, or not at all. Union wages, which set the standards for all wages in the industry, union or nonunion, are increased annually. Materials costs generally fluctuate upward as a result of the labor agreements reached, and of the worldwide pricing of materials and commodities. This results in price escalation which in the past few years has been in the range of 8 to 10 percent per year. Thus should you wish to use any of the prices you obtain now to estimate construction costs several years hence, do not fail to add this percentage to your figures and to compound it annually. You will soon come to the conclusion that you should build all you can afford to today as less will cost more tomorrow.

What the Little House represents is a way by which you, too, can have a one-of-a-kind house, the elements of which have been adjusted to your needs while at the same time embodying principals of good design, integrity of construction techniques and materials, and longevity. It is a way by which a little work on your part will bring your house in at a price you can afford. We hope you have enjoyed reading this book enough to be inspired not to buy a tract or a prefab house, but to realize the extent of your choice and your control over the space you build and live in. We hope to have given you the confidence to put together plans for your own house—even if it isn't a Little House.

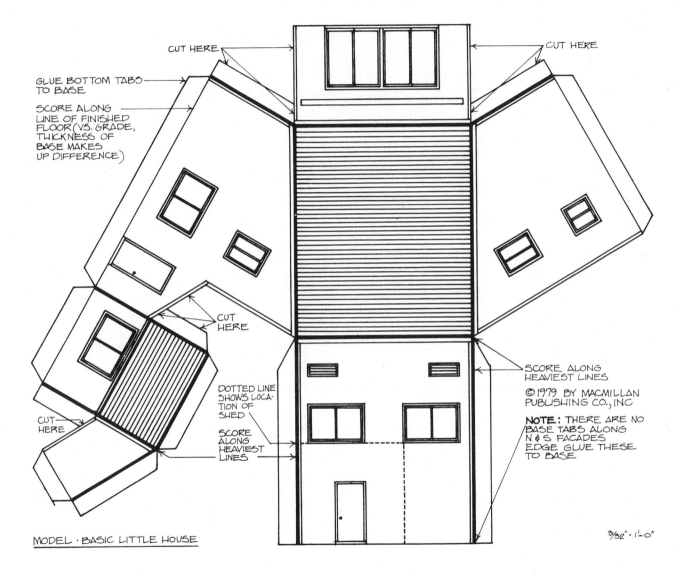

MODEL · BASIC LITTLE HOUSE

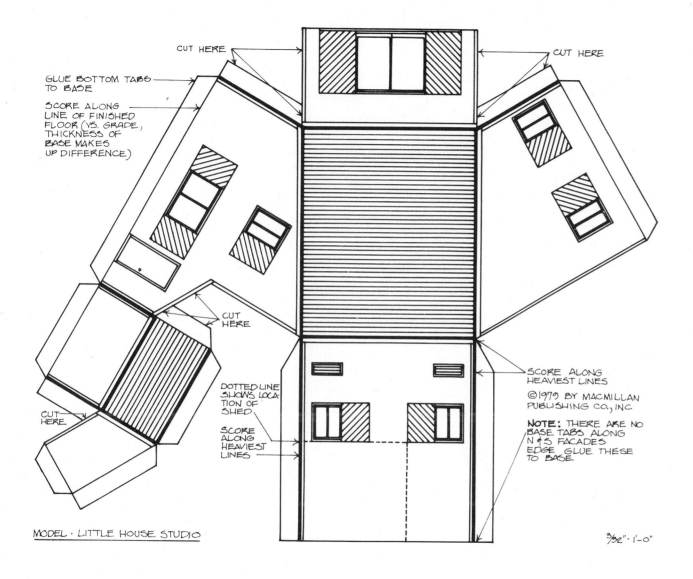

CUT HERE

CUT HERE

GLUE BOTTOM TABS
TO BASE

SCORE ALONG
LINE OF FINISHED
FLOOR (VS. GRADE,
THICKNESS OF
BASE MAKES
UP DIFFERENCE)

CUT
HERE

CUT
HERE

DOTTED LINE
SHOWS LOCA-
TION OF
SHED

SCORE
ALONG
HEAVIEST
LINES

SCORE ALONG
HEAVIEST LINES

©1979 BY MACMILLAN
PUBLISHING CO., INC

NOTE: THERE ARE NO
BASE TABS ALONG
N & S FACADES
EDGE GLUE THESE
TO BASE

MODEL · LITTLE HOUSE STUDIO

3/32" = 1'-0"

APPENDIX

Cut-out Models

Before you take to selecting a Little House most suited to your needs, modifying it perhaps, and then building it, we encourage you to play with the cut-out models we have prepared of the basic Little House, each of its variations, and a typical unit B.

If you don't want to destroy the integrity of the book, have these pages photocopied; then, with rubber cement, paste each one firmly and flatly on a piece of slightly heavier weight Bristol paper. Be sure there are no bubbles between the two pieces of paper when you start to cut the model out. Then along the edges where it says "fold here," take an Xacto-knife or matt knife blade and score the paper, i.e., scratch the paper lightly along this line using a metal edge as a guide. This will make a clean fold. Should your hand be a little heavy and your blade go through, simply tape the reverse side and proceed as instructed. Cut out whichever base is appropriate and paste it onto a thick piece of cardboard. Then cut out the cardboard as you cut out the rest of the model. Paste the model onto the base. If you are interested in making your model at a larger scale, e.g., $\frac{1}{8}$" = 1'0", have the entire page blown up to the scale of your choice.

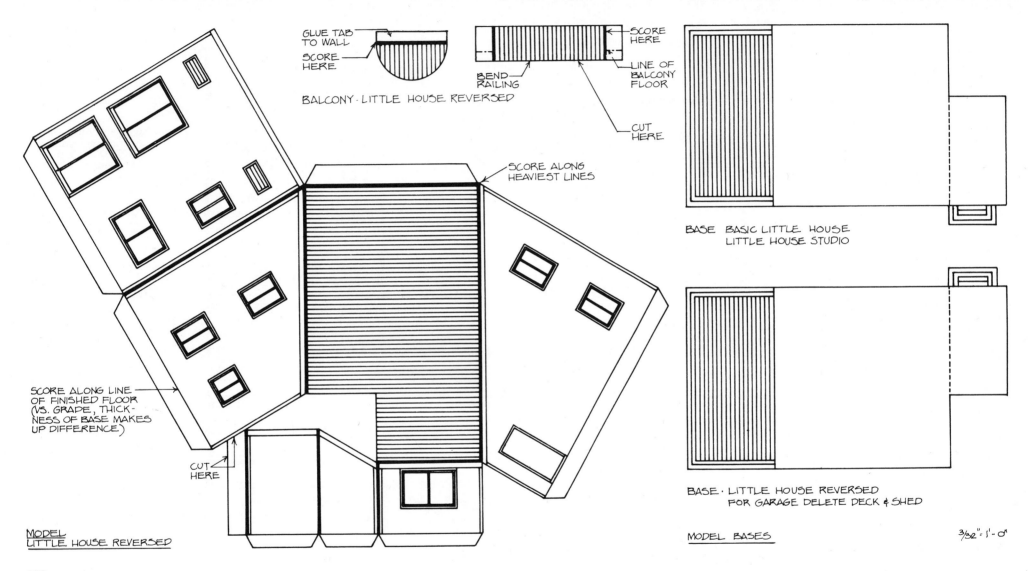

GLUE TAB
TO WALL

SCORE
HERE

SCORE
HERE

BEND
RAILING

LINE OF
BALCONY
FLOOR

CUT
HERE

BALCONY · LITTLE HOUSE REVERSED

SCORE ALONG
HEAVIEST LINES

SCORE ALONG LINE
OF FINISHED FLOOR
(VS. GRADE, THICK-
NESS OF BASE MAKES
UP DIFFERENCE.)

CUT
HERE

MODEL
LITTLE HOUSE REVERSED

BASE BASIC LITTLE HOUSE
LITTLE HOUSE STUDIO

BASE · LITTLE HOUSE REVERSED
FOR GARAGE DELETE DECK & SHED

MODEL BASES

3/32" = 1'-0"

160

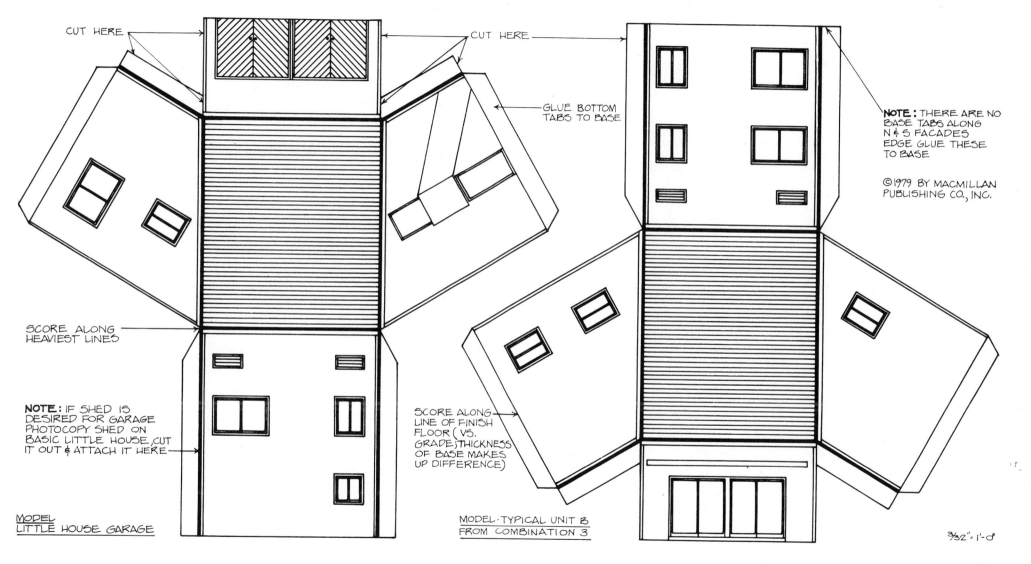

CUT HERE

CUT HERE

GLUE BOTTOM
TABS TO BASE

NOTE: THERE ARE NO
BASE TABS ALONG
N & S FACADES
EDGE GLUE THESE
TO BASE

©1979 BY MACMILLAN
PUBLISHING CO., INC.

SCORE ALONG
HEAVIEST LINES

NOTE: IF SHED IS
DESIRED FOR GARAGE
PHOTOCOPY SHED ON
BASIC LITTLE HOUSE, CUT
IT OUT & ATTACH IT HERE

SCORE ALONG
LINE OF FINISH
FLOOR (VS.
GRADE; THICKNESS
OF BASE MAKES
UP DIFFERENCE)

<u>MODEL</u>
<u>LITTLE HOUSE GARAGE</u>

<u>MODEL·TYPICAL UNIT B</u>
<u>FROM COMBINATION 3</u>

3/32"=1'-0"

161